# ENTITY AND ID
## AND OTHER ESSAYS

# Entity and Identity
## and Other Essays

P. F. STRAWSON

CLARENDON PRESS · OXFORD

*This book has been printed digitally and produced in a standard specification
in order to ensure its continuing availability*

# OXFORD
UNIVERSITY PRESS

Great Clarendon Street, Oxford OX2 6DP

Oxford University Press is a department of the University of Oxford.
It furthers the University's objective of excellence in research, scholarship,
and education by publishing worldwide in

Oxford New York

Auckland   Cape Town  Dar es Salaam  Hong Kong  Karachi
Kuala Lumpur  Madrid  Melbourne  Mexico City  Nairobi
New Delhi  Shanghai  Taipei  Toronto
With offices in
Argentina  Austria  Brazil  Chile  Czech Republic  France Greece
Guatemala  Hungary  Italy  Japan  South Korea  Poland  Portugal
Singapore  Switzerland  Thailand  Turkey  Ukraine  Vietnam

Oxford is a registered trade mark of Oxford University Press
in the UK and in certain other countries

Published in the United States
by Oxford University Press Inc., New York

Oxford is a registered trade mark of Oxford University Press
in the UK and in certain other countries

Published in the United States
by Oxford University Press Inc., New York

ISBN 0-19-825015-0

# Acknowledgements

The essays collected in this volume have, for the most part, been previously published in journals or other collections. Their original sources are listed below. I am grateful to the editors and publishers concerned for permission to reprint the papers here.

'Entity and Identity', in *Contemporary British Philosophy, Fourth Series*, ed. H. Lewis (George Allen & Unwin, London, 1976).

'Universals', in *Midwest Studies in Philosophy, Vol. 14: Studies in Metaphysics* (University of Minnesota Press, 1979).

'Positions for Quantifiers', in *Semantics and Philosophy*, ed. M. K. Munitz and P. Unger (New York University Press, 1974).

'Concepts and Properties', in *The Philosophical Quarterly* (University of St Andrews, 1987).

'Direct Singular Reference: Intended Reference and Actual Reference', in *Wo steht die Analytische Philosophie heute?*, ed. L. Nagl and R. Heinrich, *Wiener Reihe* 1986 (R. Oldenbourg K. G. Wien).

'Belief, Reference and Quantification', in *The Monist*, 1982 (The Hegeler Institute, La Salle, Ill.).

'Reference and its Roots', in *The Philosophy of W. V. Quine*, Library of Living Philosophers, 1986 (Open Court Publishing Company, La Salle, Ill.).

'Logical Form and Logical Constants', in *Logical Form, Predication and Ontology*, ed. P. K. Sen, *Jadavpur Studies in Philosophy 4* (Macmillan India Ltd., 1982).

' "If" and "⊃" ', in *Philosophical Grounds of Rationality, Intention, Categories, Ends*, ed. R. E. Grandy and R. Warner (Oxford University Press, 1986).

'May Bes and Might Have Beens', in *Meaning and Use*, ed.

A. Margalit, pp. 229–38 (Reidel; Kluwer Academic Publishers, 1979).

'Austin and "Locutionary Meaning"', in *Essays on J. L. Austin* by I. Berlin *et al.* (Oxford University Press, 1973).

'Meaning and Context', hitherto unpublished in English. A partial French translation as 'Phrase et Acte de Parole' appeared in *Langages*, 1970.

'Kant's New Foundations of Metaphysics', in *Metaphysik nach Kant*, ed. D. Henrich and R.-P. Horstmann (Klett-Cotta, 1987).

'The Problem of Realism and the A Priori', in *Kant and Contemporary Epistemology*, ed. P. Parrini, pp. 167–73 (Kluwer Academic Publishers, 1994).

'Kant's Paralogisms: Self-Consciousness and the "Outside Observer"', in *Theorie der Sujektivität*, ed. K. Cramer *et al.* (Suhrkamp Verlag, 1987).

'Kant on Substance', hitherto unpublished.

The two papers 'May Bes and Might Have Beens' and 'The Problem of Realism and the A Priori' are reprinted by permission of Kluwer Academic Publishers who hold the copyright. No part of this material may be reproduced or utilized in any form without written permission from the copyright owner.

# Contents

# Introduction

With the exception of the last four Kantian studies, all the essays in this volume are concerned with questions in the philosophy of language and logic. My aim in this introduction is to bring out the links between related essays, to qualify, and even to correct, some of the claims made, and in general to clarify the issues wherever clarification seems called for.

1. The first two essays form a natural pair. The longer and more elaborate 'Entity and Identity' was written first. The shorter 'Universals' repeats the main point of Part 1 of 'Entity and Identity', but differs from the longer article in several respects. First, in mentioning conceptual necessities, it makes an extra point on what might be called the Platonizing side of the question—a point which is not made, or appealed to, in the longer article. Second, and more substantially, 'Universals' gives a fuller, and up to a point a more sympathetic, account of the grounds for, or the explanation of, resistance to acceptance of large classes of general things or abstract entities. In referring to our natural disposition to equate existence in general with existence in nature, and to the apparent difficulty of giving any account of the relation between universals and their particular exemplification which is free from any hint of myth-making, it offers, in other words, a fuller and more understanding account of the anti-Platonizing side of the question; and this is why the article ends with the suggestion that the dispute may not be finally resolved one way or the other.

In 'Entity and Identity', on the other hand, I come down

without reservation on the more ontologically generous or indulgent side, the side of a reformed or demythologized Platonism or, as it used to be called, realism. This I do also in my more recent contribution, not reproduced here, to *Perspectives on Quine*,[1] a collection of papers delivered at a conference held in St Louis in 1988; and in the last chapter, 'The Matter of Meaning', of my 1985 book, *Skepticism and Naturalism*, I again show a qualified allegiance to the realist position—qualified by the admission, echoing the 'Universals' article, that we may have here the matter of a finally irreconcilable difference or dispute.

There are other points of difference between these two articles. The most significant perhaps, is this: that in Part II of 'Entity and Indentity' I make what is in effect a terminological recommendation. I there suggest that the application of the familiar phrase 'criterion of identity' should be restricted to those cases in which the supposed criteria can be precisely and strictly stated in a clearly applicable form; and I mention, as examples of cases in which this condition is satisfied, the classical examples of the criteria of identity for directions of straight lines and for the numbers of members of sets. This demanding condition is clearly not satisfied in the cases of ordinary substantial individuals such as dogs or men. So the suggestion has the consequence that we should, contrary to our normal practice in philosophy, give up using the phrase 'criterion of identity' in the case of such substances; though I qualify the consequence by adding that, since the possession of the relevant substance-concept, 'dog' or 'man', certainly equips us to answer identity-questions about individuals of the kinds in question it is legitimate to say that each such concept provides us with a *principle* of identity for all individuals of the kind, even though the principle is not to count as a *criterion* of identity in the strict sense recommended. In the 'Universals' article I make no such restrictive stipulation, rather avoiding the issue by avoiding the phrase 'criterion of identity' and instead using 'principle of identity' throughout.

[1] P. F. Strawson, 'Two Conceptions of Philosophy', in *Perspectives on Quine* (Cambridge, Mass., and Oxford, 1990).

Here and now, however, I wish to be more explicit, and to go further; to retract what now seems to me an excessively puritanically strict recommendation about the use of the phrase 'criterion of identity' and to endorse instead its customary more comprehensive use. It is, of course, important to be aware of the distinction I drew between those cases in which the criteria can be precisely stated and those in which they cannot; but it now seems to me both excessively fussy to try to insist that the very use of the phrase should be confined to the former cases and, moreover, pointlessly fussy since it is clear that philosophers generally are not likely to take any notice of such a recommendation. So here is a relatively minor point at which I feel that recantation is in order. I hope it does not sound arrogant to say that it is the only point.

That seems enough by way of comparative textual comment. But it is still worth rehearsing the main points of positive argument. It is conceded, in the first place, that in order to be in a position legitimately to acknowledge as a genuine individual or entity any pretender to that status, we must be in possession of a principle of identity for that individual, a principle which we can and do actually use to settle identity-questions regarding that individual. As regards ordinary particular spatio-temporal individuals, that principle is supplied by some general concept of a kind or sort under which the particular individual in question falls—and this holds good whether the individual in question is a relatively enduring substantial individual or a passing event or protracted process or a state or whatever. We need such general principles of identity for *particulars* because *particular* individuals do not have *individual essences* which could serve the relevant purpose.

But the case is different with abstract or general things. They do have individual essences. In the case of many, perhaps most, of such things which we recognize, the individual essence is captured by, is identical with, the *sense* of some adjective or common noun or verb, or with that of the relevant abstract noun if there is one. (Even if there does not exist, or we do not know the sense of, a relevant expression, the ability to recognize particular instances or exemplifications of some general characteristic as such shows that we have grasped its individual essence—and can, if we choose, introduce a word for it.) Because the individual essence of the general thing constitutes its individual identity, we have no need of a *common* general principle of identity for all the general things of some more general kind to which the given general thing belongs. I give sufficient examples of this.

Of course this is not to deny that there are *some* universals or abstract general things for which there do also exist common general principles of identity for all the things of some more general kind to which the abstract things in question belong. Favourite examples, of course, are classes and numbers. I suggested others: the members, themselves abstract, of certain art-forms such as the sonnet or sonata; and certain natural kinds, such as animal species and chemical substances, for which the development of natural science may be held to have yielded common general principles of identity. But some of the general characteristics or features which are of most interest to us are never likely to join them—notably attributes or properties in general, the targets of particular hostility on the part of the enemies of intensions. I give plenty of examples.

2. The mention of properties leads naturally to the next pair of articles, 'Positions for Quantifiers' and 'Properties and Concepts', which it is again appropriate to consider in conjunction. Any careful reader of 'Positions for Quantifiers' will find reason for suspecting me of confusion. The reason is this. I appear to be arguing among other things for the legitimacy, and indeed reality in natural language, of quantification into predicate position, while at the same time rejecting the suggestion that such quantification could at best be understood as involving objectual quantification, in the sense made familiar by Quine, over attributes (e.g. properties or action-kinds). But then, in the last section (IV) of the paper I seem to say something which is in effect inconsistent with this rejection. For I say that in using the sentences 'Socrates is brave' or

'Socrates swims' we just as surely specify or introduce the attribute, bravery, or the action-kind, swimming, as we do if we use the noun 'bravery' or the action-kind name 'swimming'. So if quantifying in the place of the names 'bravery' and 'swimming' would be objectual quantification in Quine's sense, so no less would be quantifying in the place of the adjective and the verb.

I think the apparent inconsistency is real; but also that the *confusion* is happily resolved in the later and much shorter article, 'Properties and Concepts', where the predicate expressions 'is brave' and 'swims' are resolved into a copulative element (which of course stands for nothing) on the one hand and, on the other, the adjective or verb-stem which stands for or introduces or specifies the relevant property or action-kind—so that quantification into its place is indeed in Quine's sense objectual, i.e. quantification over such items. Of course Quine has his own reasons for not welcoming such a conclusion; but that is another story, which was told and dealt with in the two articles discussed in section 1 above of this Introduction.

So, then, a good deal of the polemical heat is drained out of 'Positions for Quantifiers'—in so far as I was there arguing, in the case of quantification into predicate place, in favour of recognizing a species of quantification which was not objectual at all, was not quantification *over* anything. When I went on to consider Prior's proposal for quantification into sentence-position, I was, explicitly this time, partially on Quine's side in that I maintained that it was far more realistically in tune with natural language to recognize quantification *over* propositions than it was to accept Prior's proposal. But, again, this is not the sort of alliance that Quine would welcome, since he is no more kindly disposed to propositions than he is to attributes or properties as objects or entities.

So far, then, I seem to have settled for purely objectual quantification, even though the objects involved include many that the anti-intensionalists would refuse to countenance. But this is not the end of the story. For, in the same article, 'Positions for Quantifiers', I mentioned another class of expressions which seem strikingly parallel to such conventionally recognized natural language quantifiers as 'anything', 'nothing', 'everything', 'whatever', 'something', 'whoever', etc. These are, we might say, quantifier expressions of place, time, and manner. I listed 'somewhere', 'nowhere', 'everywhere', 'wherever'; 'always', 'sometimes', 'never', 'whenever'; 'somehow', 'anyhow', 'however'; and suggested that to recognize, as characteristic of natural language, a distinct species of quantification, into adverbial or adverbial phrase position, would be more realistic than to try to force its examples into the conventional mode of quantification over times, places, and manners. Not only do such attempts seem generally excessively artificial. The alternative suggestion here made chimes well with any proposal for understanding the logical, or semantic-syntactic, structure of sentences containing adverbial modification of action-verbs which stays close to the surface structure of natural language sentences[2]—an idea always to be aimed at if we seek to understand our own understanding of the structure of our language.

3. The next three essays are all concerned in very different ways with the topic of reference. The first is the simplest, but rates a brief summary. It begins with the assumption that definite singular terms for particular (i.e. spatio-temporal) individuals are sometimes used purely referentially or, as I express it in the paper concerned, with the intention of making a direct singular reference to such an individual. This use is characterized semantically by saying that when such a singular term, successfully so used, is coupled with a predicate to express a proposition, that proposition is true just in case the individual in question satisfies that predicate, false just in case it does not.

It follows from this characterization that the descriptive content, if any, which a singular term, so used, possesses,

[2] Cf. P. F. Strawson, 'On Understanding the Structure of One's Language', *Freedom and Resentment* (London, 1974), ch. 11, and 'Meaning and Understanding: Structural Semantics', *Analysis and Metaphysics* (Oxford, 1992), ch. 8.

while it may bear on the question, what individual, if any, is successfully referred to and hence on the identity of the proposition, if any, actually expressed, is otherwise irrelevant to the truth-conditions of any such proposition. If everything goes ideally well as far as direct singular reference is concerned in a communication situation in which a speaker intends to make such a reference, it is fairly obvious that three conditions must be fulfilled: the actual existence of just one individual item which the speaker intends to refer to; that item's satisfying the descriptive content, if any, of the term employed; and, finally, the communication situation being such that any competently equipped audience would understand the speaker to be referring to just that individual and not any other.

Now any one of these conditions may fail to be fulfilled, and there is quite a large number of possible combinations of failure. In the article in question I select and illustrate five different cases in which not all of the three conditions are satisfied, and then list three different types of possible 'theoretical' responses to these five cases. Within each 'theory' the responses to different cases may differ, and, when they do so, they differ because of the different weights attached in each theory to the fulfilment of the second and the third of the conditions mentioned. I conclude that it is futile to insist that just one type of theoretical response is right and the others simply wrong. What is necesary, in order to be clear about the facts, is simply to grasp what are the normally satisfied conditions of the successful use of directly referential terms in communication and to understand the variant reactions that may be evoked by their partial failure.

The second of these papers, 'Belief, Reference, and Quantification', is rather more complicated. It is concerned with contexts of the form 'x believes that p' (which may be taken as representative of propositional attitude contexts in general). It shares with the previous paper the assumption that definite singular terms may sometimes be employed to make direct references to particular individuals, and adds that such reference may sometimes occur within clauses following 'believes that'; from which it follows that existential quantification into such contexts is in such cases (though not necessarily in them alone) permissible.

The first question considered in the paper, however, relates to problems which arise concerning belief-contexts in general, including, but not confined to, those involving quantifying-in. These problems are solved, without implausibly multiplying senses of 'believe', if we are prepared to recognize, besides 'believe' as a two-place predicate of persons and propositions, an indefinitely numerous class of variably place-numbered *compound* predicates such as 'believes to be wise' or 'believes to love', where, in the second case, the order of the place-fillers following the predicate indicates the ordering of the pair related by the relation of loving. I have to admit, however, that while the solution is formally satisfactory and seems to me both plausible and reasonably natural, it has not evoked any noticeable positive response. So my own enthusiasm for it, never vast, has waned.

In the same article I turn next to a class of sentences which have long engaged philosophical attention, viz. identity-sentences coupling two proper names. In their case the price of taking each name to be used with the function of direct reference seems unacceptably high; for doing so would yield the result that the proposition expressed whenever such a sentence was used communicatively would, if true, amount to no more than the trivially uninformative assertion that the individual referred to was identical with itself, a result clearly incompatible with the obvious fact that the audience of such an assertion may genuinely learn something from it, may be substantially informed by it. The problem is only exacerbated when a sentence of this class is embedded in a context of the form 'A does not know (or believe) that . . .'. For the proposition expressed by the embedding sentence as a whole may well be true even though our A has a command of both names, i.e. knows, in a perfectly good sense, which individual is being referred to by each; while, of course, as a rational person, he cannot fail to be aware of the trivial necessity that every individual is self-identical.

So the search seems to be on both for the informative proposition actually expressed by such an embedding sentence and for that expressed by the embedded sentence. The point made in my article is that there is no way, in any given case, of exactly specifying any such propositions, though the point may be obscured by the nature of the over-familiar example (Hesperus/Phosphorus) usually considered in philosophical discussion of the question. So I conclude in the article that nothing more than a somewhat remote general characterization of such propositions is to be had. But even this is less satisfactory than the alternative of giving up the search for the propositions involved or even for such a general characterization of them in favour of a certain general model: namely a general model both of the information-state of someone capable of being substantially informed by an identity-statement of the kind in question and of the way in which his state of ignorance or non-belief would be transformed by being the audience of such a statement. Just such a model I offer in the book, *Subject and Predicate in Logic and Grammar*.[3]

In the last section of 'Belief, Reference, and Quantification' I revert to the assumption that definite singular terms may sometimes be used with purely referential intention within belief-contexts, and add the assumption that such terms, so used, may sometimes include definite descriptions. These assumptions raise a number of questions about the correct interpretation of utterances containing definite descriptions in the embedded clauses of belief-contexts—questions of some complexity which I there attempt to answer.

Finally, I turn to the last of the three articles directly concerned with the topic of reference, 'Reference and its Roots'. This is a critical discussion of some of the views advanced by Quine in his book, *The Roots of Reference*. Though I somewhat regret the polemical tone of my comments, I see no reason to qualify their substance.

[3] P. F. Strawson, *Subject and Predicate in Logic and Grammar* (London, 1974), ch. 2, sect. 2.

4. The next two papers form a natural pair in so far as the first is concerned with the formal constants of standard logic in general, and the second with the relation of just one of them, the material conditional, to its natural language analogue, 'if . . . then . . .'.

The nature of the logical constants of standard logic was a question that H. P. Grice and I used to discuss in the early 1950s, and I have no doubt that the present paper, 'Logical Form and Logical Constants', though written much later, was influenced by those discussions. I do not suppose, however, that Grice would have agreed with, or approved of, the position I here take up. For one thing, he was too good at finding flaws in any philosophical view to be content with this one; and for another, he would have felt little, if any, sympathy with my explicitly acknowledged debt to Wittgenstein.

There are reasons for thinking that what is here attempted, namely to find an adequate general characterization of the notion of logical or logical constant, cannot be an easy thing to do. Russell regarded it as a major unsolved problem and Quine contents himself with a list. On the other hand, when we consider Kant's view of logic or Boole's or Wittgenstein's *Tractatus*, or even Quine himself on canonical notation, we may think it cannot be quite impossible.

I mention, as others have done, two obvious features of logical constants: first, their figuring in discourse about all kinds of subject-matter; second, their bearing on necessary relations of implication or incompatibility between propositions. But these features are much too widely shared by other expressions to serve the purpose by themselves.

Then I take my text from Wittgenstein,[4] quoted and glossed in the paper; and construe it as meaning that, properly understood, the bare notion of a proposition in general (an empirical proposition about how things are in the natural world) is all we need to explain the nature of the logical constants.

This is clearly an essentialist doctrine. So we must ask what

---

[4] L. Wittgenstein, *Tractatus Logico-Philosophicus* (London, 1961), 5. 47.

is essential to the 'very nature' of propositions so understood. I distinguish two essential features. One is the excluding power of every such proposition. To say that things are *thus-and-so* is to exclude other possibilities. The other is a certain necessary duality of function which, in a way, parallels at the linguistic level Kant's epistemic duality of concept and intuition, and which consists in having the means both of specifying *general* types of situation or object or event and of indicating their incidence, i.e. of attaching these general specifications to particular instances. Finally, we add the idea, essential to any language, of identifiable linguistic devices with conventional forces or meanings.

The aim, then, is to show that the force of the forms and constants of standard logic can be wholly explained without drawing on any materials beyond what we are given with the idea of what is essential to empirical statement-making in general. Taking the aforementioned relation of exclusion as fundamental, I proceed to define in its terms certain other possible relations between statements or propositions, viz. those of incompatibility, implication, and contradictoriness; and, finally, in terms of the last two, the relation which holds between one member of a trio of statements and the other two when the first is related to the others as their disjunction. All this is done without using any idea of any statements which themselves contain any logical constants.

At this point, and with respect to the last two defined relations, i.e. those of disjunctiveness and contradictoriness, I introduce the notion of a *form-description*, which is a description of a linguistic pattern or form or schema such that its whole conventional force or function is to exhibit any statements exemplifying it as standing in just such a relation without revealing anything else about their content or subject-matter. What falls under the form-description in the two cases concerned is, of course, in the disjunctive case, the schema trio, 'p, q, p ∨ q' and, in the contradictories case, the schema duo 'p, ~ p'. The negative and disjunctive forms now available supply us, as we know, with a sufficient basis for the definition of all the other constants of standard propositional truth-functional logic. The recurrence of a sentence-letter in a schema-pattern must obviously be taken, in any exemplification of such a pattern, as representing the recurrence not merely of a sentential clause but of the proposition expressed by it.[5]

Turning from propositional logic to quantification, I simplify my task by construing the necessary duality of function referred to earlier in terms of identifying reference to particular items and predicating general concepts of them. It is then easy to set up a form description under which falls the pattern displayed by 'Fx, $(\exists x)Fx$' where the recurrence of 'F' represents recurrence of sense-preserving predicate-expression and the free 'x' in 'Fx' represents variation of name or other singular term.

It might be said that the job is still incompletely done since it does not include a characterization of the identity-sign of logic. To this I would reply that the resources for doing so are already supplied. If, as argued earlier in this Introduction, quantification into predicate-place is intelligible and legitimate, we can simply offer a definition involving such quantification, thus:

$$x = y =_{Df} (F)(Fx \equiv Fy);$$

or, if we jib at this, simply produce the corresponding unquantified schema, declaring all its exemplifications valid.

Over and above achieving its announced purpose of giving a general characterization of the constants of standard logic, the solution has other merits: first, the two obvious features of logical constants which I earlier dismissed as too widely shared to constitute a clue to their nature emerge as simple consequences of their essential character as here set out; second, the doctrine that truths of logic are analytic ceases to be merely explicative of the concept 'analytic', and gives that concept the full force of 'true in virtue of meaning alone'—a

---

[5] The point is more fully developed in my 'Propositions, Concepts and Logical Truths' (*The Philosophical Quarterly*, 1957), repr. in *Logico-Linguistic Papers* (London, 1971).

force that concept may then the more confidently retain, in the face of widely shared scepticism, in the many applications for which there is no possibility of reduction, by definitions, to truths of logic.

Two further comments are in order. Though my Wittgensteinian text contains the germ of the idea of this paper, I cannot, of course, affirm—or deny—that Wittgenstein was actually thinking on just these lines. Finally, there is no guarantee that to all the forms or particles excogitatable in the way I have set out there will be exactly corresponding expressions in natural language—nor again that there will not. This thought introduces us to the topic of the next paper: the relation between the material conditional of logic and the natural language 'if . . . then . . .'.

My object in that paper was to argue against the thesis that the conventional meaning of the natural language form is identical with that of the material conditional. In pursuit of this aim I did two things: I offered a positive account of the meaning of 'if . . . then . . .' as what I called a quasi-inference or quasi-argument marker; then, after expounding and elaborating an ingenious argument developed by Grice, though adumbrated by Quine, in favour of the view I contest, I claimed to confute its conclusion.

I shall not here summarize the course of argument I followed, for I think it is clear enough as it stands. Instead I shall consider some complications or difficulties which I overlooked or did not explicitly confront in the article in question. The first difficulty emerges from points made in the paper itself. Anyone who affirms a natural indicative conditional is thereby committed, on the view of the conventional meaning of 'if . . . then' which I advocate, to accepting the truth of the corresponding material or truth-functional conditional. But it is also clear, as my treatment of the example of Melbourne and the sea shows, that one who, *without knowledge of the truth-values of antecedent or consequent*, nevertheless comes to accept the truth of an indicative material conditional, is thereby licensed to assert what I have called a quasi-inferential conditional.

And now it may come to seem that the natural and material conditionals have been shown to entail each other, i.e. to be equivalent, which was precisely the thesis to be contested. The argument seems inconclusive. From my perspective it can be held that the mutual entailment does not really hold, since it is only in the special case considered that the move from the truth-functional to the natural conditional is licensed. But this reply can seem equally inconclusive; for, from the Gricean perspective, it can be held that the material conditional would *always carry, though not as part of its meaning*, the conversational implications which are (mis)-represented, on the quasi-inferential view, as part of the conventional meaning of 'if . . . then . . .'.

But this last Gricean move opens the way to further weighty objections to the truth-functional view. One is the general linguistic point that there are many conjunctions of which the conventional force or meaning cannot be simply assimilated to that of any truth-functional constant, although any statement containing any of them will commit its utterer to accepting a simply truth-functional conjunction as true: e.g. 'since p, q', 'p, so q', 'p, but q', and 'p, although q'. The consequentialist or adversative implications carried by these conjunctions are uncontroversially part of their conventional meaning. Since there is every reason to expect language to contain a conjunction having the conventional quasi-inferential meaning which I attribute to 'if' and since 'if' is the obvious candidate for this role, it should be equally uncontroversial that the expression has it.

There remains one more simple and familar objection to the truth-functional view of the natural conditional. If this view were correct it would seem prima facie that anyone who denies or rejects an assertion of this form would be committed to accepting the conjunction of its antecedent with the negation of its consequent, i.e. to accepting as true the corresponding proposition of the form, 'p and not-q'; whereas in fact he would not be so committed, but would more naturally express his denial or rejection by saying something like 'If p, it does not in the least follow that q' or 'It could perfectly well be the case that p and not-q' or 'It is possible that p and not-q'. Even this objection is not quite as decisive as it seems; for the Gricean, though perhaps with a slight air of desperation, could reply that one who denies the conditional has no interest in denying what it conventionally and literally means, but only in denying what it standardly and conversationally implies.

There are other complications. These concern the relations between conditional and disjunctive forms. Listening to music someone may say 'Either this piece is by Mozart or it's by Haydn' or, apparently equivalently, 'If this piece is not by Mozart it's by Haydn'. The (here exclusive) disjunctive certainly appears to be truth-functional; if so, and if the apparent equivalence is real so must be the conditional. On the other hand the conditional appears to be quasi-inferential, and if the equivalence is real, and the quasi-inferential is not truth-functional, neither is the disjunctive. The problem, in its second form, is emphasized by the apparent equivalence of 'If I don't catch that bus, I shall have to walk all the way home' and 'Either I catch that bus or I shall have to walk'.

There are several possibilities of resolution here. It would be tedious to rehearse all of them. It seems to me that the least attractive is to accept that the natural disjunctive is always truth-functional, that it always has a natural conditional equivalent and hence that the latter is truth-functional too. The next least attractive, while insisting on the quasi-inferential account of the conditional, is to accept the equivalence and to deny the truth-functionality of disjunctives. More satisfactory, I think, is to accept the quasi-inferential character of the conditional and the truth-functionality of the disjunctive and to allow that an instance of either may intelligibly *ground* a corresponding instance of the other. This seems to honour realism and to violate no cherished intuition.

I conclude with a historical note. I composed the paper '"If" and "⊃"' many years before its publication, shortly after I had the pleasure of listening to Grice expounding the essentials of his view of 'if' in a paper read to the Philosophical Society in Oxford in the late 1950s. Since Grice refrained from publishing his doctrine for many years I too held back my critique of it till the projected appearance of Grandy and Warner's book made any such restraint gratuitous.

5. The next paper, 'May Bes and Might Have Beens', stands a little aside from all the others, in that it has no obvious partners. It is concerned with modalities, in particular, possibilities. Now the field of modality in general is one of intense and enduring controversy. Yet my treatment of possibilities here succeeds, I think, in skirting or avoiding almost completely all the issues in the field which have provoked the fiercest debates. This is because the aspect or kind of possibility I here discuss is essentially epistemic. The possibilities I speak of stand in contrast, not with necessities or actualities, but with certainties. I think I have made a case for saying that this is an area in which we make serious and interesting use of the notion—or one notion—of possibility. As I remark at the end, I do not say, or think, that it is the only notion or the only use.

6. The next two papers, 'Austin and "Locutionary Meaning"' and 'Meaning and Context', are both essays in the pragmatics-semantics of language-use. They have more in common than that. They both relate to the simple threefold distinction between senses of the phrase, 'the meaning of what was said' which is set out in full in section I of the first essay and referred to repeatedly in the second. In the essay on Austin the threefold distinction is used as the basis for a thoroughgoing examination and critique of Austin's position. In 'Meaning and Context' the threefold distinction itself comes under criticism: as it stands, it is shown to be too simple to provide either for all the complexities of language-use or for all the divisions of the material of speech which may be of concern to logicians, philosophers of language, and even to linguists. Nevertheless, in both connections, the distinction is shown to be not without value; in each, it serves as

an ideal starting-point for the widely differing criticisms that
follow.

Another word about my paper on Austin is in order. The
text of *How To Do Things with Words* was carefully put
together after Austin's death from notes of lectures which he
had regularly delivered over a period of years. It cannot be
assumed, therefore, to be such as he would himself have been
quite content to publish. However, given the identity of the
editors, it can be assumed to be a reasonably accurate record
of the content of those lectures. Everyone who heard them—
as I did not myself—was greatly impressed by their original-
ity and insight, their freshness and wit. It is hardly too much
to say that in them Austin created a whole new field of
investigation in the philosophy of language and in linguistic
theory in general—a field subsequently cultivated by others
who learned from him.

It is not to be expected that one who largely originates a
field will always succeed in defining its terms and distinctions
with complete clarity. My paper is concerned with an area in
which, I think, Austin in fact failed to do this: the area,
namely, of the distinction between what he calls the 'meaning' of an utterance and its 'force' or, correspondingly, between the 'locutionary' and the 'illocutionary' aspects of the
act of making an utterance. I consider two candidate interpretations of that distinction, suggested by some of the things
he says, but incompatible with others. I then tentatively
sketch a third, also suggested by some of the things he says;
but it is clear from the text that he would not have found this
proposal satisfactory. I discuss some reasons, connected with
his views about the concept of truth, which Austin might have
been disposed to give for being dissatisfied with this proposal;
and conclude that they are bad reasons. The topic of the next
paper, 'Meaning and Context' overlaps at a number points
with the topics of this.

7. We come now to my four Kantian studies. Of these the
first two form a natural pair. Both are concerned with two

central issues in the reading or interpretation of the first *Critique*. One issue is that of the a priori status accorded to the forms of intuition and the categories. The other is the contested question of the interpretation of the notion of things in themselves or, in other words, of how we should understand 'transcendental idealism'. On the first issue, it is held in both papers that we should acknowledge a compelling argument at least quasi-Kantian[6] in favour of according a priori status to the notions of space and time; and it may be conceded that there is an equally strong case for according the same privileged status to the central categories, properly understood, of substance and cause.[7]

The second question, of the nature of things in themselves, is of a very different character. Here we are presented with a stark choice between alternative readings. On the one hand we have the possibility of an anodyne interpretation of the doctrine that things as they are in themselves are in principle unknowable, an interpretation that leaves us with a quite straightforward empirical realism about the world of things in space and time, though a realism embellished, indeed, with a brilliant account of necessary structural aspects of our knowledge of that world, and qualified only by the harmless admission that some of its features may forever remain unknown to us. On the other we have the uncompromising doctrine of things in themselves as constituting a supersensible reality utterly inaccessible to beings with our cognitive equipment, who must perforce be content with knowledge of appearances only. It is hard to render this even intelligible without so radically modifying it as to bring it uncomfortably close to the idealism of one to whom Kant patronizingly refers as 'the good Berkeley'.

It is difficult, finally, not to see Kant as torn between these two alternatives; drawn towards the first by his respect for

---

[6] The argument is also advanced in Strawson, *Subject and Predicate in Logic and Grammar*, 15–16; 'Sensibility, Understanding and Synthesis', in E. Forster (ed.), *Kant's Transcendental Deductions* (Stanford, 1989), 72; and *Analysis and Metaphysics*, 54–6.

[7] Cf. P. F. Strawson, *The Bounds of Sense* (London, 1966), Pt. Two, III, esp. 3 and 5.

natural science, and towards the second by what he conceived of as the interests of morality and rational religion.

8. The remaining two Kantian studies are concerned, not, like the preceding two, with the system of the *Critique* as a whole, but with distinct aspects of it. I find nothing to qualify in either. But there are points worth making about each.

Kant's brilliant critique in the Paralogisms of the errors of 'rational psychology' has an obvious bearing on later philosophical discussions of self-consciousness. It helps us to see clearly that if, but only if, we unwisely abstract from the platitude that the first personal pronoun 'I', in the thought of any individual human being, refers precisely to that total human being, man or woman, then we may be forced to conclude that in self-ascription in thought of states of consciousness the pronoun either has no reference at all or must be taken to refer to an immaterial substance or soul, a Cartesian ego. The first alternative was briefly favoured by Wittgenstein and later by Miss Anscombe.[8] The second may yet have a lingering appeal for those few, if any, thinkers who continue unfashionably to hanker for such an entity. What is actually demonstrated is the ineptitude of making the aforementioned abstraction. This is not a conclusion that Kant explicitly draws, for his concerns are other; but there is no reason to think he would have resisted it, and some reason to think he would have embraced it.

The unsparing criticism in the second article of Kant's official statement of his views on substance is quite consistent with the recognition that the category of substance, in the more limited quasi-Aristotelian sense, contributes essentially to the conception of the unitary spatio-temporal world of which we can and do acquire empirical knowledge.

By way of concluding this Introduction, I wish to remark on what will have been obvious enough, namely the fact that in most of the papers on philosophy of language and logic my

---

[8] E. Anscombe, 'The First Person', in S. Guttenplan (ed.), *Mind and Language* (Oxford, 1975).

stance is consistently opposed to the uncompromisingly extensionalist views associated with W. V. Quine and his followers; and to add that my opposition on this central matter detracts nothing from my admiration for the power, brilliance, and elegance with which Quine himself upholds this austere position.

# I

# *Entity and Identity*

A slogan—'no entity without identity'—and a phrase—'criterion of identity'—have achieved great popularity in recent philosophy and have been used with more freedom than caution. I shall first discuss the slogan and shall argue that it expresses no very powerful principle. In doing so I shall make an uncritical use of the phrase. Then I shall turn my attention to the phrase and shall argue that, as at present employed, it expresses no single clear idea and should either be dropped from the philosophical vocabulary or be employed only under quite severe restrictions.

I

1. 'No entity without identity.' The slogan sounds well, but how are we to understand it? Does it mean: (i) 'There is nothing which is not itself'? This seems to say too little. Does it mean: (ii) 'There is nothing which does not belong to some sort such that there is a common, general criterion of identity for all things of that sort'? This says, I think, too much. Does it mean: (iii) 'Some things belong to sorts such that for each such sort there is a general criterion of identity for all things of that sort, while other things do not: only things of the first kind are *entities* (objects), things of the second kind are not'? This sounds like nonsense or, at best, a stipulation of which one would wish to know the point.

Another possible interpretation of the slogan, less vacuous than the first, more cautious than the second, less mysterious than the third—though vaguer than any of them—might run something like this: 'There is nothing you can sensibly talk about without knowing, at least in principle, how it might be identified.' I have nothing to say against *this* admirable maxim; I shall return to it at the end of the paper.

How has the slogan been used? It has been used, for one thing, to discredit attributes or properties in comparison with classes. For the latter we have a general criterion of identity: the class of α-things is identical with the class of β-things if and only if all α-things are β-things and conversely. No such general recipe can be supplied for determining property-identity. Given the intention to discredit attributes, the comparison is unimpressive, even on its own terms. For it leaves open the possibility that properties or attributes, like, say, saleable things or things with spatial position, fall into subcategories for which, or for some of which, general criteria of identity can be given. But my immediate interest in this application of the slogan is not in its adequacy or inadequacy on its own terms but in its revelation of what those terms are. The terms are those of either the second or the third interpretation (of either (ii) or (iii) above); and presumably the third. For, as I have already suggested and shall now show, 'There is nothing (or nothing identifiable) which does not belong to a sort such that a generally applicable criterion of identity can be given for things of that sort' is fairly obviously false.

I remarked just now that the fact that there were no generally statable criteria of identity for attributes, properties, or qualities did not exclude the possibility of attributes, etc., falling into subcategories for which such criteria could be given. But in fact such criteria cannot in general be given for the subcategories either. There are no general criteria of identity for colours,[1] intellectual qualities, qualities of character, or affective attitudes. Nor are there—to extend our range—for smells, feels, timbres, ways of walking, manners of speech, literary styles, architectural styles or hair-styles. But

---

[1] There might be said to be for 'minimally discriminable shades' of colour: but even here there would be difficulties.

under all these heads there fall things we can identify or learn to identify, can recognize or learn to recognize, as the same again in different situations.

The cases differ. Suppose someone has mastered the use of the expressions 'blue', 'witty', 'cheerful', 'loves'. He knows how to apply them to visibilia, persons, and pairs. Then, and so far, he knows how to identify the corresponding colour, intellectual quality, quality of character, and affective attitude. The criterion of application of the predicate *is* the individual criterion of identity of the *individual* quality or relation. The sense of the general term gives the individual essence of the general thing. So there is no need for *general* criteria of identity for things of the kind to which the general thing belongs.

Consider next smells or musical *timbres*. There are no general criteria of identity for them. Nor are they directly named, as blue, wit, cheerfulness, and love are directly named. Yet they are often as distinctive, as easily recognizable, as anything in our experience. We borrow names for them, of course, from the kinds of things they are causally associated with: but it is only adventitiously true, if true at all, that the smell of α-kind things is the same as the smell of β-kind things if and only if α is the same kind as β. So in smells we have general things which can be ostended and recognized as the same again even though there is neither a general criterion of identity for them nor any set of names or general terms which gives for each its essence.

Consider now ways of walking, manners of speaking, characteristic styles of gesture. They can be *demonstrated* by any skilful mimic: '*This* is the way he walks.' They too are among the most readily recognizable, most readily identifiable features of our experience: how often we identify a distant friend or acquaintance by recognizing such a feature. These features again, if they have names, have in general only derived names: X's manner of speaking, Y's way of walking. But we cannot draw criteria of identity from the possibility of derived names. Not only can the mimic reproduce, but someone else (another member of the family perhaps) might untheatrically exhibit, the very manner of speaking which we first encountered in X.

I will not linger on literary styles, architectural styles, or hair-styles. There are no general criteria of identity for them either. But they are things that any trained eye or ear can recognize and any competent specialist can reproduce. Often they too have derived names, but the names indicate no exclusiveness of possession. Strawberry Hill Gothic is not found only at Strawberry Hill, and not all buildings in the Palladian style were designed by Palladio.

It will be said that the identities I have been speaking of lack sharpness of definition. And so they do—in more than one way. The extensions of the corresponding predicates have no sharp cut-off points. It is not quite clear where wit ends and (mere) sarcasm begins, where cheerfulness turns into boisterousness, when we no longer have the Transitional style, but the true Gothic. But nor is it quite clear when we have left the town or are out of the wood, where the mountain ends and the foothills begin or when the estuary becomes the sea. There is another aspect of indeterminacy, turning, not on the indefinite limits of application of a name or general term, but on variation in the fineness of discrimination required. I suppose heights, weights, and temperatures are things for which general criteria may be said at least to be stipulatable, in so far as we have balances, and measures, and in so far as we can give these quantities numerical values. But then there are variations in the sensitivity of balances and measures, variations in the degrees of deviation from indiscriminability of level which we are interested in, variations in the number of decimal places to which we are concerned to take our numerical values. And upon these variations will depend the answers we give to questions of the form: Is the weight/height/temperature of this the same as the weight/height/temperature of that? We find similar variation in the case of colours, which we learned to identify long before we associated *them* with numerical quantities. Is the colour of her eyes the same as the colour of the material of her dress? Yes, because they are both blue. No, because her eyes are a lighter blue. Is the blue of the sky in Oxford on this cloudless day in July the same blue as the blue of the sky in Florence on that cloudless day in June? Is your hair-style the same as mine? Do he and she have the same way of walking? It depends. It depends on how fine we want our discriminations to be.

2. I shall take it as agreed that the identifiability of something does not require that it be of a sort such that there exist general criteria of identity for things of that sort.[2] That is, I shall take it that (ii) is false; which leaves us to consider (iii). It may now be said that many of the identifiable things I have been discussing are really nothing but principles of discriminating among, or grouping together, independently identifiable things which do belong to sorts such that, for each such sort, there exists a criterion of identity for things of that sort. This may not be so for all the things I have been discussing— perhaps not, or not always, for colours and certainly not, in general, for smells. But though not all the things I have been discussing are merely general characters or features of independently identifiable things, many of them are: qualities of character and intellect belong to, or are manifested by, people; so are affective attitudes; manners of walking and talking are exhibited by things which walk and talk; architectural styles are exemplified by buildings, literary styles by literary works, hair-styles by heads of hair. And people, buildings, books, and heads do belong to sorts such that there exist general criteria of identity for things belonging to those sorts. Does this not begin to show a point in the third interpretation of our original dictum, the interpretation which I said was at best a stipulation, at worst nonsense?

I will return later to this thought or half-thought. First, I

---

[2] Anyone unconvinced by the examples may be invited to reflect that it would be very odd to hold that *criteria* of *identity* were not themselves identifiable. It will hardly be appealing to hold that they form a single sort with one (self-applicable?) criterion of identity for all members of the sort; and the difficulty will simply be postponed by the suggestion that they fall into subsets with a different criterion of identity associated with each subset.

want to ask a question which is not, I think, normally asked. It is agreed that some identifiabilia belong to sorts such that there exist general criteria of identity for things of those sorts, while other identifiabilia do not. Now what accounts for this difference? Why do some identifiabilia belong to the first class (the class favoured by our slogan on its third interpretation) while others do not? There is no reason to think that the explanation will take the same form for all identifiabilia of the first or slogan-favoured class.

It has been said[3] that animal species belong to a sort such that there exist general criteria of identity for things of that sort. The same has been said of chemical substances. If we imagine a primitive tribe who encounter, say, wolves, sheep, and bison, they may reasonably be supposed to distinguish and identify these animal-kinds. They have, of course and thereby, general criteria of identity for animals belonging to these kinds. But there seems no reason for saying that they have general criteria of identity for animal-kinds. They discriminate and group as they find it natural and useful to do so. That is all. We, or the experts among us, are in a different position. We have a systematic taxonomy of orders, families, genera, and species: principles for deciding whether or not to count a given plant or animal as belonging to a hitherto unknown species or as a member of an already recognized species. It is the *system* which gives sense to the idea of criteria of identity for species. It is the development of a science which underlies the possibility of such general criteria.

As in the organic, so in the inorganic realm. Our savages, no doubt, distinguish and identify various sorts of stuff. But they have no general criteria of identity for *kinds* of stuff. In the chemical notions of element, compound, and mixture, however, and the analysis of these, we find what may reasonably be regarded as such criteria. The science of chemistry supplies such criteria because it supplies systematic principles of classification.

---

[3] By Michael Dummett in *Frege: Philosophy of Language*.

Perhaps something similar now holds good of diseases and of medically interesting conditions in general. I do not know. The general point is clear enough. It is when unsystematic classification gives place to systematic classification that we can begin to make sense of talking of general criteria of identity not just for things that belong to kinds, but for the kinds themselves.

As far as *kinds* found in nature are concerned, this answers the question: what underlies the possibility of general criteria of identity? Natural history gives birth to natural science and in so doing gives birth to this possibility. But art history and literary history are not likely to have any comparable progeny; and unless they do, there will never be general criteria of identity for literary or architectural styles. The sensitive and learned discriminate and name; and the rest of us learn from them.

3. As far as universal or general things are concerned, we have, then, a partial answer to our question. General things divide roughly—only roughly—into those which belong to sorts such that there exist general criteria of identity for things of those sorts and those which do not. Styles, smells, colours, traits of intellect and character, and pre-scientifically distinguished kinds of organism or stuff are identifiable without benefit of general criteria of identity for smells, styles, traits, etc. Because biology, botany, chemistry, supply principles of systematic classification, we may say that biological, botanical, and chemical kinds *are* subject to general criteria of identity. But in spite of this difference, the cases are not really so very far apart. We might say that where the general thing is directly named, a full grasp of the sense of the name carries in every case a grasp of the *individual* criterion of identity for the general thing named; the difference is that when we have a principled system of classification, a science, a full grasp of the name carries also a grasp of the principles of classification, and hence a grasp of what we have agreed to call general criteria of identity associated with the sort to which the general thing belongs.

How different is the case of particular things, the case of spatio-temporal particulars! That particular things should belong to sorts such that there exist general criteria of identity for things of those sorts seems, on the face of it, no refinement of science but an absolute requirement of the identifiability of such things. If such a thing has a name, the fact that command of its name puts us in the way of a capacity to identify that thing (if it does) seems to depend essentially on the fact that our grasp of the name includes our knowledge of a sort to which the thing belongs and which is such that there exist general criteria of identity for things of that sort. Now what is the general principle underlying the identifiability of particular things belonging to sorts? The standard and essentially correct answer adverts to the special relationship which obtains, in the case of such things, between space and time on the one hand and some recognizable general form on the other. In the case of relatively enduring particulars—horses, men, beds, billiard balls, mountains—it is, with some familiar qualifications, some characteristic continuous manifestation of some recognizable general form through some space-time tract that yields the particular individual. So you can identify the individual because you can identify the form and, in principle, track the space-time path of a particular characteristic continuous manifestation of it. Of course there are qualifications to be made here—some beds, for example, can be dismantled and reassembled, though horses cannot; and there are many subordinate types of particular which should be distinguished and discussed in any full treatment. But if the account is *substantially* correct, there is one consequence which we should note at once—not a new consequence, rather a truth almost as old as our subject: viz. that the identifiability of a particular individual of a certain substantial sort depends upon and presupposes the identifiability of a certain general form.

This should cause us to review that half-thought I mentioned earlier. The suggestion was that, setting aside the awkward case of sense-qualia (colours and smells), those identifiabilia which did not belong to sorts such that there existed general criteria of identity for things of those sorts were all, as it were, dependent identifiabilia. They were, it was suggested, essentially general features or characters or modes of being or behaving exemplified by other independently identifiable things—people or buildings for example—which did belong to sorts such that there existed general criteria of identity for things of those sorts. Here, it was suggested or half suggested, lay a ground of preference for things of the latter kind, for awarding them the status of entities and denying it to things of the former kind. Let us distinguish these kinds by speaking of 'g-sorted' identifiabilia (i.e. those belonging to sorts such that there exist general criteria of identity for things belonging to those sorts) and 'g-unsorted' identifiabilia. Qualities of character or intellect (like cheerfulness, generosity, or wit) are g-unsorted identifiabilia, people (like Tom, Dick, and Harry) are g-sorted identifiabilia; and it is true that you can only distinguish and identify qualities of character or intellect because you can distinguish and identify people. But this and comparable facts supply no general or conclusive reason for the preference in question. For, as we have just seen, you can distinguish and identify those individuals which are preeminently g-sorted identifiabilia only because you can distinguish and identify the form of the sort. And the forms of the sorts are not, or not originally, g-sorted identifiabilia. So if we are to find any ground for the stipulation about entities—for interpretation (iii) of our slogan—it must be another ground.

A general argument to the same conclusion is this. Some sorts of g-sorted identifiabilia must themselves be identifiable as a condition of applying the criterion of identity for the sort. But on pain of infinite regress not all sorts can themselves be g-sorted. So the ultimate identifiabilia—those upon the identifiability of which the identifiability of all else depends—must be themselves g-unsorted.

I lay little weight on this general argument. It has altogether too abstract a character to be entirely convincing or trustworthy.

4. Before returning to the main line of the discussion, I should like to pursue a little further the question, why spatio-temporal particulars must be g-sorted. As I have remarked, it may seem obvious, even trivial, that they must be. For if we inquire in the most general terms into the basic nature of the particular—the nature of the primary particulars we distinguish—we must come to an answer somewhat like this: the being of the particular consists in a certain unique disposition in space and time of some general and in principle repeatable pattern or form (where we allow this notion—of a pattern or form—to include that of development over time). For any (primary) particular there must be such a pattern or form which is sufficient to yield a principle of identification for all particulars that exemplify it: it would be possible, in principle, in the case of any such particular, to give its identification, to say which or what it was, by specifying the general pattern and specifying the appropriate disposition of the pattern in space and time. Now this thought is wholly theoretical and, it might seem, *practically* empty. Yet it may have the merit of leading us to enquire what kinds of concepts of forms must be evolved if there is ever to be the practical possibility of identifying particulars as we do. It is clear, for example, that some forms must be such as to be themselves reasonably readily identifiable—and also such as to yield the possibility of relating our particulars in space and time, i.e. of supplying a space-time framework for the general determination of particular spatio-temporal dispositions of forms. Thus there emerge the sortals under which we primitively identify those particulars which supply the organizing framework of all our historical and geographical knowledge—concepts of space-occupying things, characteristically featured, some static, some mobile, with some endurance through time, concepts which allow for change in individual members of the sort and for variation of character from one member to another of the same sort. Once the framework exists, particulars of subordinate categories—notably sorts of event or process—become generally identifiable in relation to it.

This is familiar ground. I traverse it again, partly to emphasize the gap that exists between (*a*) the bare theoretical thought that the general notion of a particular already implies that of a g-sort to which it belongs, and (*b*) the make-up of the actual conceptual apparatus of sorts which we evolve to meet our needs. But, further, the question might be raised whether the bare theoretical thought is even correct. Could we not devise techniques for identifying particular space-occupying things which had histories but were not covered by any plausible sortal? Is it not clear that, even as things stand, we acknowledge particulars of which we might well hesitate to say that their being consists in a certain particular disposition in time and space of a certain general *pattern* or *form*. Particular *loads*, *cargoes*, *consignments* trace paths through space, have histories, suffer accidents. Yet we could scarcely identify a common *form* in their case. Again, for political or proprietorial reasons, we make certain divisions of the physical world which, those reasons apart, would seem quite arbitrary: the resulting *domains*, as we may generally call them, are surely particulars too. Such examples, however, do not by themselves constitute a serious objection. It is clear that these are particulars of derivative types, defined in relation to more 'natural' sorts; and there is really no reason why we should hesitate to count 'load', 'cargo', 'consignment', and various domain-terms as sortals, though derivative sortals. The examples simply show that we can frame more sophisticated concepts of particulars on the basis of more primitive ones.

Now consider what seems a more radical objection. Suppose we made a camera pan more or less at random for half an hour through the streets and countryside, and then declared that there was an individual object, lasting half an hour, composed, at any moment, of all and only what, at that moment, was being photographed, taken to a certain specified depth below the visible surface. Given suitable care in the manipulation of the camera, this object would be a spatio-temporally continuous individual with a striking enough history of development; for it would keep on gaining and losing parts. There could perhaps be other techniques for defining similarly arbitrary individuals, the common aim of all such techniques being that of detaching the idea of a spatio-temporally continuous individual (hence, *a fortiori*, a particular) from that of a covering sortal of any kind. Such individual particulars would resemble waves, or short-lived shifting sandbanks, in their successive occupation of different and overlapping parts of space and in their steady loss and compensating gain of parts; but would be covered by no such familiar sortal as waves or shifting sandbanks.

The objection fails. For we could define a sort of such particulars by reference to the technique employed in delimiting them; and this would yield a general principle of identity applicable to all the particulars delimited by a specified general technique. The case is not altogether dissimilar to that of a load or that of a domain. The major difference is that whereas there is a practical human point in distinguishing and identifying particular loads and particular domains, no point has so far been supplied for distinguishing and identifying the particulars delimited by the camera-panning technique.

Yet surely, it may be said, there are exceptions to the principle of the necessary sortedness of particulars. What of those items which some philosophers have spoken of as 'parcels' or 'quantities' of stuff, for example the gold which, as it happens, at this moment, is the gold in this room? Or the water which happens, at this moment, to be the water in this glass? Would it not be too illiberal a handling of the concept *particular* to deny such items the status of particulars? And would it not be too liberal a handling of the concept *sortal* to allow 'quantity of water' and 'quantity of gold' as sortals, either primary or derivative? For these phrases incorporate no notion of a distinctive form and none, either, of any such delimiting principle as we can find in 'load' or 'domain' or the artificial example just considered; for it is quite adventitious that the particular quantity of water in question happens just now to be all the water in this glass, and the past and future history of this particular allows for any mode and degree of scatter.

Suppose these items, then, admitted as particulars; and let us admit, too, that the relevant concepts, 'quantity of gold', 'quantity of water', are neither primary nor derivative sortals. Yet if it is insisted that these concepts are concepts of particulars which are all in principle capable of being identified as the same again, then it must be admitted that they are concepts of g-sorted particulars. Lacking sortal forms or delimiting principles, these particulars must, from the point of view of reidentifiability, be viewed simply as aggregates of the smallest portions of the relevant stuff, gold or water, of which they are constituted. So we see the identity of each as reducible to the identity of its constituent stuff-particles; and thus find a general criterion of identity, in the case of each kind of such particulars, for all the particulars of that kind. Of course, except in artificially favourable circumstances, it would be impossible to *apply* the 'criterion' with any strictness. So what is the value of the claim that it is a criterion? To this we reply: it has exactly the same value as the claim that these are genuinely reidentifiable particulars.

These last reflections gain a certain poignancy from the considerations of Part II of this essay.

5. But now I return to the main question of Part I: what justification, if any, is there for the third interpretation of our original dictum, i.e. for the doctrine that identifiabilia qualify as entities only if they are g-sorted identifiabilia? We have considered the suggestion that the identifiability of the g-unsorted always presupposes that of the g-sorted and not conversely; and found it false. I shall suggest instead that the appeal of the doctrine arises from two very different sources, the mingling of two very different kinds of consideration, which nevertheless, and not accidentally, reinforce each other in a certain way and up to a certain point. The first is the simple thought that it is the readily distinguishable material individuals of the world, the solid perceptible things, that are the real entities, the original, pre-eminent, undeniable objects: not form alone, or formless matter, but form and matter both—even though the form may simply be that of a *lump*. I have nothing to say against this ancient, earthy, and respectable prejudice. I merely wish to examine how it marries with

another thought. For the moment we are to note simply that these preferred and concrete objects are, of course, g-sorted identifiabilia, and sorted, for the most part, under the primary sortals which sort our particulars.

The second and more sophisticated thought construes the notion of 'object' or 'entity' in a different style, a logical style. Objects are, briefly, those identifiabilia which are the subjects of indispensable first-order predication: the greater the range of such predications and the more evident their indispensability, the more securely entrenched as objects those identifiabilia are. This thought yields us what we might call the 'predicate-worthiness' test for the status of entity.

It is evident that substantial objects—objects in our first and earthy sense—pass this test with flying colours. We tell the day-to-day story of our world, describe the changing postures of its states-of-affairs, essentially by means of predications of which such objects are the subjects; and we cannot seriously envisage any alternative way of doing so. What makes the story so rich in contingency, so essentially news, is just the fact that these objects, which supply, as I said, the organizing framework of all our historical or geographical knowledge, though they are essentially of this or that sort, have no *individual* essences. Each such object can be caught hold of, as it were, or identified, by this or that speaker or thinker, by this or that or the other of its unique characters or relations, but for no such object is there any unique character or relation by which it *must* be identified if it is to be identified at all. This is why it makes no sense to ask, impersonally and in general, of some individual object or person, what makes him or it *the* individual object or person it or he is; and this is why proper names for such objects or persons have no individual 'sense', though they may be said to have a general 'sense' (i.e. a sense they share with names of other objects of the same sort). And here we can see again the supreme importance of the covering sortal which links together all the uniquely exemplified characters or relations by which the particular object may be, at different times and by different thinkers, identified.

So, then, g-sortedness, predicate-worthiness, and the status of earthy or substantial object hang splendidly together. Now nobody wants (or nobody would admit to wanting) to defend the thesis that all entities are g-sorted simply on the ground that all substantial objects are g-sorted and only substantial objects are entities. And nobody, surely, wants to defend the thesis by reducing it to the truism that only g-sorted identifiabilia are g-sorted. A more interesting and attractive form of the thesis would be this: all entities (objects) are predicate-worthy and only g-sorted identifiabilia are predicate-worthy; therefore only g-sorted identifiabilia are entities (objects). But in this form the thesis seems to be untrue. What is true, as I have just remarked, and what in part, as I have suggested, accounts for the attractiveness of the thesis, is that g-sortedness and predicate-worthiness go splendidly together in the case of our model, earthy objects. But it is not true that predicate-worthiness always implies g-sortedness. I earlier mentioned styles, architectural, literary, and other, as identifiabilia which are not g-sorted. And surely styles are predicate-worthy. At any rate they are so treated in criticism, an activity which would be crippled, or at least severely handicapped, if critics were not allowed the freedom to predicate of styles. Of course it might be said that criticism is anyway a dispensable activity; for it forms no part of natural science. From such philistinism as this we can only avert our eyes.

Among other g-unsorted identifiabilia I mentioned certain sense-qualia, viz. smells and colours, and also ways of talking, walking, laughing, etc. It will hardly be denied that the former are predicate-worthy. It may be questioned whether the latter are. We say such things as: 'He has the same laugh as his father—a loud, coarse, guttural laugh.' I suppose we could say instead: 'When either of them laughs, you cannot tell (or are very hard put to it to tell), just by listening, which it is; and whenever either laughs, he always, or almost always, laughs loudly, coarsely, and gutturally.' I suppose, at a pinch, this would do. (It will be noticed that, anticipating the needs of a certain style of structural semantic analysis, I have made the *adverbial* qualifications amenable to replacement by predicates attaching to particular episodes of laughing rather than to a kind of laughter.) But it would be a pinch. And this is a particularly simple case. One should try giving the sense of 'He speaks with a Bronx accent' without reference to *ways* of talking.

The important points are these. *First*, we need only one case of an identifiable which is both predicate-worthy and g-unsorted in order to destroy the thesis in its present form; and in the face of so many challenges (I have not by any means exhausted the list) the task of defending the thesis seems hopeless. Moreover—and this is the *second* point—the effort to do so is not really worth while. For the concept of predicate-worthiness is not an absolute one. Richness of range of predications is clearly a matter of degree; and so, in those cases in which it is sensible to raise the question, is the matter of their dispensability. But do we want the status of being an object or an entity to be a matter of degree or of more or less arbitrary line-drawing? This is not, I take it, how philosophers have thought of the status.

Not only does the concept of predicate-worthiness fail to be an absolute concept. It seems plausible to hold—and this is the *third* point—that the concept of g-sortedness does so too. Games and sports, for example, I take to be predicate-worthy. Certainly we have plenty to say about them and we should find it difficult, at least, to say what we have to say without using their names. I know of no theory of games which sorts them as biology sorts species and chemistry chemical substances; and it might seem that only a mad authoritarianism would try to do so. On the other hand someone might hold that there was something like an incipient theory in our current practice of classification and naming. I do not wish to be dogmatic on the point. There is, simply, a dilemma. Either games are clearly g-unsorted, in which case we have yet another kind of example of predicate-worthy g-unsorted identifiabilia. Or they are neither clearly g-sorted nor clearly g-unsorted, in which case g-sortedness is not an absolute concept and we have an independent reason for querying the association between g-sortedness and entity-status.

We have seen, by now, a fairly complete collapse of the thesis that only g-sorted things are entities. It cannot be successfully argued for along the lines: *entity* implies *identifiability* implies *g-sortedness*; for, as we saw long ago, the last implication does not hold. It cannot be successfully argued for along the lines: *entity* implies *predicate-worthiness* implies *g-sortedness*; for again, as we have just seen, the last implication does not hold. We have also seen the interest of the thesis dwindle in the light of the fact that neither predicate-worthiness nor g-sortedness marks any generally clear or sharp division among identifiabilia. I think the moral to draw is that we should give up any attempt along any such lines as these to distinguish, among identifiabilia, between those which enjoy the privileged status of object or entity and those which do not. Belonging to all the kinds of identifiabilia I have mentioned and to many more—for example, customs, religions, social conditions (like war and peace), techniques of many sorts (for example, acupuncture, wireless telegraphy), dishes (for example, Boeuf-en-Daube, Crême Brûlée)—there will be items which we shall sometimes find it convenient or pointful to make subjects of first-order predications. We should revise our notion of predicate-worthiness and regard the capacity of an identifiable item to support a pointful predication as a sufficient attestation of worthiness to do so. Then indeed we might regard predicate-worthiness as the mark of an object. It will be a notably unexclusive mark.

Of course—the point should not need making, but perhaps it had better be made—this does not mean that we forfeit the power, or forgo the right, to distinguish between true and false existence-claims. We are no more committed, by a categorial catholicism of entities, to admitting Pegasus among the horses or the golden mountain among the mountains or the rational square root of two among the numbers or witches among the women than is the adherent of more restrictive doctrines. Exclusionists and catholics alike know how to distinguish between the names which really do name identifiabilia of a certain kind and the names which only purport, or are mistakenly supposed, to do so.

Anyone disposed to worry about inflated ontologies, proliferation of entities, and so forth will not, evidently, be pacified by this point. In so far as such a one thinks that ontological catholics are deluded into supposing that properties are like people or that objects need have anything more in common than being identifiable subjects, he does not deserve to be pacified. In so far as he simply deplores the untidy richness of the vernacular in this respect and yearns for a sparser style, he manifests a quasi-aesthetic preference which can be respected, if not shared. In so far as his point is that category-catholicism is no substitute for philosophical elucidation and that the latter enterprise may sometimes be forwarded by even partially successful efforts at analytic paraphrase, he can be agreed with; but should also be reminded that if ontological generosity is no substitute for elucidation, it is no bar to it either.[4]

II

6. So far I have taken largely for granted the connection between the idea of a (primary) substance-sort and that of a general criterion of identity for things of the sort. What is the nature of the connection? Is there one criterion of identity for dogs and another for cats? Any disposition to answer this question affirmatively receives at least an initial check in a further question: Is there one criterion of identity for wolfhounds and another for terriers? One for Scotch terriers and

---

[4] This is not to deny that there is quite a good case for a conservative reform of our terminology here, as regards both the word 'object' and the word 'ontological'. Thus we might distinguish between a 'logical' sense and an 'ontological' sense of the word 'object'. Objects in the first sense would be all predicate-worthy identifiabilia whatever. Objects in the second sense—our earthy, substantial objects—would form one ontological category among others, such as events, processes, qualities, numbers, species, states, types, etc., etc.; though, doubtless, the *first* among them.

another for smooth-haired terriers? So one may be inclined to ask whether there is not, rather, one criterion of identity for all animals, a criterion which they share with nothing else. This time the check comes from the opposite side. Why not shared with, say, plants? And if with plants, why not with some non-organic substantial things? Why not with all? Why not a common criterion of identity for all substantial things?

Wherever we set the limits for a common criterion of identity, we must be able to say what that criterion is. And a criterion is something that is *applied*. So saying what it is should reveal how it is that we are able to apply it.

We might say: if *a* is a substantial individual and *b* is a substantial individual, then $a = b$ if and only if there is a substantial kind which *a* is of and which *b* is of and there is no time at which there is a volume of space occupied by *a* which is not occupied at that time by *b*.

Could we delete the reference to kinds? One reason against doing so is this. Suppose John dies in his bed and William dies by being blown to smithereens. Then if we delete the reference to kinds, we should have to say that William is identical with his body while John is not.

The reference to kinds has another and more general importance. How could we begin to apply such a criterion as is here proposed unless we thought of any item to which it applied as occupying some more or less determinate volume of space at any time? And doing so, at least in principle, *observably* or *surveyably*? Perceiving, or thinking of, an object as falling under some substantial kind concept, we meet this requirement.

But there remains something profoundly unsatisfactory about the alleged criterion. It seems that in order to apply it we must already be operating a principle of identity: for how else could we be sure that we had the identical individual, *a*, in all those positions in which we are then to ask whether we had, at the same times, the individual, *b*? As what it is supposed to be, viz. a criterion of identity, what we are offered is otiose. All it really says is that the occupation of a given volume of space by an individual substance of a certain sort at a certain time excludes the simultaneous occupation of that volume of space by a different individual of the same sort. An important principle, certainly; but not, it seems, exactly what we were seeking.

But were we seeking the right thing? Such classical examples of clearly statable criteria of identity as those for directions of straight lines or numbers of members of sets have two features which seem quite inappropriate in the present connection. First, reference to the items for which criteria of identity are given is eliminated in the statement of the criteria: reference to lines or sets is retained, but not to directions or numbers. In fact the statements could be viewed simply as reductive analyses of the predicates 'has the same direction as' or 'has the same number of members as', two-place predicates of lines and sets. This feature seems quite alien to our present object. Second, and more vaguely, these criteria of identity have a rigidity and clear-cutness which seem equally out of place where individual substances are concerned.

Does this mean that the whole notion of a criterion of identity is here inappropriate? That might seem a desperate thing to say. At least it presents us with a quandary—or two quandaries. For in the first place we have assumed throughout that substantial individuals are prime examples of g-sorted identifiabilia, i.e. of identifiabilia belonging to sorts such that there exist common general criteria of identity for things belonging to those sorts. And in the second place we are familiar enough with perfectly intelligible discussions of questions which are at least presented as questions about the criteria of identity for men, say, or ships or buildings.

To clear a little space for manœuvre, let me revert to the point that concepts of substance-kinds range from the highly general (animal, plant) to the highly specific—of which any botanist or biologist will be forward with examples. Between the extremes lies an extensive middle ground, and in it, we may plausibly suppose, fall substance-kind concepts which are both ontogenetically and phylogenetically primitive. Such concepts as these I have already roughly characterized in a general way: they are concepts of space-occupying things, characteristically featured, some static, some mobile, with some endurance through time, capable of change in characteristic ways and exhibiting some variation of character from one member to another of the same kind. Associated with each such middle-ground substance-concept is a whole cluster of readinesses for variation *between* individual members of the kind and of expectations of typical continuities and typical modifications *in* individual members of the kind.

It is impossible to specify fully and precisely these expectations and readinesses. If we made the attempt, we should find ourselves launching into a disquisition on typical histories and varieties of organism, non-organic natural object, and artefact. A consequence is that when we attempt a reasonably brief, yet full and precise, statement of a criterion of identity for some substance-kind, we either overshoot the mark or fall short of it. We overshoot the mark when—as in the case of the general criterion for substance-identity lately considered—it would not be clear how we might apply the criterion unless the ability to keep track of the identical individual were presupposed. If we try to avoid such presupposition, we do so at the price of inadequacy. We might seek to avoid the presupposition, for example, by saying something like: we have one identical dog at all points on a spatio-temporally continuous path of manifestation of caninity (or the dog-form). But it is not clear that this excludes, as surely we want it to, some phantasmagoric sequence of transformations of dachshund into wolfhound into Pekinese, etc. Indeed it is not clear that it excludes the result that the dog at one end of a regimented line of shoulder-to-shoulder dogs is identical with the dog at the other end. Indeed, and more shortly, it is not clear at all. The difficulty is only aggravated by the substitution of a more general substance-form concept; and it is not significantly alleviated by substituting one more specific. We are not prepared for individual dogs, even of the same sub-kind, to exhibit successively the variety of characteristics which we accept with equanimity as between different individuals of the sub-kind.

What, then, of my earlier remarks about the necessary g-sortedness of particulars—g-sortedness being explained in terms of the existence of general criteria of identity? Some revision, or reinterpretation, of those earlier remarks is certainly called for. But this does not mean that we lack an explanation of our ability to identify and reidentify substantial particulars. We have only to reflect on the general character of substance-kind concepts to see that possession of any such concept necessarily carries with it the ability to distinguish one individual of the kind from another; to count such individuals (if one can count at all); and to apply the notion of 'the same one' of the kind. For they essentially are concepts of things which occupy space and endure in existence in characteristic ways. It would be harmless enough to say that each such kind-concept *is* a principle of identity for all individuals of the kind. What is mistaken is the supposition that we can analyse such kind-concepts as conceptual compounds of an identity-preserving element and something else. An example of such an attempt is the suggestion just now cited that substantial identity is to be analysed in terms of the spatio-temporally continuous manifestation of something general, say, a form. Here spatio-temporal continuity of manifestation is thought of as the common identity-preserving element in a vast range of substance-kind concepts, while the form is what varies from kind to kind. But we have no concepts of forms which will fill this analytical bill.[5]

---

[5] One source of the belief that we have may perhaps be found in the concepts of our infancy or the infancy of our concepts. It is natural to describe the responses of very young children to certain experimental tests by saying that the subjects possess powers of recognition of patterns or forms exhibited by certain sorts of objects, or even by individual objects of a sort, before they master any appropriate sortal concept; and it is natural to find in these primitive powers of recognition the germ of the power to form sortal concepts. (Cf. the discussion of the distinction between the concept of the cat-feature and the sortal concept, *cat*, in *Individuals* (Methuen, 1964), 207–8.) But to fill the analytical bill we require not only that the concept of a certain sort-form should be distinct from and theoretically independent of the concept of the sort. We require also that the latter should be analysable in terms of the former. The mental life of adults supplies no sort-form concepts which satisfy even the first of these requirements. If we waive these requirements, we can indeed maintain *a* distinction between, say, a horse-form concept and the concept of a horse. For older children, and we

Rather, in the case of a given substance-kind, the concept of the form inextricably involves expectations of characteristic modes of continuance in existence of the individuals belonging to the kind—which is not, of course, to say that we can learn nothing from experience about their typical histories. Now we are in a position to deal formally with the first of my quandaries. We can adopt either a stricter or a looser interpretation of the notion of a criterion of identity. Here is one possible strict interpretation. The notion of a criterion of identity pertains, firstly, to those things to which a certain form of analysis is appropriate. The form of analysis in question is this: the $\alpha$ of $x$ is identical with the $\alpha$ of $y$ (*or $x$* has (or is an instance or a token of) the same $\alpha$ as $y$) if $x$ and $y$ are R-related; where no expression in the analysans includes a reference to $\alpha$s and where the R-relation is not itself that of identity. The notion applies, secondly, to those things of which the identity is essentially and simply reducible, in some clearly statable way, to the identity of other, *constitutent* things. Thus it applies also to sets. (There are intended as two sufficient tests, not necessarily mutually exclusive.)

If we adopt some such strict interpretation of the notion of a criterion of identity, we shall loosen the connection between this notion and that of g-sortedness. We shall count individuals as g-sorted so long as they fall under essentially individuative concepts, whether or not we can associate general criteria of identity, *sensu stricto*, with those concepts. Thus we shall count substantial individuals as g-sorted because they fall under essentially individuative concepts of space-occupying and enduring things; each such concept *is* a principle of counting, and hence identifying, the individuals which fall under it. But we shall not count intellectual qualities or literary styles or colours or smells or ways of walking

ourselves, find *intelligible* those myths or fantasies in which something assumes, perhaps in rapid succession, a variety of forms. What, in such a fantasy, takes the form of, or appears as, a horse is not, whatever it is, a horse; even if the hero saddles and rides it. It is, perhaps, a horse-phantasm. But *this* concept of a horse-form or horse-phantasm is clearly *derivative* from that of a horse, and no more available for the analysis of the latter than that of a toy horse is.

or talking as g-sorted; because the concepts 'intellectual quality', 'literary style', etc. are not counting principles, though we can identify intellectual qualities, literary styles, etc.

The alternative is to be content with a loose notion of criterion of identity which allows us to associate the notion with any individuative concept whatever, as well as with anything which satisfies either of the two tests I have just mentioned. On this alternative we can allow the original explanation of g-sortedness and the entire terminology of Part I to stand unrevised. But I favour the first alternative. It would limit the application of a phrase which is apt to come too easily to one's lips. It would not, of course, affect the substance of the thesis maintained in Part I; only its mode of expression.

What of the second quandary? What of those discussions of problem-cases which are presented under the head of investigations into the criteria of identity of substantial individuals of certain interesting kinds? I have remarked that a substance-kind concept involves a whole cluster of expectations of typical continuities and discontinuities and, one might add, of typical terminations, to which individuals of the kind are subject. History sometimes, and mildly, and ingenious philosophers more frequently, and starkly, present us with cases in which these expectations receive a certain sort of shock. The recipe for administering the shock is to contrive some striking dislocation of normal continuities, perhaps in such a way that we may seem to be presented with rival claimants to a single identity. It is the essence of such cases that they should be quite outside the range of normal experience. Indeed, obviously, they could not have the shock-effect I have mentioned if they were not. Whatever is commonplace, or merely unusual, is taken in the stride of our normal conceptual apparatus; and the same would hold of the philosophers' imaginings if they *became* commonplace. They would be absorbed by conceptual adjustments: additions, refinements, decisions. We can amuse, and instruct, ourselves by imaginative anticipation of such adjustments; but we should recognize *this* exercise for what it is.

7. So much, for the moment, then, for substantial particulars. What of non-substantial particulars? I shall consider some examples from the large and heterogeneous class of substance-dependent non-substantial particulars: particular deaths, smiles, battles, falls, walks, etc.[6] I call these substance-dependent because they are essentially happenings to, or processes involving, or modifications of, substantial individuals, space-occupying continuants. The concepts they fall under are often directly, though sometimes rather loosely, individuative; or if, as in the case of the noun 'fall', they apply to happenings which a wide range of substance-kinds can suffer, they can be made to yield individuative concepts by appropriate substance-specification, for example 'fall of a horse'. Are we to say that the notion of a criterion of identity is in place in connection with these concepts? Not, certainly, if we take that notion in the strict sense I have mentioned. Do they present, then, a stronger case for widening the notion to embrace them than concepts of substantial individuals do?

I think this much can be said. The nature of these concepts is such that there is often a relatively standard way of giving or fixing or specifying the identity of the particular individuals which fall under them. This is particularly obvious in the case of certain kinds of event which are such that no substantial individual is liable to endure more than one event of that kind—for example a death, a destruction, a final going-hence. We often enough say what death is in question by saying who it is who suffered it. But the principle holds for many substance-dependent event- or process-kinds which do not have this once-for-all character; only in these cases an important part is often played by an appropriately precise specification of the time at which the event occurred or over which the process extended. Such time-specifications supplement speci-

---

[6] By a *particular walk*, I do not of course mean such things as the walk from the house across the fields, along the towpath and back past the Rectory—the walk we recommend to visitors and take ourselves every Sunday. The walks I mean are unrepeatable tokens rather than types. Type-walks, such as the one just described, are yet a further example of g-unsorted identifiabilia. Madder by far than any individuative principle for games would be the authoritarianism of a principle which determined how many *walks* there were in a certain district.

fication of agents or sufferers or locations of the events or processes in question to yield relatively standard ways of giving their identities.

It is difficult, however, to find in these facts a sufficient reason for discriminating in the way suggested between substantial particulars and non-substantial substance-dependent particulars. It might be said of some substantial particulars too that there exist relatively standard ways of specifying their identities. An obviously standard way of specifying identities in the case of relatively static substantial particulars such as geographical features, cities, or individual buildings is to give, with sufficient precision, their spatial location.

The issue here may be crossed by, and perhaps confused with, another issue. Suppose we could say, of some kind of particular individual, that for each such individual there was a uniquely possessed complex relational property of a certain general sort, distinguished from other uniquely possessed properties of other sorts which typically characterize individuals of that kind by being, in the case of each such individual, the property the possession of which constitute the *individual essence* of that individual or 'made it just the particular individual it was'. Then we might be inclined to think that we indeed had hold of something which deserved to be called a general criterion of identity for individual particulars of that kind. For example, suppose we thought that the individual essence of a smile smiled by a certain person at a certain moment consisted in its being smiled by *that* person at *that* moment; and that each smile had a uniquely possessed essential property of this sort. Then we might think that in the general idea of being smiled by some person at some moment we had a general criterion of identity for smiles. (I will not set it out in form: it is obvious how it would go.)

This suggestion owes such attractiveness as it has to distinguishing each such relational property, as an essence-constituting property of the smile which uniquely possesses it, from every other uniquely possessed property which the smile might exhibit (for example, being smiled at a certain time by lips occupying a certain spatial position at that time).

For it is a trivial general truth that if a property is uniquely possessed by an individual, then any individual which possesses that property is identical with the given individual; and unless we make a special claim for the property in question, it is no more than one application among others of this trivial truth to say that if a certain smile is smiled by a certain person at a certain moment, then any smile smiled by that person at that moment is identical with that smile.

Of course, it is true of any smile that it must be smiled by someone at some time, and that no other smile can possess just that particular combination of these properties that a given smile possesses. But neither this nor any other unique combination of properties constitutes the individual essence of a particular smile; for there is no such thing. The notion of an individual essence belongs not to particular things but to general things; just as the notion of an individual sense belongs not to the names of particular things, but to the names of general things. If it were the case, for some particular thing, that there was just one of its uniquely possessed properties which it *had* to be identified by if it was to be identified at all,[7] then it would be reasonable to extend the notion of individual essence to such a particular thing. I remarked earlier that this was not the case for any substantial particular. Neither is it the case for any non-substantial, substance-dependent particular. Competitions can be organized on the basis of the principle that it is *not* required that one know *who* smiled a certain smile in order to know what smile it was. The schoolmaster need be in no doubt at all as to what utterance he has in mind when he asks 'Who said that?'

There remains the point which I began this section by making. The sorts of non-substantial, substance-dependent particulars are such that there often exist relatively standard ways of specifying the identities of particulars belonging to these sorts, of saying which or what individual member of the

---

[7] Let no one say that, for any particular, there is such a property, namely the disjunction of all its uniquely possessed properties! To identify an item by means of some uniquely possessed property, you have at least to know what that property is.

sort is in question. This is less frequently true of the sorts of substantial particulars. But this difference of degree is hardly one on which we can found a case for saying that the precise-sounding notion of a criterion of identity is appropriate to the former class of individuative concepts but not to the latter.

8. I turn now to some individuating concepts of another kind, concepts of things which fall within a general classification sometimes indicated by the use of the word 'type'. The examples shall consider are those of musical or literary compositions of certain forms: for example, sonnet, ode or, more generally, poem; story or novel; song, sonata, symphony. About these I should like to make two very different points. The first is not a very serious point and perhaps could hardly be sustained. I make it by way of exaggerated anticipation of a possible objection to the second. It is that the practice of the activities of poetizing, story-telling, music-making, does not have as an immediate necessary consequence the existence of any *individuative* concepts of these kinds. I do not mean simply that certain forms might not have been devised. On the contrary the point is that the existence and practice of, for example, the sonnet-form does not strictly necessitate the existence of sonnets. We are familiar with, and can easily accommodate, the notion of different versions or variants of the *same* composition. But we can perhaps imagine this notion pushed to self-destructive lengths; to the point at which the ideas of identity of composition and hence of versions and variants of the same one are altogether lost. We can perhaps imagine a general practice of poetizing or story-telling or even sonneteering accompanied by such a habit of slight continuous variation as had the consequence that what, as things are, we should unhesitatingly describe as the tellings of two different stories or as copies of two different sonnets had a place on a continuous story- or sonnet-spectrum on which no lines of demarcation could be drawn to separate one from another.

The point, even if it could be sustained, is not to be pressed. As things are, we do have individuative concepts of these kinds. At most it has been shown that their existence and utility, as individuative concepts, rest on certain general facts about our practice in these areas.

Now for the second point. These individuating concepts, sonnet, novel, symphony, etc., strikingly emerge as far better candidates than those lately considered for the status of concepts of things for which there exist general criteria of identity in a strict sense. They pass without difficulty the first of my sufficient tests. Neglecting for the moment the matter of versions and variants, we may say, for example: *a* is an inscription of the same sonnet as *b* if *a* is an inscription of words in the sonnet-form and so is *b* and the words and their arrangement in the form are identical in both cases. We can take account of versions or variants by qualifying 'identical' with some expression like 'approximately' or 'nearly enough'—a useful reminder of the point already made. Clearly this pattern of statement of a criterion of identity can be generalized for all such types.

What of the second of my sufficient tests, the one designed for sets? Evidently, a sonnet or a sonata is not simply a set of words or a set of notes. But each is, *and is essentially*, a particular set of words or notes ordered in a particular clearly specifiable arrangement. *This* reduction is quite in order; though again minor qualifications are required to allow for versions and variants. If we interpret this second test, then, with reasonable liberality, sonnets and sonatas pass it as well as the first. We could say: the criterion of identity for compositions is their composition.

Now this might, for an unreflective moment, encourage the resurgence of a general error. It might, for example, be said: then haven't we, after all, a general criterion of identity for all material substances or bodies? For a body *a* is identical with a body *b* if *a* at any time is composed of the same material particles as *b* is composed of at that time. There are many objections to this, implicit in what has gone before. It is enough to say that a criterion is something that is *applied*. But I will add this general comment. It is futile to suppose that you can devise anything which deserves to be called a criterion of identity for things falling under some concept of high generality simply by applying the general *logical* characters of identity to any feature you happen to think of which universally characterizes things which fall under that concept. A specimen of this futility is the recent suggestion that a criterion of identity for events is to be found in the identity of their causal relations.

9. It would be instructive to consider how the notion of a criterion of identity fares in the case of yet other general sorts of individuals than those I have selected. But this paper is already long enough. I have, I think, assembled enough evidence to support the proposal that the phrase should either be dropped altogether from our professional vocabulary or be employed only under some such restrictions as I have suggested. As things are, the phrase has a spurious and thought-stopping authority. Criteria should be both clearly statable and actually applicable, actually applied. Criteria of identity are at their best in the case of certain sorts of abstract, general thing. It is pointless to extend the notion to individuative concepts in general, to all concepts of the g-sorted; it is even more futile to try to extend it to concepts—like that of an event—which are so general that they are not themselves individuative at all, although they cover a range of concepts which are.

Nevertheless useful results may sometimes be achieved with inappropriate tools or weapons; and the waving of this weapon may sometimes have forced us to a conceptual clarification, or a recognition of conceptual unclarity, which we had previously missed. These beneficial results, however, could equally well have been secured by a steady attention to that sober maxim which I suggested as an unexceptionable gloss on our original slogan, 'No entity without identity': viz. you cannot talk sense about a thing unless you know, at least in principle, how it might be identified. This principle of conceptual clarity applies equally to the g-sorted and the g-unsorted: to souls, for example, on the one hand, and to telepathy on the other. You do not know what you mean by 'telepathy' unless you know how to identify it, i.e. how you would tell that you have a case of it. You do not know what souls are unless you know how to tell one from another and to say when you have the same one again. And if someone should say that this is just old verificationism writ small, or loose, then I am quite content with that.

# 2

# *Universals*

Huizinga, noting the vogue that the problem of universals enjoyed throughout the Middle Ages and the fact that the controversy was still unresolved in his day, was disposed to find, in its persistence, confirmation of his view of philosophy as a form of agonistic play. It is certainly true that there has always been, and is still, a rough division between those who 'countenance', or take a welcoming attitude to, universals and those who would prefer to admit the existence of nothing but particular objects and events. But it may be possible to find, for this continuing division, some further explanation to supplement, at least, that which appeals to love of competition on the part of men in general and philosophers in particular.

Hostility to universals usually goes with complacency about particulars. Those philosophers who are suspicious of general properties, sorts, relations, and types usually have no doubts about the reality of people, physical objects, datable events, and tokens. This partiality of theirs has sometimes seemed paradoxical. For it has seemed unclear how they, or anyone else, could distinguish and identify the particular individuals they so readily accept unless they could distinguish and identify some, at least, of the general sorts or kinds to which those individuals belong and some, at least, of the general features that characterize them. If practical recognition of particular things entails practical recognition of general things, why should theoretical recognition, so readily accorded to the former, be given so grudgingly, if at all, to the latter?

Part of the answer lies in a certain anxiety or fear: the fear of the making of myths, objectionable in themselves and productive of absurdity. The fear has a more specific character. Let it be granted that spatio-temporal particulars—or spatio-temporal particulars of certain sorts—are model cases of what really exists or occurs. The fear is that a theoretical commitment to the existence of universals amounts to a confused half-assimilation of the general to the particular, accompanied, perhaps, by a confused analogical picture of the relations of these spurious quasi-particulars, the universals, to the actual objects to be found in space and time. Plato is represented as the prime example of this confusion; and who is to say he is free from it? The Forms are altogether too like quasi-prototypes. That the fear has, or sometimes has, this character is also suggested by the unpleasant image of a 'bloated' or 'overpopulated' universe so frequently used by those who would eschew theoretical commitment to abstract entities.

Should we not, in our sophisticated days, have progressed beyond these myths and hence beyond these fears of myth? Surely no one denies that different particular things may share identical properties, may belong to the same kinds; that different pairs or trios of particular things may stand in the same relations. And if so, what can be wrong with, what myth need attend, the admission that there *are* properties, kinds, relations that different particular things or pairs or trios of them may share? Indeed, the admission is implicit in the use, as just made, of the phrases, 'identical property', 'same kind', 'same relation'.

To this there is a stubborn, familiar reply. There is nothing wrong with saying that there *are* properties, kinds, etc., if the remark is construed as merely an idiomatically permissible way of saying that different particular things may alike, for example, be red or white or dogs or trees; that different particular pairs may alike, for example, be such that one member loves, or is larger than, the other. But the suspicion lingers that the remark is taken, by those who think it worth making, to carry some further and disputable commitment.

As for the point about practical recognition, it is again harmless to say that the ability to distinguish and identify particular individuals depends upon the ability to distinguish and identify general kinds and properties, if the remark is properly construed. We may admit that the ability to recognize a particular individual as the particular individual it is depends, in general, upon the ability to recognize it *as* a tree, say, or *as* a dog. If this is all that recognition of the general kind comes to, it may safely be acknowledged. But the ability to recognize something as a dog does not require that we have to recognize, in any sense, a further thing, the universal, *dog*.

To these replies there is an equally stubborn rejoinder. Why the reductive tone? Grant that the practical ability to recognize the universal amounts to no more than the ability to recognize its instances as being such. But note that to make the point thus generally is already to recognize, in another sense, the universal itself. Grant that the existence of universals is no more than the fact, or the possibility, that particular things do, or might, exemplify them. But acknowledge that the fact or possibility of their being exemplified is no less than the fact of their existence.

I shall suggest that the fears and tensions here recalled are likely to continue for as long as philosophical discussion of the topic continues.

Such a suggestion may appear profoundly unsatisfactory. It may be objected that we now have a clear-cut way of resolving the issue or at least of construing it as an issue that can be resolved in a clear-cut way. For the elegant and perspicuous notation of standard logic has suggested a test whereby we can determine just what ranges of items are such that we are inescapably committed to belief in their existence. The suggestion is most prominent in the work of Professor Quine, to whom it is primarily due. Quine summed up the test in a celebrated epigram: 'To be is to be the value of a variable.' It can be expressed in slightly more traditional terminology as follows: the only things we are bound to acknowledge as entities, as existing, are those that we find it indispensable, for the expression of our beliefs, to reckon among the subjects of our predications or—which comes to the same thing—among the objects of reference. To apply the test, we must submit the referential extravagance of natural language to a discipline of regimenting paraphrase that aims at maximum ontological economy. And to help us weed out the bogus pretenders to the status of entities, we have a second test: nothing is to count as an entity unless there is a clear general principle of identity for all things of its kind. Quine summed up the second test, too, in an epigram: 'No entity without identity.' To see the connection between the two tests, it is enough to recall the notation of logic. The subjects of predication are just the objects that the variables of quantification range over. Those variables are essentially such as to be able to stand on either side of the identity-predicate. If the variables purport to range over items for which a principle of identity is lacking, then the sentences containing such variables have no determinate sense.

Unfortunately the hope, which these tests might seem to offer, of clear-cut decision on our question turns out to be an illusory hope. It is true that the substantial particular individuals of the world—Aristotle's primary substances—pass both tests with impressive ease and success. And this is a satisfactory result in so far as scarcely any rational man would, even in his philosophical moments, wish to question the existence of such objects. These objects pass the first test, one might say, ahead of all competitors. They are the primary subjects of predication. As I have written elsewhere, 'we tell the day-to-day story of the world, we describe the changing postures of its states of affairs, essentially by means of predications of which such objects are the subjects; and we cannot seriously envisage any alternative way of doing so.'[1] They pass the second test too; for the common concepts under which such particular individuals are identified yield of themselves general principles of identity for their particular instances. If, for example, one has mastered the common concept 'horse', one has thereby mastered a general princi-

[1] See 'Entity and Identity', in *Contemporary British Philosophy*, 4th Series, ed. H. D. Lewis (London, 1976); included as Ch. 1 in the present volume.

ple for counting, distinguishing, and identifying particular things, namely horses.

However, when one turns to consider the case of universals or of purported abstract entities generally, disillusion sets in. One is led to question the relevance of the second test and the utility of the first. I do not mean that one is led to question the slogan 'No entity without identity'—in its strict and literal meaning; for certainly there exists nothing that is not identical with itself. But if the slogan is construed as meaning 'No entity without a *common* principle of identity for all things of a kind to which the purported entity belongs', then its relevance to the case of universals or purported abstract entities generally must come into question. For universals and abstract entities generally—if such exist—are distinguished from spatio-temporal particulars in general precisely by the fact that each has an *individual* essence which constitutes its *individual* identity. So there is no need of a common principle of identity for all universals of some kind to which the given universal belongs. To insist on this requirement would be arbitrarily to fix the rules of the game so that only spatio-temporal particulars and some favoured types of a abstract object, like sets and numbers, could win it.

To expand a little on this point. Suppose 'F' is a predicate and 'φ' the corresponding name of the universal—if such exists. Then we have

$$x \text{ is F (say, 'witty' or 'red' or 'triangular')}$$

and

$$x \left\{ \begin{array}{l} \text{is an instance of} \\ \text{exemplifies} \end{array} \right\} \phi \text{ (say 'wit' or 'red' or 'triangularity').}$$

To grasp the sense of F *is* to grasp the principle of identity for φ. It is not *eo ipso* to grasp a general, common principle of identity for things of the kind to which φ belongs. There may or may not be such a principle. In the case of intellectual qualities (the general kind to which wit belongs) or in the case of colours (the general kind to which red belongs) there is no such principle. In the case of geometrical shapes it is perhaps arguable that there is. But the point is that we do not need such a principle. For in the sense of the predicate, and hence in the sense of the associated name for the universal, we already have the essence, the individual principle of identity, of the universal thing—if there exists such a thing. The case is quite different with particular things: their names— their proper names—contain in their sense, in so far as they can be said to have a sense, no *individual* principles of identity for the individuals that bear them. When we seek a principle of identity for them, we do indeed have to have recourse to the general sort or kind to which they belong; to a sortal concept that covers them; to a general principle of identity for all things of that sort. Hence, if we amend the slogan, as just now rejected, to read 'No *particular* entity without a common principle of identity for all things of a kind to which the purported particular entity belongs', then the slogan is plausible enough. Unamended, it simply begs the general question against general things. (As already indicated, this is not to say that no abstract entities pass the test. Some do; but there is no reason why all should; and many do not.)

The first test—that of indispensability as subjects of predication—may seem at first sight a little more promising. For it is easy to think of simple cases of successful reductive paraphrase, cases in which, for example, without loss of intended sense, we can eliminate reference by name to abstract qualities in favour of general reference to particulars that characteristically have or lack those qualities, coupled with predicates corresponding to the quality-names. But to infer from such trivial successes that we could, without a crippling effect on discourse, bring about any significant reduction in the range of abstract reference by such means, is to make a wholly unjustified leap; as the study of almost any page of theoretical writing would show. And to cripple discourse is to cripple thought.

Moreover, even if the paraphrasability claim could be made good, the fact would not, by itself, serve the intended purpose. For it might be that the availability of the sentence to be paraphrased was a necessary condition of our thinking the thought to which we then try to approximate in the substitute sentence or sentences. Committed in thought to what we shun in speech, we should then seem like people seeking euphemisms in order to avoid explicit mention of distasteful realities.

The main point, however, is not that the suggested tests fail, through irrelevance in the case of the second and ineffectiveness in the case of the first, to yield any significant reduction in what adherents of the tests would call our ontological commitment to abstract entities. The point is, rather, that they fail in the more general aim of providing a clear-cut means of resolving, in any way at all, the issue that has formed the matter of perennial debate. For if it would be a mistake to think that the tests supply a clear means of limiting our ontological commitment, it would be no less a mistake to conclude that their failure to do so provides of itself a clear and final demonstration of the existence—or of our commitment to belief in the existence—of qualities, properties, types, and abstract entities generally, besides the particular events, objects, and processes that take up space or occur in time in the natural world and that *exemplify* qualities, *belong to* kinds, and are *of* types. It is not, indeed, a mistake that disappointed adherents of the tests are likely to make; they are more likely to give up their adherence. But in asking why these things are so, one may uncover the real source of the poignancy of the perennial debate.

The source lies, I suggest, in a certain inevitable tension in our thought. To locate that tension, we must first recall those considerations that underlie the whole problem, considerations of the utmost generality, relating to features characteristic of any stage of human thought and experience which deserve the names—indeed to any stage of the thought and experience of any being endowed, as Kant would say, with sensibility and understanding. At the most elementary level they amount to this: that we cannot think of, or, in a full sense, perceive, any natural thing, whether object or event, without thinking of it, or perceiving it, under *some* general aspect; as being so-and-so or a such-and such; as having some general character or as being of some general kind. Generality and particularity are alike necessary features, and mutually dependent features, of our experience; as of our speech. This being so, it is natural that we should at least be under the impression that we can distinguish in thought between particular objects and events in nature and the general characters and types that those objects and events exemplify; and indeed that we can extend our thought to embrace types and characters perhaps not exemplified at all by any particular things, or complexes of things, in nature. Should we not, then recognize that qualities, properties, types, hence universals, *exist*, as abstract objects of thought, distinct from particular objects in nature?

But here we already meet the source of tension. For when, and if, we are disposed to acquiesce in an affirmative answer to this question, we encounter the full and fierce pressure of a different disposition: a strong, natural disposition to understand by the notion of existence the same thing as existence in nature; to think that whatever exists at all exists in nature and that whatever relations hold between things are relations that are exemplified in nature. No reconciliation of the two dispositions is possible. For universals, if they exist at all, do not exist in nature. They are *incorrigibly* abstract; objects, if objects at all, of thought alone, even if indispensable objects of developed thought.

But if universals, if they exist, are outside nature, how are they related to the natural objects that exemplify or instantiate them? To repeat the professional terms, 'exemplification' or 'instantiation', seems to be to give no reply at all to this question. But it is the only reply that the believer in universals can safely give. For the question, the demand for an account of the relation, really incorporates the naturalist prejudice—if I may call it so *without* prejudice. So Plato, though right to place universals outside nature, was wrong to seek even a suggestive analogy in nature—for example, copy and original, production-line model and prototype—for the relation of exemplification. The relation of exemplification is not a natural relation and can have no natural analogues.

Aristotle was right to reject the analogy, but wrong to try, if he did try, to locate universals in nature. But it is not clear that he did try; for to say that universals are *in* particulars may not be an attempt to identify any natural relation, even by way of natural analogy; it may simply be to say that universals exist in nature only in so far as, and in the sense that, their instances exist in nature; and that they do not exist at all in any other sense.

The believer in universals, then, must be prepared to say that though instances of (some) universals are encounterable, and recognizable, in nature, the universal itself, the abstract thing, is not. The abstract thing is an object of thought alone. (The natural thing is an object of thought too, but not of thought alone.) But thinking takes place in nature. So the believer must also say that we can, in nature, think of the abstract thing which is not in nature as well as recognizing, in nature, its natural instances. (He may say that implicit in our recognition of the instance, the thing in nature, as what it is, is a capacity, even if an undeveloped capacity, to think of the abstract thing, the universal it is an instance of.)

Here he is exposed to another challenge from our native naturalism, that challenge which perhaps has more force than any other, since it covertly appeals to what seems the most fundamental dimension of natural existence, namely time. It runs. If these supposed entities are objects of thought, and objects of thought alone, are we not obliged to say one of two things: either that they come into existence when first conceived of and enjoy, while they exist, only a mind-dependent existence; or that they pre-exist their conception, waiting, in some non-natural sphere of their own, to be discovered by minds? And does not either answer seem singularly unattractive? Indeed both are unattractive, and both must be rejected by the believer; not in favour of a third temporal alternative, but on the ground that temporal predicates have no application to abstract objects, that they neither come into existence at a certain time nor exist sempiternally; that they are not in time. And here the believer has to resist the pressure of the naturalist prejudice at its strongest, the sense that whatever exists at all exists in time.

If he has stomach for this, he faces a third challenge. For it often seems that when we appear to be talking about universals, naming them and quantifying over them in such ways that we can find no plausible paraphrase, that both captures our thought and dispenses with such reference, yet we may have no further intention than to speak of what is found in nature. Should we not then conclude that even in our apparently ineliminable reference to universals we have nothing more than a feature of idiom, a *façon de parler*, an especially and perhaps inimitably vivid or economical way of suggesting, or alluding to, a more or less determinate, more or less compendious, array of natural facts—offering, perhaps, at the same time, a picture, not to be taken literally, like the personifications of eighteenth-century poetry—so that our thought has really no object other than natural things?

This is a point at which the believer can make a concession without surrendering his belief. If aggressively disposed, he may say that the occurrence of such apparent reference to universals is dependent upon the possibility of genuine reference to them; or, more bluntly, that it is only because they exist, as objects of thought, outside nature, that we can thus appear to refer to them even when we are speaking only of what is in nature. Because they exist, as objects of thought only, we can use their names to speak, picturesquely and indirectly, not of them at all, but of merely natural things that are not only objects of thought.

But the believer may not make quite so strong a claim. He may remark simply that the way just discussed is not the only way in which we use the names of universals or quantify over them. For sometimes we speak of the non-natural relations that hold between universals, or abstract entities, themselves. This we do whenever we speak of conceptual (or logical or analytic or semantic) necessities; for these are outside nature too. It is not, for example, a natural fact that scarlet things are necessarily red. When we assert, or think of, these necessities, the objects of our thought, whether they are directly named or represented by predicates, are the abstract entities themselves. It is not claimed that the existence of conceptual necessities is *explained* by a further fact, namely the existence of non-natural relations between universals or abstract entities generally. Rather, they are the same thing, neither more nor less than each other. And it is admitted that when we speak explicitly of non-natural relations between universals, the words we use are often borrowed from the vocabulary of relations exemplified in nature: for example 'includes', 'excludes', 'is incompatible with'. So we seem to picture these relations on analogy with, for example, spatial relations. Here again we see how natural is the fear that theoretical recognition of universals involves myth and confusion. The pictures seem to haunt us, however hard we try to neutralize them; and, of course, there is a quite blatant irony in the attempt to neutralize them by saying that universals are *outside* nature. But if we are to say that necessary truths are truths at all, then we must say that they are truths about objects of thought alone (concepts, universals, abstract entities); and this is why some who think that every truth must be a truth about the natural world are found to declare that all of what are called necessary truths say the same thing, namely nothing.

The more careful of committed naturalists, of course, will avoid this rather baffling epigram. He has more considered things to say. He will attempt what might be called a naturalistic reduction of our intuitions of conceptual necessity. For thinking, after all, is something that occurs in nature. So he will seek an account of these intuitions in terms of what is naturally found—in terms of this or that natural mental content or in terms of this or that natural, and socially reinforced, disposition to behaviour, especially linguistic behaviour. Talk of grasping or perceiving necessary relations between abstract objects or concepts he will see as at best an attempt to do justice to some aspects of the phenomenology of thought, but as a misguided attempt in so far as it appears to invoke objects that have no place in this, the natural, and the only, world. His opponent, on the other hand, will continue to insist that the fact that thinking is a natural phenomenon does not require that all its objects be so too; and that recognition of the full powers of thought is *eo ipso* recognition of its abstract objects.

As I have already suggested, I do not think that the dispute is finally resolvable. In saying this I do not mean that there is a right answer which will remain forever hidden from us because we lack the power to reach that impartial vantage point from which the truth can be discerned and the final judgement delivered. I mean, rather, that there is no such vantage point; neither in the natural world nor out of it; for any location of our judgement seat would be a prejudgement of the issue. If I am right in this, then the picture of a profound metaphysical disagreement should ideally be replaced by that of a choice: between the adoption of a naturalist stance, with a consequential restriction of the notion of existence to what is found in nature; and a contrary willingness to extend the notion to thought-objects, exemplifiable, but not locatable, in nature. Ideally still, it should not matter greatly which choice is made; for any pair of philosophers of opposed persuasions (or, in this matter, perhaps, of temperaments) should be able to appreciate, across their difference in idiom, the force of each other's attempts on the less general and more substantial problems that confront them both. But this *is* ideal; and it seems more likely that the old debate will continue, in variant guises and variant forms, as long as our civilization lasts. May that be long indeed!

# 3

# *Positions for Quantifiers*

I

Tom and William play follow-my-leader. William is the leader. So Tom does whatever William does. Now, as some would ask, what is the logical form of this last statement? Or—in other words—how are we to understand our understanding of the construction it exemplifies?

Someone might too hastily say that the statement is to be understood—indeed *is* understood—as involving quantification over particular actions and has the form 'For any (action) $x$, if William performs $x$, then Tom performs $x$ too'. But if by 'particular action' here we mean what, say, Donald Davidson means, this obviously won't do. For Tom *can't* perform the particular action that William performs. The best he can do is to perform another action of the same kind. So if we are to analyse our statement as involving quantification over actions, the analysis will have to be more complicated. It might, for example, run: 'For every action-kind $K$, if there is an action $x$ such that William performs $x$ and $x \, \varepsilon \, K$, then there is an action $y$, such that Tom performs $y$ and $y \, \varepsilon \, K$.' And here we quantify not only over actions, but also over action-kinds.

Now it seems undeniable that our original statement involves quantification (or something very like it). It is also undeniable that anyone who understands both our original statement and our doubly quantified analysis will acknowledge that they are, nearly enough, equivalent. But the combined force of these two truths seems insufficient to compel the conclusion that this analysis really does expose the logical form of the original. Rather, one may feel that the original statement is a good example of something for which Quine allows no place in his favoured logical grammar: namely quantification such that if we wish to represent it with the help of variables, it requires predicate-variables (or, perhaps better, a special subclass of predicate-variables). So if one were to choose a way of representing the form designed to bring out both its resemblance to, and its difference from, the kind of quantification recognized in standard logical grammar, one might write: '($\Phi$) (William $\Phi$s $\rightarrow$ Tom $\Phi$s)'.

Let us consider a comment on this from a Quinian point of view. 'There is, in this suggestion', it might be said, 'no real departure from orthodoxy, though there may well be a certain confusion—a conflation, perhaps, of two different suggestions each individually reconcilable with orthodoxy. Orthodoxy requires that all quantification be quantification over individuals (objectual, referential), *unless* it is merely substitutional. Variables of quantification can indeed genuinely fill out predicate-place; but only if they are variables of merely substitutional quantification. So if we are to take the present proposal as one according to which the variables of quantification do indeed genuinely fill out the predicate-places, then we must also take it as a proposal to view the quantification in question as merely substitutional quantification. There is, however, another alternative to the doubly quantified analysis which is also compatible with orthodoxy. We can regard our original statement as involving just one dose of quantification, and this non-substitutional quantification, if we are prepared to see the variables of quantification as ranging not over particular actions but over action-types or universals—items akin to attributes. In that case, we should make explicit in our analysis the presence of a suitable two-place predicate apt for linking the name of an actor and the name of an action-type: say 'performs' or perhaps 'exemplifies'. Indeed we might suggest that the word 'does' in our original statement has just this role. But if the proposal under consideration is to be taken in this sense, then it was confusingly presented. The presentation indeed bears all the marks of a conflation of two separately legitimate proposals.

Now let us consider a rejoinder to this orthodox comment—or, rather, two rejoinders. The first rejoinder is to the effect that neither of the so-called legitimate alternatives is realistic, that neither, therefore, is acceptable for the purposes in hand; the second, and much more important, rejoinder is that the orthodox comment has nothing but orthodoxy to recommend it and this is no recommendation, for the orthodoxy in question is not well founded.

Is either of the two so-called legitimate alternatives realistic? What of substitutional quantification? As far as I understand the matter, the criterion of *truth* for substitutional quantification is to be found in the results of dropping the quantifier and substituting expressions of the appropriate grammatical category in the place of the variables which the quantifier binds. Thus Quine writes: 'An existential substitutional quantification is counted as true if and only if there is an expression which, when substituted for the variable, makes the open sentence after the quantifier come out true'; and again 'A universal quantification is counted as true if no substitution makes the open sentence come out false.'[1] Now in the case of our universally quantified statement about Tom and William, what is here offered as a *criterion* of truth may well be a *consequence* of truth. But to present this consequence as a criterion seems quite bizarre. The criterion of truth for such a statement as is in question has nothing to do with expressions. Indeed, the criterion cannot be declared more clearly than it declares itself: Tom does whatever William does: however William acts, Tom acts thus too. William's behaviour might be indescribable without therefore being inimitable.

Perhaps I have misunderstood Quine's explanations of substitutional quantification. Perhaps the notion of a criterion of truth is out of place or unclear. But replacing it with the perhaps looser idea of an explanation of meaning, or with the

---

[1] *Ontological Relativity*, 104 (Columbia University Press, New York, 1969).

notion of explanatory paraphrase, clearly makes no change in the situation. Any paraphrase of 'Tom does whatever William does' which mentions expressions is a poor one. Substitutional quantification, if there is such a thing, must be clearly differentiated from the other sort of quantification which Quine acknowledges (quantification over individuals) without assuming the aspect of a kind of quantification of which he denies the possibility or intelligibility. But it is impossible to find in the official doctrine an account which both achieves this result and is such that our quantified statement about Tom and William can plausibly be said to be an instance of substitutional quantification. Henceforth I shall say no more about substitutional quantification.

The objection to the second proffered 'legitimate' alternative is rather subtler and more difficult to state concisely. It merges with the objection to the orthodoxy in general. If we set aside both substitutional quantification and the doubly quantified analysis, we seem to be left with two prima-facie possibilities, one compatible with the orthodoxy and one not. Consider the two pairs of statements:

1 (a) If Tom runs, then Tom is out of breath
  (b) Whoever runs is out of breath

2 (a) If William hops, then Tom hops
  (b) Tom does whatever William does.

On one view—the unorthodox view—the logical relation between 1(a) and 1(b) is exactly parallelled by the logical relation between 2(a) and 2(b). We can say 1(b) and then go on: 'For instance, 1(a)'. We can say 2(b) and then go on: 'For instance 2(a)'. The relation in each case is equally direct. There is a difference, of course: in the one case we are generalizing in name- or subject-place, in the other in predicate-place (or, perhaps better, in action-predicate-place). It is because there is the possibility of this difference that there is the possibility of this parallel. The orthodox view denies the possibility of this difference and hence the possibility of this parallel. On the orthodox view the relation between 2(a) and

2(b) cannot be direct, as is the relation between 1(a) and 1(b). The relation between 2(a) and 2(b) is mediated, on this view: it is mediated by something like a paraphrase[2] of 2(a) in which the one-place predicate occurring in 2(a) is replaced by a combination of a two-place predicate and a name. It is this paraphrase, and only this paraphrase, which stands in as direct a relation to 2(b) as 1(a) does to 1(b). If we really want a *strict* parallel to '1(b); for instance 1(a)', then we should say something like this: 'Tom does whatever William does; for instance, if Tom does hopping, then William does hopping', from which we could proceed, by paraphrase, to 'That is to say, if Tom hops, then William hops.'

Of these two views it seems to me that, while the unorthodox view yields a natural account of our understanding of the forms in question, there is nothing to recommend the orthodox view except its orthodoxy. But what is there to recommend the orthodoxy? If the orthodoxy were merely a stipulated feature of the grammar of an artificial notation, the question would have, in the present context, no interest. For our present concern is with forms of natural language. So if the only merits of the restriction in question were to be found in advantages of, say, clarity or simplicity which it secured to the artificial notation, then it would have, from our present point of view, no merits at all.

But it seems clear, or fairly clear, that Quine does not view the orthodoxy in this light. When he maintains that quantification, if not merely substitutional, is always quantification over individuals (objects), that variables of non-substitutional quantification can never fill out predicative, but only referential, position, he seems to see himself not as imposing a convenient restriction but as acknowledging a general truth. What are his reasons? One set of reasons can hardly be thought compelling. It goes like this. 'Whenever we quantify, then we can also express what we want to say by starting off with "There is. . . ." (or its negation), followed by a phrase beginning with "some" or "a" (for example, some-

---

[2] But see below, Part IV.

thing, some place, some time, some way—a thing, a place, a time, a way, etc.), followed by a relative clause. The phrase "There is . . ." is explicitly existential, and thus explicitly referential, directing us to objects, to things that exist. Names, too, direct us, in their own way, to objects; but predicates do not. Predicates are simply attached in a truth-or-falsehood-yielding way, to the referential expressions, the expressions that direct us to objects, be they names or the "some" (or "a"-) phrases of quantification introduced by the explicitly existential "There is". The availability of the "There is . . ." form makes clear, as nothing else can, what we are doing when we quantify; and *ipso facto* makes clear that, whatever the appearances, the only place for quantifiers is the referential place.'

The above is not taken from any specific page of Quine, yet seems true to the spirit of much that he writes. It can hardly be said, however, to be persuasive. Why should Quine, of all people, attach so much importance to the ever-availability in English idiom, whenever we quantify, of the 'There is . . .' form? Why not rather regard this as a trivial fact, or even as a misleading feature, of English idiom? Why not stress rather the fact of the frequent dispensability of such constructions—with or without unnaturalness? (And often without: as, for example, in my own sentence, above: 'Whenever we quantify, then . . . .'.) If we leave aside the 'There is a . . .' idiom and turn to the notion of 'object', we do not find any greater measure of clarification. Prior, who has his own reasons for rejecting the Quinian orthodoxy, remarks that the introduction of bindable variables in the place of certain expressions by no means commits us to the view that these expressions stand for or designate objects.[3] This remark would be more helpful if we were also told how to understand the notion of an object, or of an expression's standing for, or designating, an object. Quine, in a way, does tell us, but only in a way which completes the deadlock: objects (or what we take to be such) are what we quantify over, that is, take to exist.

---

[3] Cf. *Objects of Thought*, ch. 3, esp. 35–6 (Clarendon Press, Oxford, 1971).

If we get little light on the orthodoxy by way of the notions of existence and object, perhaps we shall get more by putting these notions, at least temporarily, on one side. What we are left with if we put these notions on one side is simply the notion of (singular) predication, a grammatical combination into which there enter (in the simplest case) a singular term and a predicate: and along with this the notions of position for a singular term (or referential position) and predicate-position. In Quine's ideally austere language the distinction between singular terms and predicates is *identical* with the distinction between quantifiable variables and predicates. So we must obviously look outside the limits of that language if we want to ask *why* Quine holds the general doctrine that quantifiable variables can fill out only referential position and never predicate position, that is, the doctrine that there can be singular term variables and not predicate-variables. We do not have to look very far outside. It will suffice, at least for the moment, to admit the category of names. Then we have 'Fa' as the general form of predication without quantification. And we have the question: Why is it held that quantifiable variables can fill out only the a-place and not the F-place?

Quine's answer is quite explicit, and again surprising. It is that there is no way of distinguishing the parts which enter into this general combination of predication *except* as the parts one of which occupies a position accessible to quantification while the other does not. It is not a question of specifying a certain basic grammatical combination and then advancing a certain doctrine about it; rather, it is only in terms of the doctrine that we can specify the combination. Here I quote: 'When we schematize a sentence in the predicative way "*Fa*" or "*a* is an *F*", our recognition of an "*a*" part and an "*F*" part turns strictly on our use of variables of quantification; the "*a*" represents a part of the sentence that stands where a quantifiable variable could stand, and the "*F*" represents the rest.'[4] Again, imagining a finite universe of

----

[4] 'Existence and Quantification', in *Ontological Relativity*, 95; see also 106.

named objects, in which quantification lapses, as theoretically inessential, Quine adds: 'And the very distinction between names and other signs lapses in turn, since the mark of a name is its admissibility in positions of variables.'[5] Here the orthodox doctrine is presented as absolutely watertight; for the terms in which the doctrine is stated can only be understood if the doctrine is accepted.

But is this true? Is it true that no account can be given of the distinction between the 'a' part and the 'F' part of a predication (of the subject-predicate distinction, as I shall say for short), except in terms which presuppose the orthodoxy? Surely it is *not* true. For such accounts have been given, and have not been shown to be incoherent.[6] (They—or some of them—may have been framed in terms which Quine is reluctant to employ: but that is another matter altogether.)

So in default of reasons for accepting the orthodoxy, we are released from its restrictions. We can acknowledge quantification into predicate-position as a feature of the logical grammar of natural language as freely as we can acknowledge quantification into name- (or singular-subject)-position. And we can maintain the intuitively satisfactory position earlier adumbrated on our original question: that is, that 'Tom does whatever William does' is as direct a predicate-generalization of 'If William hops, then Tom hops' as 'Whoever runs is out of breath' is a subject-generalization of 'If Tom runs, then Tom is out of breath.' Here are two convenient terminological decisions to accompany our recognition of our freedom. First: we will retain the familiar phrase 'existential quantification' for what might otherwise be called ' "some"-quantification', whether we are quantifying into referential position or not; but, second, we will restrict the idiom of 'quantifying over' to the cases where we are quantifying into referential position.

⁵ *Ontological Relativity*, 62.
⁶ Cf. Strawson, 'Singular Terms and Predication' and 'The Asymmetry of Subject and Predicate', in *Logico-Linguistic Papers*, 53–74 and 96–115 (Methuen, London, 1971).

II

Suppose we now move outside the limits of that restricted grammar which recognizes as grammatical categories just singular terms, predicates, and sentences, including open sentences; and which recognizes as constructions just predication, yielding sentences from singular terms and predicates, and a small number of constructions involving either a connective or a quantifier, yielding sentences from sentences. Our purpose is to inquire where else, if anywhere, we may quantify, besides into singular-term-position and predicate-position; or, more exactly, where else, if anywhere, it is reasonable to suppose that we do in fact quantify in our natural language. Prior has one suggestion. Indeed it seems to be primarily in the interest of this suggestion that he queries the orthodoxy just discarded. He suggests that we recognize a set of constructions which, unlike any of those just mentioned, form sentences from singular terms and sentences. 'Believes that', 'says that', and so on, would be particles entering into such constructions. He then suggests that we can quantify, not only into singular-term-place and predicate-place, but also into sentence-place: the best way of representing the logical form of 'Tom believes everything that William tells him' would be '$(p)$ (William tells Tom that $p \rightarrow$ Tom believes that $p$).' Though this freedom to quantify into sentence place is most useful in connection with constructions of this kind, it is not, of course, confined to such use. It would be suspicious if it were. The logical form of 'Some proposition is true' is '$(\exists p)$ it is true that $p$', which is equivalent to '$(\exists p)\ p$'. An important merit of this proposal in Prior's eyes is that it does not commit us to recognizing propositions as objects. Quantifying into sentence-place is not quantifying *over* propositions. It will be seen that though Prior rejects the Quinian orthodoxy as a whole, he accepts a part of it. Quine holds that whenever we quantify, we quantify into referential position and hence quantify over objects (or what we are committed to taking as such). Prior rejects the premiss, but accepts that the conclusion follows from it. When we do indeed quantify into singular-term-position, he would agree, we are committed to the view that any specifying expression, any definite singular term, which might replace the bound variable, stands for or designates an object.

Let us put Prior's proposal on one side for a moment—I will return to it later—and turn to another class of cases. Consider the following sets of expressions: somewhere, nowhere, everywhere, anywhere, wherever; always, sometimes, never, whenever; somehow, anyhow, however. Anyone who reflects on the topic of quantification should surely be struck by the parallel between these expressions and those commonly taken to be the natural language representatives of quantification into singular-term-position: that is, something, everything, nothing, anything, whatever; and someone, everyone, no one (nobody), anyone, whoever.[7] So strong is the influence of the prevailing dogma, however, that expressions of the first class have commonly been taken, like expressions of the second, as signalizing quantification into singular-term-position: quantification, that is, *over* places, times, or occasions, and perhaps manners or means. Thus 'Holmes will meet Moriarty somewhere, sometime', will become, as a first approximation—I do not wish to saddle anyone with the suggestion that this would represent a final analysis—something like 'There is a place, $x$, and a time, $y$, such that will-meet-at-at (Holmes, Moriarty, $x$, $y$).'

If, however, we are prepared to enrich our grammar— that is, in the present context to enrich our conception of our actual grammar—sufficiently to provide for adverbial phrases, and at the same time to make use of our new freedom with quantifiers, a quite different treatment may become possible. What the best account to give of constructions with adverbial phrases may be, is not an easy question. It is fairly certain that not all constructions traditionally classified as adverbial are to be handled in the same way. One way of handling some cases might be to recognize a construction involving a combination of predicate and adverb (or adverb

---

[7] Cf. Strawson, 'Singular Terms and Predication', *Logico-Linguistics Papers*, 72.

phrase) which yields a complex predicate. We might call it the modification construction. Even this might be too close to conventional models for the sort of cases that currently concern us, and it might be better to think of some kinds of adverbial modification as yielding sentences from sentences. For our present purposes the particular solution adopted in particular types of case is indifferent, so long as it involves the recognition of certain unreduced grammatical categories of adverb-phrases, including those relating to time and place. Given that this condition is satisfied and the orthodoxy regarding quantification is abandoned, there is no obstacle in principle to recognizing quantification into adverb-phrase-place wherever we find it. And of course the suggestion is that we typically find it where we find the expressions I listed just now: that is, 'somewhere', 'always', and their kin.

Parenthetically it may be pointed out that this suggestion may throw some light on Davidson's problem about action-sentences with adverbial modification.[8] He is concerned to elucidate the understanding we have of the logical grammar of natural language, which underlies our knowledge that, for example, from the proposition that Brutus stabbed Caesar in the afternoon in the Forum there follows the proposition that Brutus stabbed Caesar or from the proposition that John kissed Mary in the garden at midnight it follows that John kissed Mary. His own solution is to regard every such sentence as involving existential quantification over actions and to treat the place- and time-specifying adverbial phrases as predicates of actions; the suggestion, in the form in which he makes it, involves displacing the apparent two-place-predicates 'stab' and 'kiss' by three-place-predicates, for which relevant triples in the given cases would consist of two persons and one action. He contrasts his solution favourably with another suggestion according to which the apparent two-place-predicates 'kiss' and 'stab' are really $n$-place predicates, for somewhat indefinite $n$, with relevant $n$-tuples in-

---

[8] See Davidson, 'The Logical Form of Action Sentences', in *The Logic of Decision and Action*, ed. N. Rescher, 81–95 (University of Pittsburgh Press, Pittsburgh, 1967).

cluding, not actions, but persons, places, times, perhaps instruments, and so, somewhat vaguely, on. There is indeed little to be said for this last suggestion. But it is arguable that both it and Davidson's would seem equally unnecessary once we recognized certain categories of adverbial phrases in our logical grammar; and perhaps it would be easier to appreciate this once we recognized also the possibility of quantifying in the positions those phrases occupy. We then have 'Brutus stabbed Caesar somewhere somewhen' as a direct consequence of our original proposition; and our grasp of the fact that these quantifiers can be added to or dropped from simple ascriptions of human action without modification of truth-value rests on nothing more recondite than our grasp of the general concept of action. 'Stab', 'kiss', and so on, retain the general formal character they appear to have, namely that of two-place-predicates; which is surely one merit, on the score of realism, accruing to the present proposal and guaranteed on no other. (Of course this is only a sketch of a suggestion; and I do not suggest, or think, that it would be free from problems.)

III

We have now before us a variety of proposals for recognizing 'unorthodox' quantification, that is, quantification into positions other than referential: we have, namely quantification into predicate-place, into sentence-place and into adverbial-phrase-place. Two questions confront us, among, doubtless, many. The first is: How should we assess these proposals for realism? And here we are to remember that what we are concerned with is our understanding of the forms of natural language. For example, with reference to Prior's proposal, how are we to decide whether propositional quantification is quantification into referential position, as he says it is not, or quantification into sentence-position, as he says it is? The second question is: If we conclude in a given case that we are indeed quantifying into referential position (as the orthodoxy says we always are) what is the significance of this conclusion? What does it commit us to?

Let us take the second question first. A point on which Prior and Quine are agreed is that in general quantification into singular-term-position commits us to acknowledging a certain kind of *objects*—objects such as the attached predicates are true of, objects such as would be named or designated by any definite singular terms or specifying expressions which might occupy the place which the bound variables occupy. The commitment is said to be ontological. But is it ontological? Why should it be more than grammatical? or grammatico-logical? Quine says we are committed to a certain class of *objects*. It would be more to the point, at least at first, to say that we are committed to a certain class of *subjects*; where 'subject' is the logico-grammatical correlate of the logico-grammatical 'predicate'. Just what this logico-grammatical commitment is depends on our understanding of the significance of the correlated pair '(singular logical) subject' and 'predicate'; or 'definite referring term' and, as Quine would put it, 'general term in predicative position'. Quine, as we have seen, says that no account can be given of this correlated pair except in terms of accessibility and non-accessibility of their respective positions to quantifiers. Prior cannot share this view. He must just think it obvious that subjects stand for objects: but since he doesn't say what he understands by 'object', it isn't obvious what he thinks obvious.

Now suppose we hold, with (presumably) Aristotle, that the base class of (singular) subject-predicate-propositions are those in which an expression designating a space-occupying, relatively enduring substantial thing (personal, animal, or merely material) is coupled with an expression signifying a general character (quality or property or kind of action or undergoing, or simply kind) of such things, in such a way as to yield truth or falsehood. The first of these expressions we call the subject; the second (which may include also the symbolism of predicative or propositional coupling), the predicate. Quite apart from the location of the coupling symbolism, this combination, as I have argued elsewhere, has a profound asymmetry about it based on the difference between what the subject-terms and the predicate-terms, respectively, signify. It can be roughly expressed by saying that general characters of substantial things intrinsically enjoy logical relations with other such characters when considered in relation to any and every substantial thing they might be assigned to; whereas it is not the case that substantial things intrinsically enjoy logical relations with other such things when considered in relation to any and every general character which they might be assigned to. (Rather, they intrinsically don't enjoy such relations.) Now this relative asymmetry condition can be generalized. It can be considered in abstraction from the types or categories we start from—those of individual substances and general characters of substances. We can form the general idea of the propositional coupling of a sentence-part A and a sentence-part B where (1) A specifies an item of X type and B specifies an item of Y type and (2) X-type items stand in the same asymmetrical relation to Y-type items as substances do to general characters of substances, and (3) this logical analogy is marked in a formal grammatical way by the A-part having the form which the subjects of our basic subject-predicate-sentences have, namely the form of a noun or noun-phrase and the B-part having one or another of the forms which regularly complement a definite noun or noun-phrase to yield a sentence, for example, verb, adjective, or indefinite noun-phrase (with copula supplied in the last two cases). Then A-part and B-part stand to each other as subject to predicate. And here we have a general account of subject and predicate.

Now what of the doctrine that all subjects stand for objects and hence that all quantification into subject-position is quantification over objects? Surely 'clarity is served' by distinguishing two senses of 'object', one a merely relative, logico-grammatical sense and the other a sense which might not inaptly be called ontological. In the logico-grammatical sense some specific item is an object relative to some proposition; it is an object because some expression specifying it is propositionally coupled with another expression which, relative to the first, fulfills the conditions of being a predicate. In this sense something which is presented as object in one proposition can sometimes be presented in a quite different role in another. In this sense we quantify over objects when what the apparatus of quantification is attached to has predicate-status in relation to all the specifying expressions which might replace that apparatus. But we can and sometimes do use the word 'object' quite differently. We can and sometimes do distinguish objects from qualities, properties, relations, events, processes, species, types, and whatnot. Substances are undoubted objects in this sense. There is no grammatico-logical relativity about this sense. Rather we might say that in this sense we use the word for ontological classification or categorization; for distinguishing one ontological category from others. Never mind that it is not a particularly well-defined category. Few categories are.

Of course there is a link between the two senses of 'object'. For objects in the ontological-categorial sense are the basic objects in the logico-grammatical sense. Hard though it is to believe, it is almost impossible *not* to believe that some confusion of the two senses of 'object', or of the two ideas involved, underlies much of the persistent philosophical anxiety that goes under the name of 'ontology'. The confusion would seem too gross to be credible if it were not for the fact that in philosophy no confusion is too gross to be credible. Worries about Platonism; the talk of 'countenancing' items of this or that type or 'admitting them into our ontology'; the use of phrases like 'a grossly inflated ontology' and the rest—all of these are familiar in connection with quantification into subject-place, and the connection is very difficult to understand except on the supposition of some such confusion and quite easy to understand on that supposition.

So now back to the first of our two questions. Granted that we can ignore the bogey of ontology; granted also that we can and do quantify into places unhaunted by the bogey: How, then, should we assess such a proposal as Prior's, the proposal namely that propositional quantification should be viewed as quantification into sentence-place and not into singular-term-place?

It seems to me that the balance of realism tips against Prior and in favour of the view that propositional quantification is quantification over propositions. The language is full of what are traditionally classified as noun-phrases specifying propositions (for example, 'that it is raining'; 'this doctrine'; 'the axiom of parallels'; 'your suggestion'); it is full of what appear to be proposition-predicates (whether one-place, like 'true' and 'false', two-place, relating person and proposition, as 'believe' 'assent' 'surmise', or two-place, relating proposition and proposition, as 'implies' 'incompatible with'): and when we quantify, the apparatus of quantification is regularly attached to these apparent predicates and replaceable by those apparent noun-phrases. Both the logical asymmetry condition and the formal grammatical conditions are satisfied for speaking of propositional subjects and propositional predicates and for saying that propositional quantification is quantification into subject-place, quantification over propositions.

These remarks may not seem to be conclusive against recognizing propositional quantification into sentence-place as well as quantification over propositions. We still have before us Prior's suggestion for parsing such sentences as 'John asserts (believes) that it is raining'; and the associated suggestion that 'the proposition that $p$ is incompatible with the proposition that $q$' is simply periphrasis for 'if $p$, then not-$q$'. Have we not similarly recognized 'If William performs an action of the hopping-kind, then Tom performs an action of the hopping-kind' as a possible periphrasis for 'If William hops, then Tom hops', and associated a double quantification over actions and action-kinds with the former as well as a quantification into action-predicate-place with the latter? So may we not recognize quantification over propositions in our language without prejudice to the recognition of Prior's kind of quantification as also in the language?

Unfortunately, the parallel is seen to break down when we turn to examples. Consider 'Tom said (asserted) something incompatible with everything William said (asserted).' This is ambiguous, of course, and we can easily capture both readings in sentences in which 'is incompatible with' stands in predicate-place in relation to variables of quantification in subject-place. For these readings we can equally easily find equivalents in Priorese. Thus we have '($\exists p$) [Tom said that $p$. ($q$) William said that $q \rightarrow$ (*if* $p$, then -$q$)]' for one reading and '($q$) [William said that $q \rightarrow$ ($\exists p$) (Tom said that $p$. if $p$, then -$q$)]' for the other. The trouble is that there just are no sentences in English which the Priorese versions, with sentential quantification, can be taken as representing in the way in which sentences with quantification over propositions can be taken as representing the two readings of the ordinary English sentence we started out with.

To say the Priorese sentences do not represent the form which English sentences actually exemplify is of course not to deny the intelligibility of Priorese. Nor is it to deny ourselves any philosophical illumination we may be able to derive from our appreciation of the equivalence of Priorese sentences and English sentences. It is not even to deny that Priorese may have certain merits or advantages which English lacks, that we may perhaps be able to express elegantly in Priorese what we may be able to express only by relatively cumbrous circumlocution in English. For example '($p$) (it is true that $p \leftrightarrow p$)' is well-formed in Priorese and says neatly what we cannot say very neatly in English. All that is contended is that Priorese sentential quantification is not a realistic representation of propositional quantification in our language, even though there *are* constructions is our language which do involve quantification into positions other than subject or singular-term-position.

IV

I should not leave the subject without attempting some explanation of the restrictive doctrine regarding quantification into predicate-place. Why should it be thought that predicate-position differs from referential position in being inaccessible to quantifiers (or variables of quantification)? I have a suggestion to make, which is best reached by bringing into prominence an accepted consequence of the doctrine. The simple propositions

(a) Socrates swims
(b) Socrates is brave

yield by generalization the propositions: 'Someone swims' and 'Someone is brave' or 'There is someone who swims' and 'There is someone who is brave.' According to the doctrine in question, they cannot also yield by generalization the proposition 'Socrates does something' (or 'There is something Socrates does') and 'Socrates is something' (or 'There is something Socrates is'). The propositions (a) and (b) cannot be allowed to yield these generalizations: for to allow that they did would be to allow quantification into predicate-place. However, the sentences in question are perfectly legitimate and intelligible English sentences, generalized in form, and it must be granted (and indeed *is* granted) that there are some specifying propositions to which these general propositions stand in the same relation as the general propositions 'Someone swims', 'Someone is brave' stand in to such specifying propositions as (a) and (b). So what sort of thing *are* the specifying propositions in these cases? Well, we are offered things like:

(A) Socrates performs     swimming
          exemplifies

(B) Socrates exhibits
          possesses     bravery
          exemplifies

where the nouns 'swimming' and 'bravery' are held to 'name attributes' or 'specify concepts' and a brand-new two-place-predicate is introduced to couple the two names. Since these nouns occupy referential position, we can admit the generalizations and preserve the doctrine. But now, if the doctrine is to retain any substance there must be a substantial difference between (A) and (B) on the one hand and (a) and (b) on the other. It cannot be merely a matter of stylistic variation.

The idea, then, is that (A) or (B) *commit* us, as regards swimming and bravery, in a way in which we aren't bit committed by:

(a)  Socrates swims

or by:

(b)  Socrates is brave

I want to suggest to you, first, of course, that this is absurd; that this theory of 'commitment' by noun but not by adjective or verb is about as absolutely implausible as any philosophical view could be: that we are every bit as 'committed' by (a) and (b) as we are by (A) and (B). By all means say, if you like, that one who says

Socrates exemplifies bravery

thereby 'brings in' the attribute or concept, bravery, or shows himself as recognizing or acknowledging this attribute or concept. But then add that one who says

Socrates is brave

brings in the attribute or concept, bravery, just as much as one who says 'Socrates exemplifies bravery'.

Of course my current concern is not with the fact that the absurd view *is* absurd, but with the question why the view should be held. And my suggestion is that the fact that the predicate incorporates the propositional symbolism of the *verb* makes it easier to overlook or become blind to the fact that it also specifies a concept or attribute quite as fully and completely as any noun could. It's the former fact that makes it possible to slide away from the specificatory function of the predicate by way of saying things like: predicates are just *true or false of* what subject-terms stand for. But this soothing, pacifying, deceptive phrase, if it makes any clear point at all, simply makes the point that predicate-phrases incorporate the propositional symbolism, the symbolism of the verb.

'Predicates are wanted in all sentences,' says Quine (*Philosophy of Logic*, 28). The phrase reveals the trouble. What is wanted in all sentences is the indication of propositionality, the verb-form or whatever does its duty. It is no more necessary that sentences should contain predicates in the full sense which entails concept-specification than it is that they should contain subjects in the full sense which entails individual-specification. So 'Socrates does something' is just as good, and *just as direct* a generalization, from

Socrates swims

as 'Someone swims' is. The phrase 'does something' replaces specificity with non-specificity just as the phrase 'someone' does. It also exhibits the form of the verb necessary for sentencehood (propositionality). It is the failure to see clearly that ordinary predicate-expressions *combine* the function of concept-specification with propositional indication that leads to the queer restriction on quantification.

It might be said: granted that the predicate's incorporating the propositional symbolism makes it easier to develop a kind of blindness to the concept-specificatory or attribute-specificatory function of the predicate, the explanation still seems insufficient. Why should anyone want to slide away from recognition of this function with the help of those deceptive phrases about predicates 'being true or false of what subject-terms stand for', about their being just the other parties to predication? One answer is: because of the risk of Platonism. But what is this risk? The risk of mythologizing, of taking there to exist objects which don't exist, which it perhaps doesn't make sense to suppose do exist or which, at any rate, talking too easily of gives too easy an escape from facing problems, seems to be explanatory when it isn't, and so on. But now, and finally, what has this to do with quantification? Why should generality rather than specificity in predicate-place carry any undesirable theoretical implications? Well, putting aside the triviality that 'some' -quantification can always be expressed in English by 'There *is* something which . . .', I think I can make a diagnostic shot here, which returns us to a point made earlier in the paper. There is not, *in general*, much point in specifying a substantial particular ('Socrates') and then generalizing in predicate-place ('does something', 'is something') unless you have some higher-order concept or property in mind, some principle of collection which applies to those principles of collection which apply to particulars. But in so far as you have this in mind, then you are at least prepared for that grammatical shift which involves quantifying *over* what predicates specify as well as *into* predicate-position. But to have this preparedness is equivalent to having in mind the idea of specifiers of attributes or properties as fit occupants of subject-place. But the primary occupants of subject-place are particular-specifiers. So you are implicitly likening what attribute-specifiers specify to those honest spatio-temporal objects which particular-specifiers specify. The fear of Platonism is (at least in part) the fear of the reproach of this comparison. To that extent it is an unreasonable fear. For the likening is only a logical likening, the logical analogy already referred to. That it should ever have seemed more—in such a way as to inspire opposite emotions in different breasts—simply underlines the correctness of taking it that, in basic subject-predicate propositions, subjects stand for spatio-temporal objects.

# 4

## Concepts and Properties
### or Predication and Copulation

In a recent article[1] David Wiggins proposes a 'running repair' to Frege's doctrine of the sense and reference of predicates. The repair involves 'a plea for the copula'. While agreeing with the main contentions in Wiggins's article, I think that his repair is itself in need of a (perhaps minor) repair. I should say that in what follows I am not committing myself on any contentious point concerning the interpretation of Frege. I am concerned only with what seems to me true in Wiggins's own position and with what seems to me to need correction in it.

We are to consider simple sentences each of which contains one expression from each of the following three classes: (1) proper names, such as 'John', 'Socrates', etc.; (2) general terms (i.e. adjectives such as 'wise', 'brave', etc.; common nouns such as 'horse', 'man', etc.; verbs such as 'work', 'run', etc.); and (3) a copula such as 'is' or 'is a' or the inflections which yield a finite form of the verb.

Wiggins's position is: the name stands for, or refers to, an object; the general term stands for, or refers to, a concept; the copula does not stand for, or refer to, anything, but has an indispensable semantic role or function, viz. that of combining with the general term to form a properly predicative expression, which can then combine with the name to form a sentence, a vehicle of truth or falsity. The properly predica-

---

[1] D. Wiggins, 'The Sense and Reference of Predicates: A Running Repair to Frege's Doctrine and a Plea for the Copula', *Philosophical Quarterly* 34 (1984).

tive expression does not, *as a whole*, stand for, or refer to, anything, though it contains a part (the general term) which does. (This without prejudice to the fact that in some languages or symbolisms the copula, as distinguishable linguistic element, may sometimes be replaced or displaced 'by a convention of mere concatenation'.[2])

All this, as I say, seems to me highly plausible, indeed correct. But I have one reservation. Wiggins is willing to identify concepts (what general terms stand for or refer to) with 'forms or characters or traits or universals';[3] but he is unwilling to identify them with properties. His stated reason for this unwillingness is that whereas a general term (say, 'man') can combine with the copula to yield a properly predicative expression which can in turn combine with a name to yield a sentence, the corresponding property-name (say, 'manhood') *cannot* combine *in exactly the same way* with a copulative expression to yield an *equivalent* properly predicative expression which can in turn combine with a name to form a sentence. We can say 'Jesus is a man', but cannot, or cannot equivalently, say 'Jesus is manhood'. We can say 'Socrates is wise', but not, or not equivalently, 'Socrates is wisdom'. What this shows, Wiggins says, is that 'man' and 'manhood' (or 'wise' and 'wisdom') do not stand for the same thing.[4]

This conclusion is what I want to question. I should emphasize that, in questioning it, I am not questioning something else that Wiggins says, which seems to me perfectly true. The thing he says that seems to me perfectly true is that the general term is more fundamental than the corresponding property-name, or, as he puts it, that 'concept-words are more fundamental than property-designations'.[5] This is surely correct in that the abstract nouns which name properties are *linguistically derivative* from the corresponding adjectives, common nouns, or verbs. Thus—to quote Wiggins—he says, of the expression 'manhood', that 'surely it is synonymous with, or an alternative form of, the nominalization "be-

² Op. cit., 327.      ³ Op. cit., 323.      ⁴ Op. cit., 320.
⁵ Op. cit., 323.

ing a man", which presupposes the unsaturated [i.e. properly predicative] expression "ξ is a man" which (in my story, at least) presupposes the Fregean concept *man*'.[6]

However, neither this point about the linguistic derivativeness of the property-name nor the associated earlier point that the property-name is grammatically debarred from playing exactly the same role as the associated general term seems to me to warrant the denial of the identity of concept (as understood by Wiggins) and property. To think otherwise is to attribute to a purely formal, syntactical matter a categorial or ontological significance it does not have.

There is perhaps another line of reasoning involved in Wiggins's position—a line of reasoning which goes as follows. In the case of properties, the expressions which (appear to) refer to or stand for them also (appear to) *name* or *designate* them. So properties—if there are such entities at all—are *objects*. But in the case of concepts the expressions which refer to or stand for them do not name or designate them. They are not abstract nouns or nominalizing phrases; they are general terms. So concepts are not objects. This is why Frege was right, according to Wiggins, to say that the concept *horse* is not a concept. For the expression, 'the concept *horse*' is designative, a name; it refers to an object. So concepts and— if they exist—the corresponding properties, so far from being identical, belong to entirely different categories.

If this is indeed a part of Wiggins's reason for denying the identity of concept and corresponding property, then he is false to his own position. For Frege's reason for saying that the concept *horse* is not a concept, and in general for distinguishing so sharply between concepts and objects, is that expressions referring to concepts are, in his view, essentially unsaturated, i.e. essentially properly predicative; but this is precisely the view which Wiggins, in making his repair, rejects, insisting (in my view rightly) that it is only the *combination* of general term (concept-referring expression) and copula that is properly predicative. So this line of reasoning

---

[6] Op. cit., 320-1.

(quite apart from the strains it reveals in the strictly Fregean concept of a concept) is not available to Wiggins. In implicitly endorsing it, it appears that he has allowed to remain in place too much of the original structure which he sets out to repair. With this obstacle removed, I see no remaining impediment to identifying concepts with their corresponding properties—if, that is, we are prepared (unlike, say, Quine) to countenance the latter at all. If we seek a neutral term, indifferent to variations in grammatical category, for the relation which abstract noun and corresponding general term alike have to the one item concerned, the relevant property or concept, I suggest (indeed have elsewhere used) the term 'specify'[7] or the term 'introduce'.[8] Thus we avoid both the perhaps overloaded 'refer to' and 'stand for' and the perhaps too restrictive 'name' or 'designate'. Alternatively, or in addition, and by way of maximum concession to difference of grammatical category, we could, if we liked, adopt the to my mind unnecessary and idiosyncratic ruling that the one item in question is to be *known as* as a property when specified by an abstract noun or nominalizing phrase and as a concept when specified by a general term.

But this ruling would be merely eccentric or pious. There are indeed grounds for distinguishing the uses of the expressions 'concept' and 'property'; but they are quite other grounds. Thus, to have, or to exhibit, the *property* of courage is to be courageous or to behave courageously. To have, or to grasp, the *concept* of courage is to know or come to know what courage is or what it is to be courageous or behave courageously; and to exhibit the *concept* of courage would perhaps be to give a lecture on the subject. Again, philosophers speak of something's falling under a concept; but nobody speaks of something's falling under a property (unless, perhaps, it is a piece of stage property). Or again, one can perhaps say of a concept that it is clear or incoherent or confused; but one cannot say of a property that it is clear or incoherent or confused. In the context of the present discus-

[7] In *Subject and Predicate in Logic and Grammar* (London, 1974).
[8] In *Individuals* (London, 1959).

sion, these differences are nothing to the purpose. But if it is insisted that they be taken account of, then we seem forced to conclude that the difference between concepts and their corresponding properties consists in this: that to talk of the concept is to talk of the *idea* or *thought* of the thing, the property, whereas to talk of the property is to talk of the thing itself. And if this is so, then it would seem better to have said at the start that what the general term, like the abstract noun, normally refers to or stands for or specifies or introduces is the property, not the concept.

Enough, for the moment, about the expressions 'property' and 'concept' and the difference in meaning or use which they actually have in standard English usage. These differences, as already remarked, are nothing to the present purpose. Wiggins significantly makes no appeal to them; and indeed they seem quite irrelevant to *his* use of the expression 'concept', as I take it they are to Frege's also. Consider, instead, two groups of sentences, in the members of the first of which there occurs what Wiggins calls a concept-word (i.e. a word standing for a concept) and in the members of the second of which there occurs the corresponding property-name. We are to imagine the sentences being used to report a saying of some speaker, X.

I
$$
\text{X said, of Socrates,} \left\{ \begin{array}{l} \text{that he was wise} \\ \text{that he fell under the concept, } \textit{wise} \end{array} \right\}
$$
$$
\text{X} \left\{ \begin{array}{l} \text{described} \\ \text{characterized} \end{array} \right\} \text{Socrates} \left\{ \begin{array}{l} \text{as wise} \\ \text{as being wise} \end{array} \right\}
$$

II
$$
\text{X said, of Socrates, that he had} \left\{ \begin{array}{l} \text{wisdom} \\ \text{the property of wisdom} \end{array} \right\}
$$
$$
\text{X} \left\{ \begin{array}{l} \text{ascribed} \\ \text{attributed} \end{array} \right\} \left\{ \begin{array}{l} \text{wisdom} \\ \text{the} \\ \text{property} \\ \text{of} \end{array} \left\{ \begin{array}{l} \text{wisdom} \\ \text{being} \\ \text{wise} \end{array} \right\} \right\} \left\{ \begin{array}{l} \text{to} \\ \text{Socrates} \end{array} \right.
$$

The variations between these reports are merely verbal. The content of them all is effectively the same. They all say the same thing about X and all report him as saying the same thing about Socrates. For they all report him, in a more or less straightforward, or a more or less stilted, style, as characterizing Socrates in the same way. But if we agree with Wiggins *both* in saying that the general term 'wise' stands for a concept while the abstract noun 'wisdom' names a property *and* in refusing the identification of concept, so understood, and property, then we shall also have to say that the reports of group I and the reports of group II say quite different things about X and report X as saying quite different things about Socrates; for we shall have to say that while, in all these reports alike, reference is made to X, to Socrates, and to one other item, the third item is, in some of these reports, a concept and in others, something quite different, a property. Surely it is more plausible to say—to change and simplify the example—that the two members of the pair

>  Socrates is courageous
>  Socrates has courage

say the same thing about Socrates; and that, if anything, besides Socrates himself, is referred to in each case, it is one and the same thing in each; and hence that the expression, 'concept', as understood in the present context (i.e. by Wiggins) and the expression, 'property', are simply alternative expressions for classifying things of that kind. When a thing of that kind is predicatively copulated, then, if it is specified by an adjective, it is normally copulated by the use of the verb 'to be', and it if is specified by an abstract noun, it is normally copulated either by the verb 'to have' or by some variant (e.g. 'possesses', 'exemplifies', 'instances', etc.).

Of course there are those who would junk the whole apparatus of concepts, properties, etc. These remarks are not addressed to them. There are also those who would junk properties while preserving, out of piety perhaps, concepts as understood in the present context. These last, if I am right, are in an impossible position. Finally there are perhaps some who, from one ontological perspective or another, or perhaps from none, think that there is no serious purpose served by abstract nouns (or equivalent nominal phrases) or by quantifying in their places that could not, *theoretically*, be equally well served without them, i.e. by the use of general terms and by quantifying in *their* places. But either the qualification 'theoretically' here alludes to some underlying *philosophical* theory which should be explicitly stated and independently argued for on its own merits, or what is envisaged is a capricious attempt at a reform of language—an attempt which, seriously undertaken, would render discourse intolerably cumbersome, if it didn't, at any sophisticated, generalizing, or theoretical level, cripple it altogether. But this party does not really concern us.

# 5

## *Direct Singular Reference: Intended Reference and Actual Reference*

Reference is a large subject with many aspects. In a short paper it is impossible to deal adequately with more than one of them. I shall be concerned with the pragmatics or, perhaps better, the pragmatics-semantics of what I shall call 'direct singular reference'.

I am, therefore, making the barely controversial assumption that direct singular reference sometimes occurs, i.e. is an actual feature of some linguistic communication. I characterize it semantically, or in terms of truth-conditions, as follows: when a direct reference is successfully made, by the use of some definite singular term, to some particular individual, then the coupling of that term with a predicate results in *something said* about that individual (i.e. a proposition about that individual) which is true just in case that individual satisfies that predicate, false just in case it does not.

I shall make also the more controversial assumption that some definite singular terms with explicit descriptive content (with or without explicit demonstrative or indexical elements also present) may sometimes be used to make direct references. Of course such terms as these are not always or only so used; they may, for example, be used for what Donnellan has called 'attributive reference' or in the spirit of a Russellian analysis. But it follows from the semantic characterization just given that, when definite singular terms with explicit descriptive content *are* successfully used to make direct references, their descriptive content does not enter into the statement of the truth-conditions of *what is said*, i.e. of the proposition which is affirmed, or otherwise expressed, by the speaker.

To say this is not to say that the descriptive content of the singular term does not enter into the characterization of the speaker's current *thought*, of the mode in which he is *thinking* of the individual he refers to. That it may well do; or, again, it may not, or not straightforwardly, for he may select his term in, for example, a vein of irony. But the *primary* purpose, in selection of his singular term, on the part of a speaker intent on direct reference, must be to select a term which will enable, or cause, the members of his audience to identify, as the subject of what he says, just the particular individual he intends to speak of—to select a term, in other words, which will get them to know which individual he means—let *their* mode of thinking of that individual be what it variously may. If he is successful in this, then what is common to his own and each of his audience's grasp of what is said will be grasp of the truth-conditions specified in the simple characterization already given. In the case of successful direct reference, then, the identity of the individual referred to determines, as far as reference is concerned, the identity of the proposition expressed. This way of putting it is adequate; there is no need to go as far as Russell sometimes did and declare the particular individual in question to be a constituent *part* of the proposition or to represent the latter as—in appropriate cases—an ordered couple of individual and property. These further steps, though perhaps permissible, can only be an embarrassment for those who prefer to think of propositions as purely abstract entities.

I have spoken, so far, of successful direct reference. But not all attempted direct reference is successful or wholly successful. My purpose (in this paper) is to enquire what happens when a speaker thinks he is in a position to make a direct reference to a particular individual, and uses a term with that intention, but one or more of a variety of things goes wrong. In order to see in what ways things may go wrong, let us first consider more fully the normal case in which, at least as far as reference is concerned, everything goes well, the case in which there is no question but that the speaker does succeed in making just the direct reference he intends to make, so that his intended and his actual reference unquestionably coincide.

A speaker, S, intending to make a direct reference, uses a definite singular term with some descriptive content, D. In the normally satisfactory case a number of conditions are fulfilled. First, I mention what may be called *the minimal condition*, (a). This condition is satisfied when there does exist just one particular individual such that the speaker meant (i.e. intended, by the use of his definite singular term to refer to, and to be taken as referring to) that individual. It can be expressed briefly as follows:

(a)                    $(\exists x)(S \text{ meant } x)$.

(There is no need to write in an explicit uniqueness condition, since, by hypothesis, we are dealing with intended singular reference.)

This is a condition that *could* fail, though it rarely will. But it *could* be the case that there really wasn't anything or anybody at all that the speaker had meant, though, of course, he thought there was. That is, it *could* be the case that, were he fully informed of the relevant facts, he would recognize that what he had regarded as, for example, the central, indispensable core of his reference-fixing beliefs or capacities just did not apply to anything at all; that there was nothing, no actual individual, which he could honestly say he had meant. (He was deceived or confused or deluded or self-deluded.)

Of course this is not the normal case. Normally the minimal condition (a) is satisfied. But not condition (a) alone. In the normal, satisfactory case, it will not only be so, that there is an individual the speaker means, it will also be the case that that individual answers to the descriptive content, D, of the singular term employed. So we expand (a), the minimal condition, to (b), *the expanded condition*, which can be expressed as follows:

(b)　　　　　　　　$(\exists x)(S \text{ meant } x \cdot Dx)$.

For example, if the term the speaker uses is 'your wife' or 'your husband', then, if all goes well, there is not only someone the speaker means, but that person is, also indeed married to the person the speaker is addressing. But of course *this* condition *can* fail.

These two conditions are obvious. There is a slightly more complex condition to be added. It will not only normally be the case that there is an individual whom or which the speaker means and who answers to the descriptive content of the singular term the speaker uses, it will also normally be the case that, in the physical and social context of the speaker's utterance, any linguistically competent and reasonably informed audience which took the speaker to be speaking conventionally in that context, would take the speaker to mean that individual in that context. Of course there may not in fact be such an audience. But it will normally be the case that, *if* there were, it would take the speaker to mean the individual he does mean. We may express this condition by expanding (b) to *the full condition*, (c), as follows:

(c)　　　　$(\exists x)(S \text{ meant } x \cdot Dx \cdot S \text{ putatively meant } x)$

where 'S putatively meant x' is short for 'S, if taken by a linguistically competent and reasonably informed audience to be speaking conventionally in the physical and social context of his utterance, would be taken by that audience to have meant x in that context'.

The fulfilment of the expanded condition (b) does not guarantee the fulfilment of the full condition (c). The last added requirement could fail independently of the other two. Here is an example. At a party, a speaker might say to his host: 'Your brother is very charming.' As it happens, a brother of the host has been at the party and has just left it, having behaved very charmingly. It is a large party and the speaker is unaware of this latter fact; but has met another brother of the person addressed (the host) earlier in the day. This other brother has not been at the party. The host naturally takes the speaker to mean the brother who has just left. The speaker actually means the other brother.

Philosophical debate may arise over the question what reference, if any, the speaker has actually made, what proposition, if any, he has actually asserted (i.e. over what— whatever he *meant* to say—he has *actually* said) in cases where one or another or some combination of the listed conditions fails to be satisfied. Of course there is no debate when all the conditions are satisfied. In that case the speaker has asserted, or otherwise expressed, a proposition about the individual which he meant, which answers to the descriptive content of his definite singular term and which he putatively meant; and the proposition is true if that individual satisfies the predicate attached to the definite singular term, false if it does not. From the point of view of reference all has gone well: intended and actual reference are the same. But what about the deviant cases?

Well, I shall list some deviant cases; and then, in relation to them, I shall list three types of possible answer to the question; three theories, one might say, of direct reference, actual and intended. But, as you will see, I shall not exhaust the possibilities, either of deviance or of theory.

First, then, five deviant cases:

(1) There is no individual which S meant and there is no individual which is such both that it satisfies the descriptive content of the singular term employed and that S putatively meant it.

$-(\exists x)(S \text{ meant } x) \ \& \ -(\exists x)(Dx \cdot S \text{ putatively meant } x)$

(2) There is no individual which S meant, but there is an individual which satisfies the descriptive content of the singular term employed and which S putatively meant.

$-(\exists x)(S \text{ meant } x) \ \& \ (\exists x)(Dx \cdot S \text{ putatively meant } x)$

(3) There is an individual which S meant but which does not satisfy the descriptive content of the singular term employed and there is also an individual which does satisfy that content and which S putatively meant.

$(\exists x)(S \text{ meant } x \cdot -Dx) \ \& \ (\exists x)(Dx \cdot S \text{ putatively meant } x)$

(4) There is an individual which S meant but which does not satisfy the descriptive content of the singular term employed and there is no individual which satisfies that content and which S putatively meant.

($\exists$x)(S meant x $\cdot$ $-$Dx) & $-$($\exists$x)(Dx $\cdot$ S putatively meant x)

(5) There is an individual which S meant and which satisfies the descriptive content of the singular term employed and there is another individual, not identical with the first, which also satisfies that content and which S putatively meant.

($\exists$x)($\exists$y)(S meant x $\cdot$ Dx $\cdot$ S putatively meant y $\cdot$ Dy $\cdot$ x $\neq$ y)

(The case of the two brothers mentioned above is an example of (5)).

Next, I list three types of theoretical response to these cases. Adherents of the first type of response demand no more and no less of direct reference than satisfaction of the minimal condition (a). That is, they attach exclusive importance to the question of what item, if any, was the intended object of S's reference. Consequently, they rule that, in the first two cases, where there is no such item, no reference is made and no proposition expressed; whereas, in the remaining three cases, where there is an individual which S intended to refer to, even though the situation is less than normally satisfactory in other respects, S is deemed to have referred to that individual and to have said something—expressed a proposition—about it or him (or her). Theorists of the second type, though sympathetic in part to the views or prejudices of type 1 theorists, are made of sterner stuff, holding that fulfillment, not of the minimal condition (a), but of the expanded condition (b) is both sufficient and necessary for direct reference. Consequently they declare that in all of the first four cases S's utterance is void for lack of reference: no reference is made, no proposition expressed; and only in the last case is S deemed to have made reference to, and expressed a proposition about, the item he meant. Theorists of the third type share type-2 theorists' insistence on satisfaction of the descriptive content of the singular term employed, but differ from theorists of both other types in attaching less importance to the question, what reference the speaker intended to make, and more to the question, what reference, if any, he would normally and naturally be *taken* to have made. So, while agreeing with both other theorists that no reference is made and no proposition expressed in case (1) and with the theorist of type 2 that the utterance in case (4) is similarly void for lack of reference, the theorist of type 3 will hold that in cases (2) and (3) the speaker actually referred to, and expressed a proposition about, the individual item he *putatively* meant; that in these cases he succeeded, indeed, in making a reference, but not to the item he intended to refer to—either because there was no such item (case 2) or because, though there was such an item, it did not answer to the descriptive content of his singular term. However, the type-3 theorist graciously joins hands with his two rivals in respect of case (5), allowing that where both the intended and the putative objects of reference satisfy the descriptive content of the term employed, the speaker's intention shall be deemed to turn the balance in favour of actual reference to the former. So agreement between all three is achieved in cases (1) and (5), though in none of the others.

As I remarked, I have not exhausted the possibilities either of deviance or of theory. It would be a modest, and modestly appealing, exercise to add to them both; though its modest appeal would be confined, at most, to those who accept my initial assumptions, viz. that direct reference occurs and may sometimes be effected by singular terms with descriptive content.

As far as the three theories regarding my five deviant cases are concerned, my intention so not to choose between them, but to suggest that there is no need to choose; that it is sufficient to note the different possibilities and the reasons for them and to leave it at that. In so far as one is impressed by the difference between 'what the speaker meant to say' and 'what he actually said', one might incline towards theory 3. But to incline is enough. Far more important for the understanding of the actual use of directly referential terms in communication is a grasp of the normally satisfied conditions of their successful employment.

I set out below the three theories of deviance, applied to the five cases, in tabular form:

|       | Theory 1 | Theory 2 | Theory 3 |
|-------|----------|----------|----------|
| (1)   | UV       | UV       | UV       |
| (2)   | UV       | UV       | PRA      |
| (3)   | IRA      | UV       | PRA      |
| (4)   | IRA      | UV       | UV       |
| (5)   | IRA      | IRA      | IRA      |

UV ...... utterance void (i.e. no reference, no proposition),

IRA ...... intended reference = actual reference (i.e. reference to, and proposition about, the item S meant),

PRA ...... putative reference = actual reference (i.e. reference to, and proposition about, the item S putatively meant).

# 6

# Belief, Reference, and Quantification

1. For the purposes of this paper I shall assume that some definite singular terms for individual particulars are sometimes used purely referentially or, as I shall say, with the function of direct reference; and that they sometimes occur, so used, in the belief-specifying clauses of belief-attributing sentences. Direct reference can be characterized semantically, or in terms of truth-conditions, as follows: When a direct reference is made, by some term, to a particular individual, in an utterance in which that term is coupled with a predicate, then there is uttered a proposition which is true if that individual satisfies that predicate, false if it does not. A full account of the pragmatics of direct reference would be a much more complicated matter; I shall refer briefly to just one aspect of the matter towards the end of the paper.

To say that some definite singular terms are sometimes used purely referentially is not to say that all are sometimes so used or that any are always so used. Especially in the case of definite descriptions, something like the Russellian model of analysis may often be nearer the mark. For those who accept my starting assumption this will be one reason, though not the only reason, for agreeing that we do not know the logical form of a given English utterance if all we know is that it consists of, say: the phrase 'Philip believes that' (or 'Philip does not believe that'); followed by some definite singular term or other which is such that it might, in some suitable context, apply to some one individual particular; followed by some predicate of particulars. To all who accept the starting assumption it will be common ground that there are *at least* three types of case falling under this general description of a class of English utterances. (There are indeed more, but I shall not consider further cases till later.)

First is the case in which the definite singular term is being used to make a direct reference. We may provisionally represent its form by:

(1) Philip believes that $Gf$

when the lower-case '$f$' represents the definite singular term. An utterance of this form permits the inference to the corresponding utterance of the form '$(\exists x)$ (Philip believes that $Gx$)'.

The forms of the other two cases can be represented by:

(2) $(\exists x)$ (uniquely-$Fx$ and Philip believes that $Gx$)

and

(3) Philip believes that $(\exists x)$ (uniquely-$Fx$ and $Gx$).

It is worth sparing a word here for the expression 'uniquely-$F$'. Suppose the definite singular term in cases of types (2) and (3) is 'the Liberal candidate'. Then context will make it clear that it is *with reference to a certain constituency* that the proposition that there is just one Liberal candidate is being represented by the speaker as true in a case of type (2) and as being believed by Philip in a case of type (3).

Now cases of types (1) and (2) resemble each other, and differ from cases of type (3) in a familiar and important respect. In both the former the function, as we may call it, of *objective* or *external* reference is performed by the speaker in the specification, complete or incomplete, of what is being said to be believed by Philip; by direct reference to a particular actual individual in case (1) and by quantifying over the domain of particular actual individuals in case (2). In a case of type (3), on the other hand, no objective or external reference of either kind is made in the specification of what is being said to be believed by Philip. This has the familiar consequence that, in the case of utterances of type (1) or type (2), but not in the case of utterances of type (3), any utterance which is made in the same context as the original utterance and which repeats the original utterance save for the substitution of a different singular term having, in context, the same unique application as the original singular term, will preserve the truth-value of the original utterance.

2. This, however, is not the consequence that immediately concerns me. My immediate question concerns 'quantifying in' to belief-contexts, i.e. the phenomenon of which examples are provided by utterances of type (2) above and by legitimate inference from utterances of type (1) above.

Why should the phenomenon have seemed to present a problem? I approach the question by considering first the case in which there is neither the fact nor the possibility of quantifying in: e.g. any utterance of type (3) above or any other belief-attributing utterance which is such that what follows 'believes' is quite sealed off from any possibility of first-order quantification into it from outside.

Clearly theorists of meaning in general have to give some account of these belief-sentences containing 'sealed-off' belief-specifying clauses. Some analysis or account of their semantics or logical form is called for. Thus, if one were perfectly happy with propositions as intensional entities, one could say that 'believes' is a two-place predicate of persons and propositions, the person in our case being referred to by the name 'Philip' and the proposition being specified by the 'that'-clause which follows 'believes'. Or, if one were a follower of Davidson, one might say that 'believes' means something like 'would be disposed to assent to a suitable utterance same-saying with'; that it is indeed a two-place predicate, but one apt for joining a name denoting a person to a demonstrative pronoun which in turn refers to a following token-sentence.

Whatever the merits of these and related views which represent 'believes' as a two-place predicate, they have seemed to pose a problem when we turn from sealed-off belief-specifying clauses to those which exhibit or permit quantification into themselves from outside the belief-context. It has seemed difficult, on the propositional view, to see how a quantifier from outside the belief-context could succeed in capturing a variable *inside* the second term of the two-place predicate; while on the Davidsonian view, as stated, any such thing is clearly quite impossible, since the second term of the two-place predicate is an unstructured demonstrative. Both views of course permit the inference to: 'There is something which Philip believes'; but this is not what is in question.

One familiar suggestion for solving this problem is that we should recognize a sense of 'believes' in which it is a relational predicate with more than two places, not relating a believer to a proposition or a demonstrated utterance, but to other particular individuals and their properties and relations. (There is a variant form of this suggestion which speaks of linguistic expressions rather than properties or relations; but since the difference is irrelevant for present purposes, I shall continue to use the intensional terminology which is the more convenient for informal exposition.)

If we adopt this suggestion, then the true form for interpretations of type (1) will be

$$(1')\quad B\,(ph, f, G)$$

where '$B$' abbreviates 'believes', '*ph*' abbreviates 'Philip', and '$G$' represents a property-name corresponding to the predicate represented in (1) by '$G$'. 'Believes' appears as a three-place predicate, and we can intelligibly quantify into the position occupied by the term, represented by '$f$', which directly refers to the particular individual. Hence '$(\exists x)(B(ph, x, G))$'

Similarly the true form for interpretations of type (2) will be:

$$(2')\quad (\exists x)\,(\text{uniquely-}F\,x \text{ and } B\,(ph, x, G)).$$

We could produce an English reading which would reveal the form more clearly than our ordinary style of expression by introducing, instead of 'believes', some such phrase as 'mentally ascribes to'; so that we have, for example, for (1′),

> Philip mentally ascribes to $f$ the property $G$

and for (2′)

> There is something which uniquely-$F$ and to which Philip mentally ascribes the property $G$.

(We could similarly give English readings to the linguistic variant on the lines of, e.g.

> There is something which uniquely-$F$ and of which Philip is prepared affirmatively to predicate an expression synonymous with '$G$'

where '$G$' now represents the mention of a predicate.)

No less familiar than this suggestion are certain difficulties which have been found in it; and scarcely less familiar than these difficulties are the technical devices which have been proposed to overcome them. Nevertheless it is relevant to my purpose to rehearse these difficulties once again. So I hope I may be forgiven for doing so.

The first difficulty is that whereas one extra sense of 'believe' may seem tolerable—(I shall later suggest that we do not need even this)—a plurality of extra senses seems less so. But suppose it is said that Philip believes that John loves Mary, where John and Mary are directly referred to; or, more generally, that there is someone whom Philip believes that John loves. The form of these propositions will be given by

$$B\,(ph, j, m, L)$$

and

$$\exists x\,(B\,(ph, j, x, L))$$

So now 'believes' appears as a four-place predicate. And if it is said that there is something which Philip believes John gave to Mary, the belief-predicate required has five places.

This is disturbing because the idea of the same predicate having a variable number of places is something quite undreamt of in our philosophy of logic; so we shall have to admit different predicates in these cases, a plurality of more-than-two-place belief-predicates. But this seems very implausible. For surely we want to say that 'believes' is quite univocal in all such cases; that we have one and the same predicate throughout.

There is another and more impressive difficulty pointed out long ago by Russell. If we adopt the proposal in question, then what follows 'believes' in the relevant cases is never a sentence or a sentential clause, not even an open sentence or sentential clause; for it contains no verb; or (what is the same thing) it contains no predicate.[1] It consists of a set of terms, either standing for particular individuals or properties or relations or, if the terms are variables, ranging over particulars or properties or relations. Hence, whereas the ordinary English, 'Philip believes that John loves Mary', by preserving the verb inside the belief-context, indicates the order in which the loving-relation is said to be believed by Philip to hold between John and Mary, no such indication is provided by the proposed analysis. The terms are ordered with reference to the belief-relation but not with reference to the loving-relation. So we do not know whether Philip is being said to believe that John loves Mary or that Mary loves John or, indeed, that their love is mutual.

The technical device proposed to deal with both these difficulties at one blow is familiar. The proposal is to construe 'believes' in all such cases as signifying a triadic relation which holds between believers, relations, and *sequences* of individual particulars instead of individual particulars themselves. Thus in the simple case before us the Englishing of the proposal would yield something like 'Philip mentally ascribes the relation of loving to the ordered pair, John and Mary' and in the more complicated case it would yield something like 'There is some individual such that there is an ordered pair consisting of John and that individual such that Philip ascribes the relation of loving to that ordered pair.'

---

[1] Of course, in the linguistic version, it contains a *mention* of a verb or predicate.

I do not question the formal adequacy of this proposal. But it is not clear to me that it is either realistic or necessary; while it is clear that it leaves us with two senses of 'believe' or two belief-predicates, the dyadic and the triadic, on our hands. So I want to make a modest alternative suggestion which, if unobjectionable on other grounds, is no less successful in coping with the difficulties noted; which is (I think) more realistic; and which does not require us to recognize more than one sense of 'believes'.

3. Consider some ordinary belief-attributing sentences apt for utterance in cases in which the definite singular terms inside the belief-specifying clause are performing the function of definite reference; e.g.

> (1) Philip believes (that Mary is a scholar
>                (Mary to be a scholar

> (2) Philip believes (that John loves Mary
>                (John to love Mary

If we knock out 'Mary' from (1) and replace it by a free variable, we have a form which yields truth for some fillings by a directly referring term and falsity for others, viz.: 'Philip believes that $x$ is a scholar'. We have in fact, I shall suggest, a one-place predicate, albeit a complex or compound one. If we knock out 'Philip' as well, obtaining '$x$ believes that $y$ is a scholar', we have a two-place non-symmetrical predicate, albeit, again, a compound one: to be written, if desired,

> believes to be a scholar $(x, y)$.

Knocking out both 'John' and 'Mary' from (2), we have a form which will yield truth for some fillings by directly referring terms and falsity for others and perhaps truth for one order of filling of two given terms and falsity for the other ordering of the same terms. We have in fact a non-symmetrical two-place predicate, albeit a compound one, viz.: 'Philip believes that $x$ loves $y$.' Knocking out 'Philip' as well yields us the compound three-place predicate, '$x$ believes that $y$ loves $z$' or, if desired, believes to love $(x, y, z)$.

If we are justified in recognizing these putative compound or complex predicates as such, it is clear not only that they permit quantification into any of their places, but also that they give rise to neither of the difficulties we have just been considering. The resulting multiplicity of compound predicates, each with a different sense, imports no multiplicity of senses of 'believe'; neither does the fact that some of these predicates have a different number of places from others entail the consequence that we must recognize different unitary 'believe'-predicates with different numbers of places. Finally, the ordering difficulty does not arise, since this kind of compound predicate preserves the ordering force of the verb as it figures in the clause which follows 'believes' in the ordinary English sentence. In fact no departure at all from ordinary language is called for.

But are we justified in recognizing these putative compound predicates as such?

Before attacking the question directly, let us notice how strong the prima-facie case in favour of them is. What we have here, it might be said, is not just a device for avoiding difficulties. Indeed it is not a device at all. What is proposed is simply the recognition of what is there. In exactly the same way as an ordinary two-place predicate, say 'loves', can be used to collect and order pairs by way of the question 'Who loves whom?', so the compound two-place predicate '. . . is believed by Philip to love . . .' or, in its equivalent form, 'Philip believes that . . . loves . . .' can be used to collect and order pairs by way of the question 'Who does Philip believe loves whom?' Or, to go a step further, the three-place predicate '$x$ believes that $y$ loves $z$' can be used to collect and order triples by way of the question 'Who believes who loves whom?' So these compound predicates have just as good a right to be counted as *bona fide* predicates as any others. They signify what is common to the members of certain sets of ordered couples, triples, etc. just as ordinary undoubted multi-placed predicates do. Thus our last mentioned three-place predicate collects such triples as Philip, John, Mary and Othello, Desdemona, Cassio, just as '*x* gives *y* to *z*' collects such triples as John, Fido, Mary and Lear, Cordelia, the king of France.

The reason why we cannot rest content with the prima-facie case is, of course, precisely that the predicates in question, if they are such, are compounded. They are formed by some construction out of simpler elements. So we ought to be able to give some account of the construction in question, some account of the principles of composition of these compound predicates, which explains how we can understand them as such. Now the invariant element in all these compounds is the element—presumably itself a unitary, i.e. non-compound, predicate—'believes' itself. So we ought to start with an account of 'believes' itself and explain how we can form the compound predicates which contain it.

Earlier on we had before us two accounts of 'believes' as a single, unitary two-place predicate. One was the Davidsonian account. This will not help us. The other represented 'believes' as signifying a relation between persons and propositions. I did not linger over it at the time, but went straight on to consider the theory of a special 'transparent' sense of 'believes' as a more-than-two-place predicate. But let us consider it now.

Our problem is: How can a two-place predicate of persons and propositions enter into or yield different compound predicates of two or more places which are all predicates of (pairs or trios or quadruples, etc. of) particular individuals?

The answer resides in the two facts: (a) that the proposition being said to be believed itself has structure and the grasp of what is being said to be believed involves grasps of that structure and of the structured elements; and (b) that terms can figure with direct reference inside the belief-specifying clause of the belief-attributing utterance.

Consider a belief-attributing statement made in the words

> Philip believes that John loves Mary

where the terms 'John' and 'Mary' make direct references. What we have to show is that the statement *both* has the form

(3) Believes [Philip, that $F$ (a, b)]

where the predicate, the simple two-place predicate, is unbracketed and its *two* place-fillers (specifying, respectively, a person and a proposition) are put in square brackets and *also* has the form

(4) Believes that $F$ [Philip, $a$, $b$]

where the predicate, this time the compound predicate, is again unbracketed and its *three* place-fillers (each specifying, this time, a particular individual) are put in square brackets.

I said that this is what I have to show; and really 'show' is the operative word. For this is a point at which argument comes to an end; or almost does. I think it is really obvious that to grasp the statement (to grasp what is said by the whole utterance) viewed as having the form (3) is the same thing as to grasp what is said viewed as having the form (4). For to grasp what proposition is being asserted to be *believed* (by Philip) is the same thing as to grasp which individual is being asserted to be *believed* (by Philip) *to love* which other individual. These two different descriptions of one and the same 'act of understanding' are tailored respectively to viewing what is said as having the form (3) and to viewing what is said as having the form (4).

If this is right, then there is really no problem about how the two-place predicate 'believes' can yield the compound predicates I have been speaking of. These compound predicates can be primarily discerned in those cases in which the propositional term of the two-place relational predicate 'believes' contains, in referential position, only terms performing the function of definite reference—as in my example. Once discerned there, they are established as predicates in their own right; and all their places can be occupied by variables of quantification, as in the case of any other multi-placed predicates. Thus we have not only the form (4) but also the forms

(5) $\begin{cases} (\exists x) \text{ (Believes that } F \text{ (Philip, } x, b)) \\ (\exists x) (\exists y) \text{ (Believes that } F \text{ (Philip, } x, y)) \\ (\exists x) (\exists y) (\exists z) \text{ (Believes that } F \text{ (}x, y, z)) \end{cases}$

Of course, in these cases, where we have quantification into one or more of the places of the compound predicate other than the first, we can no longer see 'believes' as having the double role of *both* two-place predicate *and* element in a compound; for there is neither discernible quantification over propositions (as in 'Philip believes something') nor any complete proposition left to serve as the second term of the two-termed relation. Thus if we say 'There is someone who Philip believes loves Mary', no part of what we say specifies any proposition that Philip believes; and though what we say has the strict consequence that there is some appropriately related complete proposition which Philip does believe, we do not explicitly say this and there is no standard formal way of deriving it from what we do say.

None of this, however, constitutes a problem. The point can be put generally as follows. We can discern the *compound* predicate in every case in which the function of objective (or external) reference is performed by the speaker in the specification, complete or incomplete, of what is being said to be believed by Philip. This function can be performed either by direct reference to a particular actual individual or by quantifying over the domain of particular actual individuals. If it is performed only in the former way, then we can discern both the compound predicate and the two-termed simple 'believes' predicate in the sentence. If it is performed partly or wholly in the latter way, we can discern the compound predicate but not the two-termed simple 'believes' predicate.

If there is no objective or external reference involved in the specification of the believer's belief, then of course we cannot discern the compound predicate. We simply have the two-termed 'believes' predicate. Such is the case, for example, with any statement of which the correct form of interpretation is as given at 1 (3) above: 'Philip believes that ($\exists x$) (uniquely-$F\,x$ and $Gx$).' In such a case the speaker, in specifying Philip's belief (which he does completely) makes no reference, either direct or by way of quantifiers, to actual individuals external to Philip's belief-world or belief-scheme.

No direct reference figures in the specification; and all the quantification is internal to Philip's belief-world. So the speaker makes no use of the compound predicate which would be represented by 'Philip believes that G . . .'. He neither applies it directly to something nor says that there is something to which it applies, nor denies this, nor even asserts or denies that it does or would apply to any actual individual which satisfies or would satisfy the predicate represented by 'uniquely-*F* . . .'; though he could, of course, quite consistently with making the statement in question, go on to make a further statement, using the compound predicate, in which he asserted or denied any one of these things. (He might, for example, think that Philip was such a poor confused creature that, though there is nothing in fact which satisfies the predicate represented by 'uniquely-*F* . . .', yet if there were such a thing, Philip would not believe that it satisfied the predicate represented by '*G* . . .'; and in stating this thought, he would use the compound predicate represented by '. . . believes that G . . .'.)

So we need to distinguish three cases:

(a) What I shall call the primary case: the case of complete specification, involving objective reference, of what is being said to be believed. In this case all objective reference included in the specification will be direct.

(b) The case of incomplete specification, involving objective reference, of what is being said to be believed. In this case not all objective reference included in the specification will be direct; and it may be that none is.

(c) The case of complete specification, not involving any objective reference, of what is being said to be believed.

Wherever we have complete specification, we have 'believes' as a two-place predicate of believers and propositions. Wherever we have objective reference, we have 'believes' as an element in a compound predicate. And wherever we have both—i.e. in what I called the primary case—we have both—i.e. 'believes' both as a two-place predicate and as an element in a two-or-more-place compound predicate.

If we accept this account we have no need at all to recognize a special 'transparent' sense of 'believes' (let alone a plurality of them). We have just the one sense in which, in the primary case, the expression both functions as a two-place predicate of believers and propositions and *at the same time* enters into or yields a compound predicate of particular individuals. Then these two roles can come apart, as in the other two cases.

4. A question naturally suggests itself at this point. I have argued that the alleged problem of 'quantifying in' to belief-attributing contexts is scarcely a problem at all; or, if we are to call it a problem, that the solution lies plainly there, for all to see, on the surface of language. If this is really so, it will naturally be asked, why has it *seemed* such a problem? Why has it been thought that quantification into such contexts is either quite unintelligible or, in order to be shown to be intelligible, calls for a distinction of senses of 'believes' and for the adoption, in the analysis of one of the resulting two classes of belief-attributing sentences, of the counter-intuitive view that an expression which appears as a verb in the ordinary English of these sentences is not really understood by its users as functioning there as a verb at all?

I suggest that the answer to the question lies in the fact that the construction upon the recognition of which my simple surface solution depends—the compound predicate which includes a subordinate predicate—cannot be directly represented in standard logical notation and cannot be simply and perspicuously accounted for in terms of that notation. The conventional grammatical categories of standard logic do not allow for it. I do not mean that they exclude such a construction. They simply do not provide for it. Hence if we start with the prejudice or presupposition that all intelligible constructions can be accounted for in their terms, we shall inevitably overlook the construction in question.

It will help to make the point clearer if I contrast our compound predicates with other such predicates which can be accounted for in the standard way. For instance, we frequently encounter in ordinary discourse conjunctive or disjunctive predicates: as in 'Pam is *fat and happy*', 'Anyone who *both hunts and shoots* is a sportsman', 'Anyone who thinks that *is either a knave or a fool*.' We can certainly discern such compound predicates as these: they collect individuals as other one-place predicates do, they can figure straightforwardly in arguments as one-place predicates and so on. But the construction which yields them is not felt as constituting any problem; because the sentences containing, say, conjunctive predicates can easily be seen as abbreviations or transformations of sentences containing sentence-conjunction (including open sentence conjunction) which is of course allowed for in standard logic. (I do not say it is *right* to see things in this way in these cases. I am disposed, rather, to think it unnecessary. But at any rate this way of seeing things is available.)

Some constructions yielding compound predicates are, then, simply *accountable for* in terms of the standard notation. Others are more or less *directly representable* in those terms. Such is the case, for example, with 'loves Mary' or 'loves some girl'. Neither is the case with the putative compound predicate obtained by, say, knocking out the names from the English sentence 'Philip believes that John loves Mary.' It might be objected that this is not so; that to adopt the analysis proposed in terms of the 'transparent' sense of 'believes' precisely *is* to reveal the underlying logical character of the merely surface-predicate '... believes that ... loves ...'. But this seems to me merely a reiteration of the prejudice referred to above, a prejudice which may promote ingenuity, but not necessarily understanding. I see no reason to think that all the constructions which figure in natural language can establish their claim to recognition only by being paraphrased or reconstructed in terms of standard logical notation. I suggest that the informal account which I earlier gave of the construction in question is perfectly intelligible and captures the way we think quite accurately, though it does not conform to the requirements which the prejudice would insist on.

Before I leave this point, I should like to mention two side-symptoms of the fact that our construction eludes logically conventional representation. The first I have already alluded to, but not dwelt on. The second has not surfaced before.

Earlier I distinguished three cases: (a) that in which specification of the attributed belief is complete and includes external reference (all of which must therefore be direct); (b) that in which specification of an attributed belief includes external reference but is incomplete (i.e. includes an externally bound variable); (c) that in which specification of an attributed belief is complete but includes no external reference.

In all three cases the belief-attributing statement has the strict consequence that there is something (some proposition) which the believer believes. In cases (a) and (c) this is a formally validated consequence. In case (b) it is not; for, formally speaking, 'believes' is here completely absorbed into the compound predicate and does not retain a formally independent role as a two-place predicate. Yet the word is said to be quite univocal throughout. If we insist that all structurally valid inference shall be, in the restricted sense concerned, formally valid, we shall find the combination of these theses unacceptable. If not, not.

Of course we have a parallel situation in the case of the alleged 'transparent' sense of 'believes' as well. But this will not be found unacceptable precisely because 'believes' is here seen as a different predicate from the two-place 'believes'. If desired, an axiom can be introduced to link the two.

The second symptom is more striking. Consider a case in which the specification of the attributed belief is complete and contains external (hence, since we have complete specification, direct) reference, but also contains internal quantification: e.g. 'Philip believes that there is someone who loves Mary.' Since it is a case of complete specification with external reference, we should be able both formally to isolate the two-place predicate 'believes' and also to discern an appropriate compound predicate into which 'believes' enters as an element. And so we can. The appropriate compound predicate is '. . . believes there to be someone who loves . . .'. If we forget that these predicates are not constructed on a logically conventional model and try to write down the form of the sentence as if they were, we find it cannot be done. All we can produce is something ill-formed, like:

> *Believes that (∃x) (loves (x* [Philip, Mary].

So then, here as elsewhere, we have a choice: either we recognize that there are constructions which can be intelligibly characterized, though not in conventional terms, and which, therefore, a systematic semantics must be ready to allow for; or we can deny ourselves the simple solution to our present problem (and others) which this recognition makes possible and persist in looking for something more elaborate which will answer to conventional requirements. A choice between liberating heresy and constricting orthodoxy.

5. I want now to turn to two further questions, both of which are related to what has gone before, though my treatment of them does not depend on the correctness (if it is correct) of the main point I have argued for up to now.

I consider, first, the class of English utterances which consist of the name of a person followed by 'believes that' (or 'does not believe that') followed by a definite singular term followed by the identity-predicate followed by another definite singular term. It is sometimes suggested that even if definite singular terms can sometimes figure with direct reference within the scope of the verb 'believes', they cannot be seen as doing so in such utterances as these. This view, thus generally stated, is easily rebutted. For example, a speaker who says 'Philip believes that Tom is the only man who refused to sign' produces an utterance of the kind just described. And it seems plain that if ever definite singular terms can figure purely referentially within the scope of 'believes', then it could be true of the given utterance that 'Tom' is used to make a direct reference while the definite description is not so used. (The form of the statement could be either 'Philip believes that (∃x) (uniquely-*F x* and *x* = Tom)' or '(∃y) (uniquely-$Fy$) and Philip believes that ($\exists x$) (uniquely-$Fx$ and $x = $ Tom)'.)

The view in question, however, seems much more firmly based if it is restricted to utterances in which both the definite singular terms which follow 'believes' are proper names. And indeed, so restricted, it is very firmly based indeed. One argument commonly used in support of it is the following. It could very well be the case both that a statement made in the words 'Philip does not believe that Cicero is (identical with) Tully' was true while a statement, not differing from it in form, but made in the words 'Philip does not believe that Cicero is (identical with) Cicero' would be false. Since Cicero *is* identical with Tully, this could not be the case if all the names concerned were used purely referentially. Hence they are not so used in statements such as these.

This is a sound argument and quite strong enough for its purpose. But two points about it are worth making. First, it is sometimes credited with a super-strength which it neither has nor, for this purpose, needs. For it is sometimes thought that if someone, say Philip, has command of a certain name, say 'James', as applied to a particular person, then an utterance made in the words 'Philip believes that James is (identical with) James' could not fail to be true. But this is false and easily seen to be so. (Imagine an ill-fated Jacobite expedition in which Philip, a rather naïve member of the court in exile, is a participant and in which the king, cleverly disguised as valet to another Jacobite gentleman, travels under the name of 'James'. It might come as quite a shock to Philip to be told that James is James.)

The second point to be made is this. The argument does not in fact show that the directly referring use of the relevant names in such utterances is logically excluded. It shows only that they never would in fact be used in this way in such utterances; for such uses would always be, in a pragmatic point of view, pointless or absurd. (The only *information* that could be gleaned from such uses, if they occurred, would be that the believer has *some* beliefs or other about, or some acquaintance or other with, the named individuals.) So we must look for another way of construing the use of the names in such utterances.

We might begin our search with the odd little example about Philip and James. The situation can be described baldly, but for ordinary purposes clearly enough, by saying that, before his enlightenment, Philip does not know (indeed does not believe) that James, the (pretended) valet, is James, the (pretender) king. There are two complex properties, each, in the limited setting, uniquely instantiated and each of which Philip believes to be, in that setting, uniquely instantiated. They are: being (or acting as) a valet, bearing the name 'James'; and being (or claiming to be) a king, bearing the name 'James'. Writing in the uniqueness-condition, let us represent them by 'uniquely-$V$ "James"' and 'uniquely-$K$ "James"'. Now there *is* someone, namely James, of whom Philip believes both that he uniquely-$V$ 'James' and that he uniquely-$K$ 'James'. But it does not follow that Philip believes that there is someone who both uniquely-$V$ 'James' and uniquely-$K$ 'James'. And indeed it is just this last belief-attributing proposition which a speaker effectively denies in saying that Philip does not know (does not believe) that James is James. So here we have a plausible shot at the form of this denial.

Let us turn from this particular case with its oddities and its simplicities. What in general is someone concerned to say when he asserts or denies a belief-attributing proposition with two names coupled by the identity-predicate in the clause that follows 'believes'? We confine our attention to those cases in which the two names, as used by the speaker, in fact apply to the same thing or person—to say which is not, of course, to say that the speaker uses them with the function of direct reference to that thing or person. Even so we must distinguish cases. Sometimes the speaker may be concerned with the relation between the believer's (Philip's) knowledge of the individual in question and his (Philip's) command of the two names (say 'N' and 'M') for that individual. What he has in mind in saying that Philip does not know/believe that N = M may then be the fact that Philip does not believe that there is anyone who both has the identifying properties of the individual concerned which he (Philip) crucially associates with the name 'N' and also has the identifying properties of the individual concerned which he (Philip) crucially associated with the name 'M'. (By 'identifying property' here is meant any property which is, uniquely instantiated: e.g. *being a philosopher usually referred to by the name 'N' in such-and-such a circle* might be such a property.) But sometimes the relation of Philip's knowledge of the individual concerned to Philip's command of the two names might not be in question. It may be that the two names commonly, or customarily, or in the minds of the speaker and his audience, have different associations without its being the case that they have these associations for Philip, who may, indeed, have no relevant command of either name; yet that Philip knows *of* the individual concerned in both these connections without knowing that there is just *one* individual concerned. Then just this will be the point which the speaker is effectively making in saying that Philip does not know/believe that N = M. We can perhaps bring both cases under a common formula by replacing the embedded reference to Philip in the first case by a general notion of *relevant* association; so that what is effectively said is that Philip does not believe that there is anyone who both has the identifying properties *relevantly* associated with the name 'N' and also has the identifying properties *relevantly* associated with the name 'M'.

This does not boil down to any neat and perspicuous little formula; but there is really no reason to expect that it should. And it leaves us with a metalinguistic element in the account; but this seems to me unobjectionable in these cases.

Of course, it should finally be added, this way of using names inside belief-contexts is not *confined* to cases in which the embedded clause is an identity. If Philip believes that Cicero denounced Catiline, then he also believes, whatever he may say, that Tully denounced Catiline. And it is also true that there is something which has whatever identifying properties are relevantly associated with the name 'Tully' and which Philip believes denounced Catiline. But it by no means follows from either of these truths that Philip believes that there is something which has the identifying properties relevantly associated with the name 'Tully' and which denounced Catiline. And the words 'Philip does not believe that Tully denounced Catiline' may be used to make this point.

In general it seems that the endless discussion of these issues would have been greatly curtailed if it had been firmly and continuously borne in mind that from the fact that one single individual is believed by Philip to have both of two properties (or to satisfy both of two predicates) it does not follow that Philip believes there to be one single individual who has both of those properties (or satisfies both of those predicates); yet that one English sentence may be used to say either of these different things.

6. So now to my last question. I take it as clear that English sentences of the kinds we have been concerned with, which contain a definite singular term for a particular individual in the belief-specifying clause may, on different occasions of utterance, be assigned different interpretations or readings. My last question is: what considerations determine which of the possible readings it would be correct to assign on any particular occasion of the utterance of such a sentence? And in raising this question I want to introduce an assumption I have so far made no use of, viz. that among the definite singular terms which may sometimes be used purely referentially in the belief-specifying clauses are included some definite descriptions. That is to say that in some utterances which, as made in ordinary English, exhibit the form 'Philip believes (does not believe) that the $F$ (is) $G$', the expression represented by 'the $F$' is used to make a direct reference.

Now let 'the $F$' represent, say, the phrase 'the Liberal candidate' and, correspondingly, let '$F$' by itself represent 'is standing as a Liberal candidate'; and let '$G$' or 'is $G$' represent the predicate-phrase 'will be elected' or 'will win the election'. Then at least five possibilities of interpretation are in principle open for an utterance of the English sentence

'Philip believes that the Liberal candidate will be elected.' There are the three I originally listed and for which we may use the same forms of representation as before (taking now, for the first form, the lower-case '*f*' to represent a directly referring use of 'the Liberal candidate'). These are:

(1) Philip believes that $Gf$
(2) $(\exists x)$ (uniquely-$Fx$ and Philip believes that $Gx$)
(3) Philip believes that $(\exists x)$ (uniquely-$Fx$ and $Gx$).

There are also[2] at least two others, which may be represented as follows:

(4) Philip believes that uniquely-$Ff$ and that $Gf$
(5) $(\exists x)$ (uniquely-$Fx$ and Philip believes that uniquely-$Fx$ and that $Gx$).

I think there are in fact more, but I shall neglect them. So far I have neglected (4) and (5) as well.

It might seem that the question, what determines which interpretation is correct in a given case, is very easily answered. For the forms as listed display the variant truth-conditions for the different interpretations; and the speaker himself, if he knows what he is saying, knows what the truth-conditions of what he is saying are. So we can elicit the answer from him by asking a series of questions. Thus, first: Could what you say be both true and free from any kind of deviance if there were no Liberal candidate? Only if the answer is 'Yes' can reading (3) be correct; for if there is no Liberal candidate then (2) and (5) will be straightforwardly false and (1) and (4) will at least be deviant cases. Assuming the answer to that question is 'No' and thus limiting ourselves to the remaining cases, we ask: Can what is said be true if, though there is someone of whom Philip believes that he will win the election, it is not the case that Philip believes that he is the Liberal candidate. The answer 'No' leaves us with (4) and (5) as possible correct readings and knocks out (1) and

---

[2] See B. Loar, 'Propositional Attitudes', *Philosophical Review*, 1972.

(2). The answer 'Yes' knocks out (4) and (5) and leaves us with (1) and (2).

One more question settles the choice of reading as between (1) and (2) and as between (4) and (5). Supposing again that there was indeed some individual of whom Philip believed that he would win the election, but that this individual was not the Liberal candidate, then would what was said be plain false or would it be a case of some other kind of deviance? If the answer is 'plain false', then we have either (2) or (5); if 'some other kind of deviance', we have (1) or (4). In other words, if the correct answer to the last question is 'some other kind of deviance', we know that the speaker is using the definite singular term (at least in intention) as a vehicle of direct reference; if it is 'plain falsity', we know he is not. But now the answers simply invite the further question: What determines whether the speaker is using the term as a vehicle of direct reference (at least in intention) or not?

This is a question in the pragmatics of direct reference. It is distinct from the question, what puts a speaker in a position to make a direct reference to a particular individual, and distinct again from the question of the kinds of deviance to which a speaker's utterance is subject when he thinks he is in a position to make a direct reference and intends to do so, but one of a variety of things goes wrong. It is simply the question: Granted that a speaker is, or thinks he is, in a position to make a direct reference by the use of a certain definite singular term, under what conditions will it normally be correct to say that he is, in a given case, actually (or at least in intention) using the term in this way?

I think we can answer this only by taking account of the speaker's view of the information-state of his *audience*, of the person or persons he is *addressing*. If, taking himself to be in a position to make a direct reference to a particular individual by means of a certain definite singular term (whether name or description), he takes the audience *also* to be in a position to make (and hence to understand) the same direct reference by the same term, then a necessary condition of his so using the term is fulfilled. That this is not a sufficient condition of his using the term *merely* in this way is clear from case (4), where the term fulfils a double function: though used to make a direct reference, it is *also* so used that its descriptive content enters into the truth-conditions of the utterance. And that the condition is not *in general* a sufficient condition of a definite singular term's being used even partly in this way is clear from the cases of belief-clauses containing names which were considered in the previous section. Where the belief-specifying clause contains two names coupled by the identity-predicate it will normally, for the reasons given, be unrealistic to take either name as used to make a direct reference; and when the belief-specifying clause contains a name not so coupled, it will sometimes be correct to take the name as used purely referentially and sometimes not. But there is no reason at all to suppose that a case in which it would be incorrect to take a name as used to make a direct reference must be a case in which our necessary condition of so using it is unfulfilled.

# 7

# *Reference and Its Roots*

It is impossible to write about reference without referring to Quine. He who does the first does the second. I myself have done both often enough and am now to do both again. But I need have no fear of repeating myself. The appearance of *The Roots of Reference*, packed with fresh thoughts brilliantly phrased, supplies enough, and more than enough, new matter. What follows is concerned solely with that book, is a critique of certain aspects of it. Only of certain aspects. On set theory, for example, the hot-house of reference, I have nothing to say. I am concerned only with the roots and the natural growths, the common or garden flowers.

I begin with (I) a few general reflections on Quine's reform of epistemology and his shunning of the mentalism that haunted its classical forms; there follows (II) the substance of my critique; I end with (III) a short defence against a possible charge of misunderstanding.

## I

Classical empiricist epistemology took the way of ideas and the way branched into different familiar paths. One led to scepticism about the objects of natural science, others to idealist interpretations, others to a laboriously argued realism. A reformed epistemology, Quine suggests, will take science for granted and ask, given its results, how we came to achieve them. The question itself belongs to natural science. Impingements on the human exterior progressively modify

the inner constitution in such a way that yet further impingements produce a behavioural output which counts as mani-
festing command of scientific theory, including, crucially, the
apparatus of objective reference. Just what are the mechanisms involved? That is the question.

Or is it? As the story develops, as the explanation of early
learning and later elaboration of language and theory gets
under way, physiological mechanisms recede into the background. They may, someday, be isolated (27).[1] It is a comfort,
perhaps, to be confident they are there, to be assured that all
the terms used in the course of the explanation have corre-
lates of enormous complexity in the realm of receptors, neu-
ral paths and fibres of striped muscle. But it is the various
terms of the explanation that do the explaining, not this
perfectly general assurance, invariant in form at all stages. It
is the melody, not the ground-bass, we attend to.

When mentalism is forsworn, it is important to be clear just
where, and within what limits, it is being forsworn. As theorists we investigate the acquisition of theory, beginning with
the acquisition of speech. We are not to speculate about
inaccessible goings-on in our subjects' minds. We are to attend to what is observable, including utterances of words,
'out where we can see and hear them' (35). Thus the language-learning process is 'a matter of fact, accessible to empirical science' (37). So the theorist *observes* the teacher's
conditioning of the child to utter an observation sentence in
appropriate *observable* circumstances: to utter 'red', say, in
the conspicuous presence of red. But how does the theorist
come to treat the occasion as one for learning about the
learning of 'red'? Surely the theorist of theorizing here tacitly
credits the observant theorist with the full mentalistic load of
perceptual-conceptual experience: with *seeing* what *he* sees
*as* red, *hearing* what *he* hears *as* 'red'. And how does the
theorist—the first theorist this time, not his meta-half—how
does he suppose the teacher knows when to teach? Without
the tacit appeal to mentalism at some point, the explanation

---

[1] Numerals in parentheses refer to pages in *The Roots of Reference* (La Salle,
Ill., Open Court, 1974).

could never start, could never count as explanation, could never be understood.

However it may be with theorists and teachers, can we not still avoid mentalism in our account of the learning subject, the child? What he goes through falls 'within the scope of standard animal training' (42). When we say that 'the learning of an observation sentence amounts to determining ... the distinctive trait shared by episodes appropriate to that observation sentence' (43), this is to be construed as referring to the bringing about in the child, by a combination of impingements, of an internal modification which itself results in a selective response to further impingements. But the child is father of the man, the learner of the teacher and even of the theorist of learning. In the end he must be viewed as mentalistically as his mentor; and *this* end is not far from the beginning. Before long the pupil shares the teacher's understanding; knows when to respond just as teacher knows when to encourage; says as teacher says because he sees as teacher sees.

So much mentalism is elementary, a fairly easy consequence of the emphasis on externality commended as observable. What of the psychogenetic stages that carry us ultimately to 'the advancing front of natural science'? Surely it is right to conceive the stages, as Quine does, in terms of 'analogical extension' or 'natural if not inevitable continuation of what is already at work at lower language levels' (121), to think of steps in the development of system as a 'series of short leaps each made on the strength of similarities or analogies' (138). At the advancing front itself we are said to go forward with our eyes open: 'the minds at the advancing front are themselves aware of what they are doing' (130). Before we reach it, that front, we jump and stumble forward in the dark, with but a dim consciousness, if any, of the analogies which guide our steps. But it is the retrospective discerning of the guiding analogies which yields the understanding of the forward movement; and this we elicit from ourselves by a variant of that species of self-conscious reflection on our own practice and its rationale which is characteristically philosophical. Certainly we should check with the psycho-linguists; but the categories we use in submitting the story to check, and in interpreting the psycho-linguists' independently advertised results, these categories belong to logical reflection. We need the perspective of minds that know what they're doing to appreciate the stages by which they reached the point of knowing.

These points have further connections, connections, in particular, with the attempt to understand our *developed* understanding of the semantically significant structural features of language; for a theory of development is an ingredient in a theory of developed understanding. We handle our structural forms with unreflective expertise just as we handle the items of vocabulary which fill them with unreflective expertise. Reflection may suggest principles of handling which the more reflective handlers may recognize and acknowledge; and they will be the readier to do so in proportion as they can see more sophisticated styles of thought as emerging, by analogy and extension, from more basic styles.

We may perhaps hope, in the end, for a physiology of mental development, disclosing the underlying mechanisms, the adjustments of micro-functioning; but the logical reflection, the critical self-consciousness, comes first.

II

When does objective reference emerge? It stands forth in its clearest, uncluttered form, Quine holds, in the apparatus of quantification and variables; and so he suggests that we could 'approximate to the essentials of the real psychogenesis of reference' (100) by a plausible account of the steps which could lead the child or the primitive to quantification. But 'quantification, in the form in which we have come to know and love it, is less than a hundred years old' (100). Science is not so young; and even now the knowing lovers form but a small minority of those whom science would not blush to acknowledge as her own. So it might be wiser not to confine ourselves to checking the steps of the Quine-child, but rather to allow ourselves and our subject to make free with 'the less tidy referential apparatus of actual English' (100).

There is a certain wavering over the characteristics of this last or a certain reluctance, perhaps, even to concede the character of 'referential apparatus' to any forms other than the canonical. Predication goes hand-in-hand with reference. The forms 'An $\alpha$ is a $\beta$', 'Every $\alpha$ is a $\beta$', are put forward as forms of predication on p. 66 and firmly denied to be such on p. 93; 'This is not a predication. It couples two general terms.' Again, plural endings are mentioned on p.84 as a feature of the referential apparatus of English, but no single instance of their functioning as part of that apparatus is allowed a mention in these pages; notoriously, 'Many $\alpha$s are $\beta$', 'A few $\alpha$s are $\beta$', etc. are not very easily or simply accommodated in the favoured idiom.

It seems best explicitly to acknowledge the distinction between a wider and a narrower notion of a form of predication. In the narrower notion all predication, whether under quantification or not, joins a general term in predicative position to a singular term in referential position and hence is grammatically singular, creating no role for plural endings. The wider notion allows general terms, with or without plural endings, into subject-position. Shall we say: into *referential* position? or restrict that title to a place occupied only by a singular term, whether name or variable? It hardly matters. It does matter that we should see 'the referential apparatus of actual English' as at home with the wider notion. One thing we may helpfully notice as common to both conceptions of predication, a bridge between them: the proper name of the bodily individual, the singular term *par excellence*, is admitted by both as a prime occupant of subject- or referential position. It is not the only thing; some singular pronouns, too, are, on both conceptions, equally admissible occupants of the place.

So what is the path to predication? How does our child, or primitive, make his way to the referential apparatus? Quine envisages a pre-predicative situation of language-learning and language-use, where all sentences are occasion-sentences and all terms observation-terms. He distinguishes, initially, three classes of observation-terms. To the first belong 'red', 'water', 'sugar', 'snow', 'white'; 'Fido' and 'Mama' are examples of the second; 'dog', 'apple', 'buckle', 'woman' of the third. For the learning child all are alike in so far as it is the recurrence of some recognizable circumstance that prompts utterance, or assent to utterance, of any of them. Still, there are general differences, in the bases of his recognition, between the three classes. Red can manifest itself in simultaneous scattered portions, as can water; and shape has nothing to do with the recognizability of either. But Mama is neither scattered nor amorphous; 'Mama' names a body. Terms of both these classes, however, 'share a certain semantic simplicity' (55) which does not belong to terms of the third class. These last are more sophisticated. 'Dog', 'buckle', etc. have built-in individuation and to learn them the child must master their individuative force: he can be 'confronted by many dogs at once' and has to learn 'what to count as one dog and what to count as another' (55).

With later developments in mind (Quine says), we can categorize 'Fido' and 'Mama' as singular terms and 'apple', 'dog', etc. as general terms. But 'our categorizing them as such is a sophisticated bit of retrospection that bears little relation to what the learning child is up to' (85); for the terminology of 'general' and 'singular' terms is appropriate only at the level of objective reference and the child has not yet reached that level when the limit of his achievement is utterance, or assent to utterance, of observation terms on appropriate occasions. This holds good whatever the class of the term, although (Quine adds) the learning of terms of the third class brings the child a step nearer to objective reference 'because of the individuation' (85).

There is much to pause over in this. Consider first the claim that 'Fido' and 'Mama' are semantically simpler than 'dog' and 'woman', together with the claim that the first pair are nevertheless what in due course we may classify as singular, the second pair what we may in due course classify as general, terms. The simplicity-ordering is backed by the observation that to learn the name 'Fido' the child has only to appreciate the similarity of Fido-presentations whereas to learn 'dog' he 'has to appreciate a second-order similarity between the similarity-basis of "Fido" and the similarity-bases determining other enduring dogs' (56). But the child is said to be learning 'Fido' and 'Mama' *as singular names* or what will eventually qualify as such. If this is so, it is not enough that the child should not in fact encounter, or be confronted by, a plurality of simultaneous but spatially separated presentations sufficiently similar for them all to count for him as Fido-presentations. It must be part of his mastery of 'Fido' that Fido is unique. A plurality of Fidos simultaneously soliciting his attention must be ruled out by his understanding of the term—semantically ruled out. If it is not ruled out, then 'Fido' is semantically on a par with 'dog', deserving just as much as the latter to be called a general term, though doubtless more specific. But if it is ruled out, then what becomes of the claim that 'Fido' is semantically simpler that 'dog'? The answer at least is simple: we just reverse the terms. Fido is not just *any* Fido-like creature, though he is that; he is the one and only Fido.[2] 'Fido' is a more, not a less, sophisticated acquisition than 'dog'. 'Dog' has individuation; 'Fido' has individuation plus.

Let us consider, second, the thesis that the learning of 'dog', for all the built-in individuation and for all that it is a step on the way, has not yet brought the child to the point of objective reference. Why not? What must he do to qualify? Would it be enough if he said 'dogs' in the presence of a plurality? But he is supposed already to have mastered the individuation, to be able to tell one dog from another; 'dog'

---

[2] It is worth recalling here an experiment recorded by Bower in the course of his studies of the intellectual development of very young children. With the help of mirrors the child is surrounded with a plurality of Mama-presentations, moving and smiling together. The very young child is unbewildered, indeed delighted, at being confronted with many mamas at once. It is the somewhat older child who shows signs of distress (Bower, *Scientific American*, Oct., 1971).

Doubtless the result admits of more than one interpretation. My argument, of course, is quite independent of it.

for him, as occasion sentence, has the force that 'a dog' has for us. Of course he hasn't mastered the *whole* apparatus of objective reference. But why hasn't he wholly mastered a part of it?

It is difficult to find in Quine's text an explicit answer to this question. But the text strongly suggests the following answer: that no one has reached the stage of reference unless he has at least reached the stage of predication. A predication, on any view, must be a joining of terms, capable of yielding truth or falsity according as the terms are aptly or inaptly joined. But the child's primitive observation sentences consist only of one term, of whichever of Quine's three classes. There is, of course, a certain implicit duality about the utterance, a duality which makes it capable of being right or wrong, as-sessable for truth-value. For we have both what he says and the when-and-where he says it. We can represent this duality to ourselves by tacking on to the term an explicit 'here-now', or we can think of the 'here-now' as implicit in the very utterance of the term. But the implicit 'here-now', an invari-ant feature of the observation-sentence, does not qualify as a term in a predication. No doubt a grown-up who says 'A dog is here' or 'At least one dog is here' or (more plausibly) 'There's a dog here' may be allowed to have exercised the power of objective reference, in that the adult utterance can be both grammatically and psychologically grouped with others of which the adult is capable but the child is not. But it would be a misrepresentation of the stage of development our child is at to make any such assimilation of *his* one-term observation sentence.

This, then, I suggest, is Quine's answer to the question why the child who has learned the individuative 'dog' has not yet reached the point of objective reference. Given my earlier point about 'Fido', the same question arises, with even greater force, about the child's mastery of that singular name; and it must receive the same answer. That this is the answer Quine would give is strongly borne out by his treatment of what he calls 'observational compounds' (59–62); but that treatment also suggests that he is wedded to a very much stronger, and highly questionable, thesis about the conditions for achieving true predication and objective reference. These points I now proceed to develop, beginning with a sketch of Quine's position.

The child who has learned 'yellow' and 'paper' as observation terms, i.e. has learned to utter, or assent to, each as a one-term observation sentence, is well placed to be taught an observation term of a new kind—'yellow paper'. 'All our mentor has to do to perfect our training in the compound' is to encourage assent when the yellow and the paper coincide and 'to discourage assent in those less striking cases where the yellow and the paper are separate' (60). Given the learning of a few more such compounds, one by one, the child cottons on to the general principle: he learns to form new compounds of his own and to respond correctly to new ones proposed to him. But he is not yet at predication, not even when one of the terms is individuative, as in 'brown dog', or a name, as in 'wet Fido'. He has not learned to couple terms (predicatively) to make a sentence, he has only learned to couple terms to make a term—which can serve as a sentence. The other element of the duality which yields truth-valuedness is still what it was before, the implicit 'here-now' of the utterance of the observation-sentence-term.

What of 'The dog is brown', 'Fido is wet', uttered or assented to in the conspicuous presence of a brown dog or of wet Fido? These have the grammatical form of predications and, spoken by an adult, even in these circumstances, may (doubtless? perhaps?) be accounted such. But for our child, at the present stage of his learning Odyssey, they could only be pointless variants on his pre-predicative one-term observation sentences where the term is a compound term; and variants which the teacher would do well to withhold from his pupil if he wants to bring the child to the point of true predication, the point of objective reference (67).

For to reach that point, Quine holds, the child has to cross a gulf—a gulf that separates all the learning he has done so far (the learning of occasion sentences) from the learning of the standing or 'eternal predicational construction' (65). This

gulf is bridged, Quine suggests, by a quite different mechanism of learning from any put to work hitherto. The correct
assent to, or assertion of, an observation term as occasion
sentence requires the presence of the relevant feature or—in
the case of an observational compound—the present coincidence of the relevant features. Correct assertion or assent
just *is* assertion or assent on an occasion of such presence or
coincidence. Correctness or incorrectness is wholly occasion-
dependent. But correctness of assertion or assent in the case
of a standing or eternal sentence is quite a different matter.
Correctness in occasion-independent, assent is—subject to
actual change of mind—once for all. So the mechanism of
learning must be quite a different matter too.

Quine has a suggestion about this new mechanism of learning. In the conspicuous or ostended presence of snow, the
child has already learned occasion assent not only to 'snow'
but also to 'white'; in the presence of Fido, he has learned to
assent not only to 'Fido' but also to 'dog'; in the presence of
dog, not only to 'dog' but also to 'animal'. The mechanism
proposed is that of transfer of conditioning, transfer of response from, e.g. 'the snow stimulus to the associated verbal
stimulus, the word "snow" ' (65). From the stage at which the
presence of snow is sufficient to induce assent to 'white' the
child moves to the stage at which the presence of 'snow' is
sufficient to induce assent to 'white', irrespective of the presence or absence of snow. From assenting to 'dog' on seeing
Fido he moves to assenting to 'dog' on hearing 'Fido'. Thus
he learns to assent to queried eternal sentences, 'Snow is
white', 'Fido is a dog' (65–6); and thence, by a psychological
mechanism of generalization, he moves to the point of pro-
ducing such constructions on his own. (One sees why the
formally predicative variants on observation-compounds had
better not reach the child's ears too soon. Too early an exposure to them would at the very least necessitate a painful
process of re-education—if it didn't dish the child's chances
of learning predication for ever!)

Quine shakes his head a little over the murkiness of this
transition, with its more-than-hint of confusion of sign and

object, use and mention. But we should rejoice, he says, in the final outcome, science, rather than dwell on its dubious antecedents (68).

Still, there are other things to pause over in this account; and to pause over, this time, for rather longer. It is not the reputability, nor even the credibility, of such a way of 'bridging the gulf' between observation sentence and eternal predication that need detain us. There is a prior question. Predication, for Quine, predication with objective reference at least, is like the soul of Adonais: it beacons from the abode where the eternal (sentences) are; between that abode and the lower regions of occasion-bound utterance there is a gulf to be bridged, or leaped; on the further side of the gulf stands predication, the joining of terms to make a sentence; on the hither side we have, at best, the joining of terms to make a term—an observational compound—which can serve as a sentence. The prior question is whether this picture is realistic.

Surely it is not. Predication does not stand on the further side of such a gulf. There is no such gulf. Several features of Quine's presentation may combine to mask from us, and from him, the realities of the case. One is the extremely confined range of examples of forms of predication considered at the point of transition: the two forms mentioned are the universal categorical 'An (i.e. any) α is a β' and the traditionally associated singular categorical exemplified by 'Fido is a dog'. Another is a striking omission from the range of observation terms considered: with one exception they include no words for types of happening or change. A third is an unrealistically sharp-edged conception of an 'occasion' or an 'occasion-sentence'.

Let us see how these work in together. Recall, first, Quine's account of the learning of attributive observational compounds. 'Yellow' and 'paper', already learned separately, provided good material: all we need is a coincidence of what could also occur separately and be verbally responded to separately, viz. yellow and paper. We need 'an intersecting of the pertinent saliences' and the stage is set. Suppose, now, our child has learned 'dog' and 'cat' and, perhaps, 'Fido' and 'Felix'. Before his eyes a dog chases a cat. Perhaps Fido chases Felix. Another teaching opportunity. But what are we teaching him? We can scarcely have taught him 'chase' already, and separately, as an observation term all on its own, the pertinent salience now happily intersecting with dog-and-cat-saliences so that we can seize the opportunity to introduce him to the observational compound 'dog chase cat' (or 'Fido chase Felix'). So the standard account doesn't fit. Are we then teaching him a predicational construction already at this tender stage, with full objective reference and no 'hanky-panky over use and mention' (68)? Why not?

At one point Quine himself seems to waver, to forswear the theory of the gulf; notably enough, at the point where there figures the one exception or near-exception to my remark about the exclusion of happening-words from the list of observation-terms. Thus he says: 'Attributive composition affords access to a rich vein of predications' (61); and immediately afterwards offers 'Mama is smiling' or 'smiling Mama' as an instance of attributive composition. But the wavering is only apparent. The doctrine is that we still have at most a 'mere variant' (67) of the observational compound; that there is as yet no need to distinguish a genuinely different mode of composition.

What, then, of the point that the standard account of the learning or framing of observational compound doesn't fit the case of 'dog chase cat' or 'Fido chase Felix'? It doesn't really fit 'Mama smiling' either; much less the contented observation, 'Spoon gone', emanating from the child who has just pitched the instrument off his high chair.

Quine's answer emerges fairly clearly on pp. 61–2. Attributive composition, so clearly exemplified by the case of 'yellow paper', is not the only mode of constructing observation-terms from observation-terms. There are others. Quine mentions the '. . . in . . .' construction, which yields such terms as 'Mama in garden' and the '. . . -like' construction which yields 'dog-like', 'tree-like' etc. as further observation-terms. No doubt the '. . . chase . . .' construction and the '. . . gone' construction could be added to the list. It would be quite a long list. Too long surely. But the doctrine must be that all the phrases that can be formed by means of such constructions are sufficiently like a simple observation term to be themselves classified as observation terms—which can serve as sentences. 'They can be viewed indifferently as terms or sentences' (62).

Or to put the point negatively: there is as yet no sufficient case for distinguishing any one part of such a phrase as having an essentially predicative role in relation to some other part or parts to which a referential or subject-role can be assigned. A gulf still divides these constructions from predicative constructions proper.

The doctrine rests on a notion of sufficient likeness. But what is the respect of likeness? The answer, like the question, imposes itself. Every one of the complex terms yielded by these modes of composition is available as an occasion-sentence, available for utterance with that implicit 'here-now' which makes them subject to assessment as correct or incorrect, true or false, on any occasion of utterance. The underlying idea is still a little elusive. But it seems to be the thought that it is this combination of a situation-description, in itself truth-valueless, on the one hand, and the implicit 'here-now', on the other, which makes the utterance assessable for truth-value in the light of what goes on—so that there is no occasion to find, in the composition of the situation-description itself, a structure which confers assessability for truth-value on the utterance. But how important is implicit 'now' as opposed to implicit 'a moment ago'? implicit 'here' as opposed to implicit 'near by'? 'dog chase cat' happily murmurs the child when the chase has taken both of them out of sight or 'Cat drink milk' he remarks to Mama as she enters the room to find the saucer indeed empty and the cat licking his fur. Surely the child is not in error; and equally surely he has not, just by the timing of the announcement, taken so portentous a step as that from compound term construction to genuine predicative construction with objective reference.

But if he has not taken it now, when *does* he take it? Observe the formidable ambiguity of the phrase 'occasion-sentence'. Most of the sentences we utter outside our studies and seminars, however complicated their construction, depend, for assessment of their truth-value as uttered, upon account being taken of the *occasion* of utterance. They are sprinkled, you may say, with indicator-words, explicit or implicit. Some of them, numerous enough, yet but a small proportion of the whole, relate to what is within the range of direct observation at the very moment of utterace. These last are occasion-sentences in the narrow sense. I have just suggested that it would be absurd to hold that a structural revolution occurs when the child edges reminiscently (or anticipatorily) outside this narrow range. But if we agree that this is absurd, if we abandon the narrow sense, then we are on a slide which carries us smoothly down the whole range of occasion sentences in the broad sense, i.e. of all sentences which depend for their evaluation, as uttered, on account being taken of the occasion of utterance.

So shall we, after all, make the structural break only when we reach the end of the slide and are deposited on the secure terrain of the eternal sentence? More strictly, perhaps: Shall we hold that the child makes *his* structural breakthrough when he steps, at any point, off this slide on to that terrain for the first time—thereafter predicating in occasion-dependent sentences too? But this would be, if possible, even less acceptable. It would seem bizarre to maintain, for example, that no sentence containing the first-person pronoun or possessive really exhibits predicational structure in the fullest sense of that phrase—unless its speaker has mastered some eternal sentence as well. Moreover, some of Quine's claimants for the status of eternal sentence—those which 'gain [their] specificity through explicit use of names, dates, or addresses' (63)—are not, on any realistic view of the matter, eternal sentences at all, place- and person-names being what they are. It is quite unrealistic to say of such sentences that 'their truth-values are fixed for good, regardless of speaker and occasion' (63). We could, indeed, within the limits of a language, remove or minimize speaker-and-occasion relativity by, e.g. adding dates and places of birth, if we knew them, to personal names. An unpromising route to logical metamorphosis. Better to say straight off that the goal is reached only when the sentences 'most characteristic of scientific theory' (63) appear, the completely general sentences. Reviewing his review of the genesis and development of reference, Quine comes near to saying just this: 'An early phase of reference, *perhaps the earliest worthy of the name*, was the universal categorical, as in "A dog is an animal"' (123).

There is surely confusion of aim here. 'When and how do we achieve objective reference?' is one question. 'When and how do we achieve that complete generality of utterance which frees our sentences, as regards truth-value, from any dependence on utterance-occasion?' is another question. There is no profit in conflating them. Objective reference and context-free, or setting-free, generality are doubtless alike 'central to our scientific picture of the world' (89). But the achievement of setting-free generality is not essential to the achievement of objective reference. To legislate to the contrary is to obscure the understanding of both.

Back, then, to the starting-point—painful as it is to retrace one's steps. Back, in particular, to Quine's acknowledgement that the learning of individuative terms like 'dog' is a first step towards objective reference—'because of the individuation' (85). Make this acknowledgement more generous; allow that step to take the child all the way to objective reference, though not indeed to mastery of all its modes (i.e. of all its apparatus); and the slippery questions we have been toying with appear as spurious as they really are. Let us by all means recognize, or at least allow for, a pre-referential and pre-predicative stage of language-learning. I myself used to call sentences (or terms) which might figure at this stage 'feature-placing' sentences (or terms).[3] There is nothing in that conception which excludes composition of terms to form compound feature-terms. These would correspond, within limits, to Quine's observational compounds. Only within lim-

---

[3] See *Individuals* (London, Methuen, 1959), ch. 6, sect. 6; also 'Particular and General', *Proceedings of the Aristotelian Society,* 1953–4, repr. in *Logico-Linguistic Papers* (London, Methuen, 1971).

its; for what the conception of a feature-placing sentence does exclude is individuative terms. The decisive conceptual step, the transition from the pre-referential to the referential stage, is the step to individuative terms. Individuation delivers individuals, and language which relates to individuals is referential. With individuative terms in general, and *a fortiori* with individual names, we have reference. I postpone for a moment the question whether we also have predication.

Consider, first, that the child who has taken the decisive conceptual step, who has learned 'dog', say, as an individuative term, has thereby learned to distinguish one dog from another from a third, to identify a dog as the same again. (Not that he never makes mistakes—the important thing is that he is able to make *such* mistakes.) He is poised, thereby, for the mastery of much of the referential apparatus of ordinary English, and for its employment in what we call noun-phrases containing the individuative term—the apparatus, e.g. of pluralization, numeration, determiners, more or less vague quantifiers like 'a few', 'several', 'lots of'. I earlier issued a caution against neglecting, or bypassing, this ordinary apparatus in order to construct a speculative path by which the Quine-child could climb to mastery of canonical notation. It is not a path that any of us followed. Instead, we should recognize that wider notion of reference and predication, or subject and predicate, in which subject- or referential position is occupied not only by singular names or variables but also by noun-phrases consisting of general terms together with determiners, vague quantifiers, or number words. When we review our topic from this position, then—however much we may value the notation of logic—we must surely find it misleading to rule *both* that reference requires predication *and* that predication consists solely in coupling general term in predicative position with singular name(s) or variable(s) under quantification in such a way as to yield truth or falsity. Yet at least the hint of such a rule may be thought to underlie the reluctance to concede to the decisive step its full decisiveness.

The subjacent rule would encourage the reluctance in

more than one way. 'A dog chases a cat', for example, with its English unreformed, would fail to qualify as referential since the terms in subject-position, the noun-phrases, though grammatically singular, are neither names nor variables. 'Here's a dog' or 'Two dogs are here' are in even worse case; not only do the putative subject-terms, the noun-phrases 'a dog' and 'two dogs' fail to qualify, the second more drastically than the first, but the indicator-word 'here' is at best a dubious candidate for the role of general term in predicative position. Yet it would be strange to maintain that the appropriate utterance of these sentences does not show, whereas utterance of, say, 'Something (here) is such that it is a dog' would show, that the utterer had got hold of the trick of objective reference. The latter, artificial form indeed satisfies the rule's requirement for predication—it has an undoubted general term, 'dog', in predicative position; whereas the ordinary 'A dog is here', with the noun-phrase, 'a dog', as putative subject-term, does not. But surely it matters not a straw whether we *call* 'A dog is here' or 'Two dogs are here' predications or not. Traditional grammar sanctions it; and if we insist that there is no such thing as objective reference without predication, we had better follow traditional grammar.

I have already referred to another way in which the subjacent rule might operate to delay recognition of objective reference. It seems sufficiently important in Quine's thinking to deserve mentioning once more. This is the idea that where there is objective reference, it is the predicative or predicative-cum-quantificational combination of terms *and this alone* which yields as outcome something assessable for truth or falsity. Or rather, since this description is ambiguous, it is the construction put on this condition which is responsible, a construction which turns it into a condition satisfiable by eternal sentences alone, a condition disqualifying all dependence, explicit or implicit, on indicator-words, ruling out any degree of determination of the truth-value-assessable outcome by the circumstances of utterance, including time, place, identity of speaker, and other less obvious features of the utterance-setting. A mild symptom of this effect I noted in referring to Quine's readiness to multiply constructions yielding complex observation-terms rather than acknowledge predication and reference at the level of occasion-sentences in the narrow sense. I speculated on his readiness to add the 'chase' construction to the list to deal with 'dog chase cat' or 'Fido chase Felix'. But surely good sense must quickly call a halt. What a complication of term-yielding constructions would be necessary to deny the status of full objective-reference-cum-predication to such a simple observation as 'Fido is fighting two other dogs in the garden'.

### III

It may be felt that much of the foregoing misses the essential point of Quine's position; that it is not by any sort of oversight that he defers recognition of the achievement of objective reference; that he really holds that objective reference in the fullest sense (101) is not achieved until we reach the level of general theory and until our theories are couched, in effect, in terms solely of predicates, truth-functions, and quantification (139). But if this is to be more than an idiosyncratic definition, if it is to be a thesis, it needs defence. And how should it be defended? Not on the ground that such is the language of science. The language of science is simply this or that natural language, enriched, sometimes, by the symbolism of mathematics; differing from the language of law reports or Parliamentary debates only in descriptive vocabulary, not in grammatical structure; but when we speak of the apparatus of reference, it is grammatical structure, not descriptive vocabulary, that is our topic.

Is it claimed, rather, that the range of our references stands forth more clearly when we effect (where we can) the paraphrase into the quantificational notation as we now have it? If this is the claim, it should be noted, first, that it is a different claim. It is no longer disputed that we who are content with the 'less tidy referential apparatus of actual English' are as fully engaged in objective reference as the purist of logical language; it is claimed merely that we are not so clear about what we are referring to.

But there seems to be no reason for conceding even this claim. There is nothing intrinsic to the spare apparatus of variable and predicate which makes it any better an index than the less tidy, i.e. richer, referential apparatus of actual English. It is true that we deploy the referential apparatus of actual English with a lavishness which may offend nominalistic scruple. But, again, there is nothing in the formal structure of quantification which inhibits a quite parallel lavishness in *its* deployment. We may have, or think we have, reasons for wishing to check, or limit, this lavishness. Some may, in particular, insist that no deployment of referential apparatus, rich or spare, tidy or untidy, shall count as comporting objective reference (or even, in strictness, be admitted at all) unless either a general principle of individuation or a general 'criterion of identity' is forthcoming for the sort of thing to which the putative objects of reference belong. This is an issue I have discussed elsewhere,[4] arguing, in effect, that though individuative principles are integral to the birth of reference (to reference to spatio-temporal particulars), it is gratuitous, and would be crippling, to insist that they be forthcoming at every stage through which, by logical analogy, reference evolves. The issue itself is not now to the point. The point is that whatever stand we take on the issue we must take on its own philosophical merits. The referential forms themselves, rich and familiar or spare and strange, make no metaphysical claims and impose no ontological limitations. It is we who do these things, if we do them at all—and for diverse reasons. What can be conceded, perhaps, is a certain harmony between a taste for spareness in the forms of reference and a distaste for luxuriance in the range of categories of items referred to. But now we are outside the range of reasons. As Quine remarks in another connection, *de gustibus non disputandum est* (50).

---

[4] See 'Entity and Identity', in *Contemporary British Philosophy*, 4th Series, ed. H. D. Lewis (London, Allen & Unwin, 1976), 93–120; included as Ch. 1 in the present volume.

# 8

# *Logical Form and Logical Constants*

I want to consider, with respect to standard logic, whether it
is possible to give an adequate general characterization of the
notions of logical form or logical constant. There is some
reason to think that it is not an easy matter to do so. Russell,
in 1937, represented it as a major unsolved problem in the
philosophy of logic.[1] Quine finds it easy enough to explain the
allied notion of a truth of logic; but his definition[2] contains
and depends on the notion of a logical particle; and of that
notion he gives no general explanation whatever, contenting
himself with a selective list, ending with the phrase *etcetera*.
Later, in *Philosophy of Logic*,[3] he suggests that the matter is
to some extent at the discretion (or whim) of the logical
grammarian; but apart from a reference to the indifference to
subject-matter, and the ubiquity of employment, of the forms
of logic, he gives no indication of how that discretion should
be exercised. Finally, it is just worth mentioning, for the sake
of its weakly despairing quality, Pap's suggestion that 'we can
give no better general explicit definition of a logical constant
than "constant occurring essentially in *most* of the necessary
inferences in which it occurs"'.[4] This is weak indeed. Even if
the given characterization happened to be historically true
of all and only those elements which are distinguished as
logical particles, it would be absurd to represent it as the
explanatory principle of their being thus distinguished. If we

---

[1] Russell (1937), Introduction.    [2] Quine (1953), Quine (1952).
[3] Quine (1970).    [4] Pap (1958), 161.

could really do no better than this, we might as well give up the attempt.

However, if there are reasons for thinking the problem difficult, there are also reasons for thinking that it cannot be quite intractable. All the attitudes just illustrated—Quine's caution or indifference, Russell's sense of a large unsolved problem, Pap's despair—must seem a little surprising when we consider that there is a large measure of interdefinability among the constants of standard logic. At most, then, we must be dealing with a rather small number of fundamental ideas, and it should surely be possible to explain what in general makes just these ideas the proper material of the science of logic.

There is another and somewhat vague indication that the problem ought not to be so very intractable. Though it is expressed in different idioms at different times and at different stages in the history of the subject, it is nevertheless possible to find a certain community of attitudes to formal logic in the work of a number of philosophers: in Kant's view of logic, for example, as the completed science of the pure forms of the understanding: in Boole's and others' account of it as the study of the completely general laws of thought; and above all, perhaps, in the way of thinking about logic which dominates Wittgenstein's *Tractatus*[5] and is made by him the subject of retrospective analysis in the *Investigations*.[6] That way of thinking might be expressed in some such words as these: 'Logic reveals the general essence of all thought and all (developed) language.' (We may even think that Quine's claims on behalf of canonical notation belong essentially to the same family of attitudes.) If such attitudes are well founded, if such views have any truth in them, we should be able to discover what it is.

Before making any such attempt, let me refer to two thoughts both of which have obvious relevance to the subject, but neither of which, by itself, gets us very far. The first is the thought of that feature of subject-matter-indifference or

---

[5] Wittgenstein (1961).    [6] Wittgenstein (1953). See esp. paras 89 to 108.

ubiquity of employment to which Quine refers and which Ryle more elegantly named 'topic-neutrality'. It would plainly be inadequate to characterize logical particles as expressions exhibiting this feature. The idea is too vague, for one thing, and its coverage much too comprehensive; there are many prepositions (to, for, with, by, at), conjunctions (for, since, as, although), adverbs (very, much, rather) which possess topic-neutrality if anything does but which we should certainly not wish to count as logical particles. To attempt to remedy this deficiency, to narrow down the field, simply by specifying further criteria, besides being an inelegant procedure, would tend only to emphasize the major deficiency of the whole approach, which is that it is insufficiently explanatory. Surely the feature of topic-neutrality, a feature shared by so many expressions, must be no more than a consequence of some more central fact about logical particles,and a really good explanation of their nature would show it as such and not take it as a starting-point.

The second thought, which clearly underlies Pap's suggestion, is that of a peculiarly intimate connection between logical form or logical particles on the one hand and, on the other, such necessary or intensional relations between propositions as those of necessary implication, deductive consequence, contradiction, and incompatibility. That there is such a connection seems evident enough. The difficulty is to state it without falling into obvious falsity or equally obvious circularity. If we say, as some used to say, that deductive or necessary inference depends on logical form alone, i.e. that logical particles are just those elements in statements in virtue of which they necessarily imply, or are implied by, or are incompatible with, other statements, then we encounter the obvious objection that such relations without number are generated by the descriptive or non-logical words in sentences. We can perhaps save the doctrine by placing a sufficiently restrictive interpretation on the notion of *deductive* inference or *logically* necessary implication, etc.; but how to do this without rendering the doctrine trivially circular is just the problem we started with, the problem of characterizing logical particles or logical form.

A different objection to any such approach would come from those who question the intelligibility of any such intensional notions of necessity or impossibility as are employed in it; who think they are quite empty notions. Since I am quite unconvinced by arguments to this effect, I shall disregard this objection; except, perhaps, to suggest at the end that it has been implicitly answered.

Since both these approaches, as so far described, seem to run into trouble, I shall enquire whether there is any illumination to be gained from the imprecisely expressed idea, already mentioned, that logic—or standard logic—somehow reveals or contains the general essence of propositional thought and language. Of course it is quite unclear what this means. So I shall take as my text a particular formulation of the idea: a quotation from Wittgenstein's *Tractatus* (5.47). It runs:

One could say that the sole logical constant was what *all* propositions, by their very nature, had in common with one another.
But that is the general propositional form.

Elsewhere Wittgenstein says that the general propositional form is: 'This is how things are.' What this means, I think, is that when he talks of propositions, he has in mind the sort of sentences we frame when we state, or purport to state, *facts* about the natural world—whether these sentences, as used, relate to particular episodes or objects or states of affairs which have dates or places in the world; or are commonplace generalizations about kinds of such episodes or objects; or are relatively high-flying theories about the way things go. He has in mind sentences such that, if we affirm them, we are saying *things are in fact this way*—even though they might have been otherwise. For short, we can say that he is concerned with the domain of empirical statement—though 'statement' must not be taken too literally here, since the sentences in question could of course be used by way of expressing surmise or hypothesis as well as in the way of definite affirmation.

But how are we to interpret Wittgenstein's remark about the sole logical constant? Clearly he does not mean that there is literally only one logical constant. He may perhaps be taken to mean that the forms and constants of logic are somehow implicit in the bare notion of a proposition in general. Or, to attempt a paraphrase which comes closer to our problem: what is distinctive about the forms and constants of logic is that their whole force or meaning can be explained without drawing on any materials other than those which we are *given* with the notion of a proposition. What we are invited to consider is 'the very nature' of a proposition, the essence of (empirical) statement. We are invited to find the solution to our problem just here.

I propose first to sketch, very quickly and roughly and perhaps objectionably, one way of following up this clue; and then to trace a rather more careful, or at least more elaborate, route. It is clear that if we are to follow up the clue at all, we must enquire what *is* essential to statement, to saying how things are in the world. One thing often remarked upon is the necessity of a certain duality of function whereby we are able, on the one hand, to specify certain *general types* of situation or thing or event and, on the other, to attach these general specifications to *particular cases* or *items*: i.e. to indicate some *particular* item and characterize it as being of some *general* sort. Evidently in so characterizing some particular item or situation, we implicitly exclude certain other possibilities regarding that item. And here we touch on a necessary general feature of *all* statements of how things are in the world. For *every* such statement, not merely those which exhibit the duality of function I have just mentioned, must exclude *some* possibilities. It must not be compatible with any and every conceivable state of affairs whatever. For if it excludes nothing, it says nothing.

Now it is simply to express the necessary excluding power of every empirical statement in another way, to say that every such statement must admit of the two mutually exclusive possibilities of being true or being false. Because it excludes, it *can* inform, i.e. be a vehicle of truth; because it *can* inform, it *can* misinform, i.e. be a vehicle of falsehood.

So we have at our disposal the notions of specifying a general type (or introducing a general concept) on the one hand and indicating a particular instance or case of it on the other; and also the notion of every statement's admitting of the two exclusive possibilities of truth and falsity. We have only to add the idea, inseparable from that of language in general, of identifiable linguistic forms or devices with conventional forces or meaning—and we have all we need.

First: the idea of a plurality of statements, each the possible possessor of one of the two mutually exclusive truth-values, truth and falsity, carries with it the idea of different possible *combinations* of truth-values for pairs or sets of statements; and nothing more is needed for the explanation of the force of those forms or schemata which represent different modes of truth-functional composition. The familiar truth-tables display this fact in the most striking way. It should be noticed that I have not claimed that it is an essential feature of empirical statement that every empirical statement must *possess* one or the other of the two mutually exclusive truth-values. I have only said that they must *admit* of either and cannot admit of both. In this way a controversial issue is avoided without prejudice to the programme. The force of the truth-functional constants is explained by exhibiting the consequences of attaching them to propositions which do actually possess one or other of the two mutually exclusive truth-values. We do not have to rule on the question whether these are all propositions or not.

Next: the idea of introducing a general concept and attaching it to a particular case carries with it the idea of a range of statements in which the *same* general concept is applied to a plurality of different particular cases, one in each statement. So much is given with the very notion of the *generality* of a concept or type: the general type is something repeatable in different cases. Combining the notion of a range of statements in which the same general concept is applied to different particular cases with the thought of every statement as a possible possessor of one of the two mutually exclusive truth-values, we obtain once more the thought of different possible combinations of truth-values among the members of such a set of statements. Many of such combinations will evidently include at least one case of truth. The thought of a linguistic form or schema *representing* this last idea is the thought of the existentially quantified form.

The foregoing is not intended as an exposition of Wittgenstein's own thought. It is no more than a rough sketch of one possible way of following up the hint contained in his remark. Now I shall sketch another way of doing the same thing. The aim, as before, will be to show that the force of the forms and constants of standard logic can be wholly explained without drawing on any materials other than what we are given with the idea of what is essential to empirical statement-making. We begin directly, this time, with the thought that if anything is to qualify as an empirical statement, as potentially informative about the world, it must exclude some possibilities. We take this notion of exclusion as fundamental. We proceed to define, in terms of this notion of exclusion, certain possible relations between statements. We do not have to claim that it is essential to any language in which empirical statements can be made, that it *must* contain statements standing to each other in these relations; though we shall certainly find it natural that it should. It is enough that we can explain the ideas of these relations in terms of the truly essential feature of the excluding force of empirical statement. It is enough that the *possibility* of statements related by these relations is given with the idea of empirical statement in general.

The other idea we need is the idea of linguistic forms or devices of which the whole conventional force or meaning is *exhausted* by *exhibiting* certain statements as standing in these relations. Such devices or forms will serve not to *state*, but to *show*, the statements in question to be related in the ways in question without revealing anything of the content of the statements, without, indeed, revealing anything else about them at all. One more, we do not have to claim that it is an essential feature of a language in which empirical statements can be made, that it should contain such forms or devices. It is enough that the idea of such devices, and their force, can be explained in terms of our permitted materials: i.e. in terms of what *is* admitted to be essential to empirical statement-making.

To begin, then, with some of the relations I spoke of. One of them is the relation between two statements each of which excludes what the other affirms, i.e. each of which excludes the possibility which is realized if the other is true. Any such statements are related by the relation of *incompatibility*. Next, suppose we have two statements one of which excludes everything that the other excludes and perhaps more; then we shall say that the first *implies* the second. Next, suppose we have two statements which are incompatible with each other and which are also such that neither excludes anything which the other also excludes. Then we shall say that they are each other's *contradictories*.

We can define more complicated relations in terms of these. Suppose we have three statements related in the following way: two of the statements form a pair such that each member of the pair by itself implies the third statement, while the third statement, taken together with a contradictory of each member of the pair in turn, implies the other member of the pair. Then we shall say that the third member of the trio of statements is related to the other two as their *disjunction*.

I pause to note that it is *not* the case that in framing the ideas of statements related in these ways we have *ipso facto* framed the idea of statements containing any particular logical constants. (Here, for example, is a trio of statements standing in this last relation explained which do not, however, contain any disjunctive particle:

John's father is a brother of one of William's parents
John's mother is a sister of one of William's parents
John's and William are first cousins.)

And now for the next step. We take the relation just illustrated and form the idea of a trio of statements which are related by this relation *and which are expressed in accordance with a linguistic pattern or schema of which the whole force or function is to exhibit any statements exemplifying it as standing in just this relation without, in itself, revealing anything else about their content.* We then frame a corresponding idea for the relation of contradictoriness; i.e. we form the idea of a pair of statements which are each other's contradictories and which are expressed in accordance with a linguistic pattern or schema of which, again, the whole force or function is to exhibit *this* relationship between statements without revealing anything else about their content. Now we ask what linguistic patterns or schemata, if any, answer to these descriptions. The answer is, obviously, that the first description fits *what is common* to all trios of statements exemplifying the schemata of propositional logic

$$p, q, p \vee q$$

and the second description fits what is common to all pairs of statements exemplifying the schemata

$$p, \sim p.$$

We can express these descriptions of linguistic patterns or schemata in a slightly different way. In the first case, the description could be paraphrased as follows: it is a form or schema such that given any pair of statements, a third statement related to them in the way described (i.e. as their disjunction) can be framed in accordance with this schema without any knowledge of what the given statements state. Correspondingly for the second case: it is a form or schema such that, given any statement, a statement related to it as its contradictory can be framed in accordance with the schema without any knowledge of what the given statement states.

These descriptions of linguistic patterns do not exceed the permitted materials. They are framed exclusively in terms of ideas which are themselves explained in terms of what is essential to empirical statement in general. They mention only statements, relations between statements which are themselves definable in the permitted terms, and linguistic forms and forces. Since there could evidently be no language at all without linguistic forms or devices having conventional forces or meanings, we seem to be well within our limits. Let us call descriptions of forms or devices framed in these terms '*form-descriptions*'. We may now provisionally define logical constants as the constant expressions in statement-sets exemplifying either schemata falling under form-descriptions or schemata definable in terms of schemata falling under *form-descriptions*. Since negation and disjunction provide together an adequate basis for the definition of all other constants of standard propositional logic, we have at any rate a definition which covers the forms and particles of that part of logic.

There are several points to note about form-descriptions before we proceed.

1. The first point has already been implicitly made, but is worth repeating. As regards propositional logic, what falls under a form-description is not just the isolated schema of the constant itself, but that schema taken together with the representation of those identities which are represented in the symbolism by *recurrence* of sentence-letters. What falls under a form-description, that is to say, is not just, for example, '$\sim p$' or '$p \lor q$' but '$p, \sim p$' or '$p, q, p \lor q$'. This is an advantage, since it keeps forcibly before our minds the importance of the identities represented by sentence-letter recurrence. (A constant-description is easily obtainable from a form-description.)

2. This first point leads directly to a second point of some importance, which arises as soon as we ask what exactly *is* represented by sentence-letter recurrence in the schemata-sets which fall under form-descriptions. We cannot answer that recurrence of sentence-letters in these schemata sets represents *merely* the recurrence of identical type-sentences or sentential clauses. We have to say, rather, that sentence-letter-recurrence represents sentential clause recurrence *under certain conditions*: viz. under just those conditions, whatever they may be for different types of case, under which identity of sentential clause guarantees identity of proposition expressed by the clause. We could indeed rest content

with the simpler answer for the case of an idealized language which was completely free from both indexicality and ambiguities of sense; but only because these freedoms together *would* constitute conditions under which sentential identity guaranteed identity of proposition expressed. But natural languages exhibit both indexicality and equivocality. As far as natural languages are concerned, there are no particles, natural or symbolic, such that the occurrence of these particles together with mere sentence-recurrence as represented in our schemata-sets would alone be sufficient to guarantee that the statements these sentences were used to make had to each other the relevant relations. So we have to insist explicitly on the condition mentioned: which amounts to the requirement that recurrence of the same general-concept-specifying expression in any two occurrences of the same type-sentences should preserve identity of sense and recurrence of the same indexical expressions (including proper names) in any two occurrences of the same type-sentence should preserve identity of reference.

3. There is a third point which is perhaps just worth making about form-descriptions. I began by explaining certain possible relations between statements in terms of the notion of exclusion. The relations I chose to define were respectively the two-termed relations of incompatibility, implication, and contradictoriness and the three-termed relation which holds between statements when one has the force of the disjunction of the other two. (The definition of this last was given in terms of implication and contradiction.) In the case of the last two of these relations, i.e. the three-termed relation and the two-termed relation of contradictoriness, I then gave descriptions of linguistic patterns of which the whole force was to *exhibit* statements as standing in such relations without revealing anything else about them, descriptions which were seen to fit certain schemata-sets of logic. I gave no such form-descriptions for the first two of the defined relations, namely incompatibility and implication. Suppose someone were to ask: Why not? The answer, of course, is that given a so far (implicit) requirement on schemata-sets under form-

descriptions, it is impossible; it can't be done. But this might prompt the further question: Why not?

The answer turns once more on the notion of propositional identity. It demands that a little more should be explicitly said about what is to be required of schemata-sets falling under form-descriptions. Such a set contains either one or two isolated sentence-letters and a schema in which the isolated sentence-letters recur together with a constant. So in any exemplification of the schemata-set, the statement containing the constant is represented as some kind of function of the identities of the statement or statements which replace the isolated sentence-letter or letters. The requirement to be made explicit on schemata-sets falling under form-descriptions is the following. In every exemplification of such a set, the total logical powers, i.e. the total excluding force, of every constant-containing statement should be determinate, given the identities of the isolated statements which are repeated as clauses in the constant-containing statement. In the case of a statement which has the force of the disjunction of two others and in the case of a statement which is a contradictory of another, this condition is satisfied. For, as will be evident from the definition of these relations, any statement which is a contradictory of a given statement will have exactly the same exclusion-range as (i.e. will be equivalent to) any other statement which is a contradictory of the given statement. Similarly any statement which has the force of a disjunction of two given statements will be equivalent to any other such statement. But the condition is obviously not satisfied in the case of the incompatibility-relation in general or in the case of the implication relation. For any given statement there are many statements which are incompatible with it but which are not equivalent to, and indeed may be incompatible with, each other. Similarly for a given statement and the statements which imply it or the statements which it implies. Suppose, for example, we tried to mimic, for the case of the incompatibility relation, the procedure followed in the cases of the contradictory relation and the disjunctive relation. We could introduce a special symbol, say '*x*', and then try to stipulate that in any exemplification of the schema-set '*p, xp*', the two exemplifying statements would be exhibited as incompatible with each other. The trouble with this is that the identity of the proposition exemplifying '*p*' would not determine any definite logical force, and definite identity, for the statement—or rather the pseudo-statement—exemplifying '*xp*'. Similarly we might introduce upward and downward arrows '↑' and '↓' and try to stipulate that in any exemplification of the schema

$$p, \downarrow p$$

the statement exemplifying '↓ *p*' was exhibited as *implied by* the statement-exemplifying '*p*' and in any exemplification of the schema

$$\uparrow p, p$$

the statement exemplifying '↑ *p*' was exhibited as *implying* the statement exemplifying '*p*'. The trouble, as before, would be that the identity of the given statement exemplifying '*p*' would not determine any definite logical force (any definite exclusion range) for the pseudo-statements containing the pretended logical constants.

It should be clear, I think, that the requirement made explicit in dealing with this point was really implicit in the mode of introduction of the notion of schema-sets falling under form-descriptions.

It has been shown, then, that we can, in the permitted terms, cover precisely the field of standard propositional logic. Now to turn to quantification. In dealing with propositional constants, the only essential feature of empirical statement which was invoked was the excluding power which any such proposition must possess. To cope with quantification we must invoke also that necessary duality of function which I mentioned at the outset. But that duality demands a slightly more critical look. In introducing it, I said that it was essential to the possibility of empirical statement that we should have the means of specifying general types of situation, thing, etc., i.e. of introducing general concepts into discourse, and also of attaching these general specifications or general concepts to particular cases. And it might be objected that this condition *could* be satisfied without there being any possibility of explaining objectual quantification on its basis. For we might imagine—as Quine imagined in *The Roots of Reference*[7] and, indeed, as I once imagined myself— a very primitive pre-predicative level of discourse at which there was no such distinction among terms as we make by speaking, say, of general terms and singular names; at which, rather, all our general concept expressions are such feature-terms as 'water' or 'red', and at which all statement-like utterances would simply consist in the enunciation of such a term on what was, or was represented as, an occasion of the presence of water or red.

On this I have two comments. The first is that the programme could in fact proceed, if in a rather limping and unsatisfactory way, on this basis. We could get, not exactly *objectual* quantification, but something analogous—say, occasion quantification. For all that is absolutely needed is the right to speak of two distinguishable functions, namely the specification of some kind of *repeatable* feature and the indication of its incidence; and both functions are clearly performed in the primitive utterances envisaged. Even these primitive utterances indicate *both* the occasion—the occasion of utterance itself—*and* what it's supposed to be an occasion *of*.

My second comment is that, though it might be possible to proceed on this basis, it seems unnecessarily puritanical to restrict ourselves in this way; for it seems reasonable to allow, as essential to any *developed* language in which empirical statements are made, not merely this function of indicating occasions for the application of terms, but the function of indicating *particular* individuals, particular items, to which *general* terms are applied. So we proceed on the more generous assumption that the two functions of identifying refer-

---

[7] Quine (1974).

ence and of predication are to be admitted among the features in terms of which we are to be permitted to define, or explain, other notions. There must be means of showing what general concept is being predicated and what it is being predicated of. Without exceeding our permitted materials, then, we can frame the idea of a set of statements in each of which the same general concept is predicated of a particular item, but a different particular item in each case. And then we can frame the further idea of a statement with the following characteristics:

(1) It is implied by any member of a certain given set of statements of the kind just mentioned.

(2) It is not implied by any member of any other such set, unless, of course, that set is such that any member of it implies a member of the original set.

A statement so related to statements of a given set may be said to express the highest common factor of such a set of statements.

Next, we frame the idea of statements of such a set, on the one hand, and their highest common factor statement on the other, being expressed in accordance with a pattern of linguistic forms of which the force or function is simply to exhibit the relationship between them which I have just described without, in itself, revealing anything else about their content. This description, of course, is designed to fit the common features of sets of statements such that one member of the set exemplifies the schema of existential or particular quantification, '$(\exists x)(Fx)$', while each of the others exemplifies the schema '$Fx$' with constant replacement for '$F$' and varying replacement for '$x$'.

The description is subject to similar comments to those which apply in the case of descriptions of propositional schemata. Thus:

(1) The description fits not just the schema of the existential quantifier itself, but the whole pattern displayed by '$(\exists x)$

(*Fx*)' and '*Fx*', taken together, where the recurrence of '*F*' in both schemata represents *recurrence* of predicative phrase, while the free '*x*' in '*Fx*' represents *variation* of name or other referring expression.

(2) We must regard predicate-letter recurrence as representing not merely predicate-expression recurrence, but predicate-expression recurrence under the condition that identity of sense is also preserved.

(3) As before we can easily extract from our description a description of the device of quantifier and bound variable itself as opposed to the whole pattern.

(4) As before there is no need to find another such description for the form of universal quantification, since that form is definable in terms of forms already described.

A further comment seems called for to which there is no parallel in the previous account of propositional constants. The description as I have given it fits only monadic schemata of quantification. But it is easily extended. Having allowed the functions of reference and predication as essential to statement-making, we can frame the idea of multi-place predicates (without having to declare such predicates essential to statement-making) and then proceed, by similar, though more complicated, steps, as before.

Now to stand back and review the course that has been followed. We begin with the idea of certain powers or functions as essential to empirical statement-making, to saying how things are in the world: viz. the power of exclusion and the functional duality which we consider in the form of identifying reference and predication. We proceed to define, in terms of these powers and functions, certain relationships which statements might have to each other. We then frame, as it were, certain specifications of linguistic forms or devices. They are to be forms or devices whose force can be wholly explained in terms of the ways in which they exhibit or indicate (though they do not affirm) the incidence of certain of these relationships. They are to be essentially forms and devices which, as it were, display these relationships on the surface of language without, in themselves, revealing anything more about the content of the statements exemplifying these forms than their possession of these relationships. And we find that the forms and particles of standard logic are just such forms and devices as these. The form-descriptions or form-specifications which we frame in our permitted terms fit these logical forms and constants exactly.

The result obtained harmonizes with that way of thinking about logic which was epitomized in my text from Wittgenstein; for though I certainly cannot claim to have been expounding Wittgenstein's actual thought at the time of the *Tractatus*, the result *was* obtained by following up that clue—in a certain way. We might say that the result allows us to think of standard logic as something in principle excogitatable, though not of course actually excogitated, by pure reflection on the general nature of statement, on what is the least that is necessarily involved in the making of empirically informative statements.

It should be noted as well that the result also harmonizes with—and clarifies—those two abortive approaches to the problem which I mentioned earlier. First, the topic-neutrality, the indifference to subject-matter, manifested by the forms and particles of logic, emerges as a consequence of their force being explicable without reference to anything but the idea of a statement in general. And second, the nature of the peculiarly intimate connection between form on the one hand and the relations of necessary implication, incompatibility, etc., on the other, now becomes clear. It is of course *not* true that all the implications and incompatibilities of statements depend on their logical form alone; but it *is* true that the whole force of these forms is exhausted in determining, in exhibiting, more or less complex relations between statements, relations which are definable in terms of such relations as implication and incompatibility, i.e. ultimately in terms of the notion of exclusion. It is false that form alone determines *all* such relations; but it is true that form alone determines *nothing but* such relations. In the slogan 'Deductive relations are revealed by form alone' we have either a falsehood or a triviality; in the slogan 'Deductive relations alone are revealed by form' we have a mnemonic for the truth.

One other consequence is worth mentioning. If the account I have given of the force or meaning of logical forms and particles is in general correct, then it is also correct to say that the logical relations determined by those forms are determined by meaning alone; and this is as much as to say that logical truth is determined by meaning alone. So the disputed notion of analyticity—understood as truth in virtue of meaning alone—together with the associated range of notions of intensional relations, such as that of necessary implication, is vindicated for the case of logical truth, logical implication, etc.

Now it might be said that this result is not particularly impressive since the *general* acceptability or validity of the notions of such intensional relations was assumed at the outset when definitions of such relations were offered in terms of the notions of exclusion. To this I am tempted to answer that the argument can in fact go through without any such initial assumption. We can insist on the excluding power which statements must possess without insisting on any particular *account* of this power: and so for the other relations defined in terms of exclusion. That is to say, we need not *initially* speak of such relations as holding in virtue of meaning alone. We can delay the introduction of *this* notion till we reach the point of introducing forms or devices of which the meaning is given by saying that their force is precisely that of exhibiting propositions as standing in such relations. Relations so exhibited do hold in virtue of the meanings of such forms. So what we self-denyingly eschew at one level we are given at another, and then, being given it at this level, the level of strictly *logical* truth and strictly *logical* relations, we should be the less reluctant to admit it at other levels, to allow, that is, that such relations may depend on meaning alone without depending on, and being exhibited by, logical form. However, since I have never been touched by a generalized scepticism about analyticity, etc. I feel no need to press this reply.

One final comment. The point of the procedure followed has been to exhibit the forms and particles of standard logic—with the force they have—as something obtainable or excogitatable by pure reflection on the general nature of the proposition, of empirical statement-making, without reference to anything else such as the subject-matter of statements or the specific practical problems and purposes of statement-making, not, of course, that we could eliminate reference to purposes altogether: it was on the fact that statement-making includes the purpose of informativeness—of saying how things are—that we based their essential characteristic of excluding something. But this was as far as we went in reference to purposes. Now two comments on this general procedure immediately suggest themselves. First even if the forms and particles of logic can plausibly be represented as obtainable by pure reflection of this kind on the nature of statement-making in general, they obviously weren't in fact excogitated or obtained in this way, but were rather obtained by refining on what is to be found in natural languages. Second, the fact, if it is a fact, that the force or meaning of the forms and particles of logic can be thus explicated purely in terms of what is essential to statement-making in general, gives *in itself* no decisive reason to expect that forms and particles with exactly their character should actually be found in natural languages. Obviously the explanation of what, if anything, actually *is* found corresponding more or less closely to the ideally excogitatable forms will turn on more points about the needs and purposes of speech than (1) the general need for a statement to have some power of exclusion and (2) the duality of reference and predication—which are all that have been invoked in the course of the argument. It cannot be simply assumed that the pragmatic pressures which shape language, even though they may be expected to yield some forms corresponding more or less closely to the ideally excogitatable forms, will invariably yield forms which are precisely identical in force with these. Continuing discussion of the relations between natural language 'if . . . then . . .' and the material conditional of logic suggests that there is still some life in this issue.

## REFERENCES

Pap, A. (1958): *Semantics and Necessary Truth* (New Haven, Yale University Press, 1958).

Quine, W. V. O. (1952): *Methods of Logic* (London, Routledge & Kegan Paul, 1952).

——(1953): *From a Logical Point of View: Logic Philosophical Essays* (Cambridge, Mass., Harvard University Press, 1953).

——(1970): *Philosophy of Logic* (Englewood Cliffs, NJ, Prentice-Hall, 1970).

——(1974): *The Roots of Reference* (La Salle, Ill., Open Court Publishing Co., 1974).

Russell, B. (1937): *The Principles of Mathematics* (London, Cambridge University Press, 1903; 2nd edn., 1937).

Wittgenstein, L., (1961): *Tractatus* (D. F. Pears and B. T. McGuiness (trans.)) (London, Routledge & Kegan Paul, 1961).

——(1953): *Philosophical Investigations* (G. E. M. Anscombe (trans.)) (Oxford, Blackwell, 1953).

# 9

# 'If' and '⊃'

The object of this paper is to bring about a confrontation, at a fairly general level, of two views about the meaning, or conventional force, or sense, of 'if . . . then . . .'. I do not suggest that these two views exhaust the possibilities.

One of these views may be called the truth-functionalist view. On this view, 'if . . . then . . .' really has precisely the same meaning or conventional force as '⊃'. If we are prone to think otherwise, it is, according to this view, because we are tempted to count as part of the *meaning* of 'if' certain features which do not belong to its meaning, though they are characteristic of central cases of its *use*. (Let me remark how the wider bearings of this particular conflict are indicated here.) A view of this kind is succinctly expressed by Quine as follows:

> Only those conditionals are worth affirming which follow from some manner of relevance between antecedent and consequent— some law, perhaps, connecting the matters which these two component statements describe. But such connection underlies the useful application of the conditional without needing to participate in its meaning. Such connection underlies the useful application of the conditional even though the meaning of the conditional be understood precisely as '~(p. ~ q)'. (*Methods of Logic*, London, 1974: 16)

The most powerful arguments I have heard employed in this cause are due to Paul Grice. I shall refer to them in what follows.

The view that 'if . . . then . . .' is identical in conventional force with '. . . ⊃ . . .' is sometimes accompanied by reserva-

tions about counterfactual conditionals.[1] But if it is to be
attractive, I think it will have to be forced through for coun-
terfactuals as well. For if (*if*) the right way of tackling the
whole question of conditionals is, among other things, to try
to settle the question of the meaning, or meanings, of the
expression 'if . . . then . . .', then we are faced with the alternative of saying either that 'if . . . then . . .' has the same
meaning, or that it has different meanings, in such cases as
the following—I go back a little in recent history for my
example:

> (1) Remark made in the summer of 1964:
>     'If Goldwater is elected, then the liberals will be
>     dismayed.'
> (2) Remark made in the winter of 1964:
>     'If Goldwater had been elected, then the liberals
>     would have been dismayed.'

It seems obvious that about the least attractive thing that one
could say about the *difference* between these two remarks is
that it shows that, or even that it is partly accounted for by the
fact that, the expression 'if . . . then . . .' has a different meaning in one remark from the meaning which it has in the other.
So I shall assume that the truth-functionalist view must somehow be extended to cover the counterfactual cases, and shall
suggest a way in which this might be done.

The other of the two views to be brought into confrontation with each other might be called the consequentialist
view. It is the view that 'if . . . then . . .' is first cousin in
conventional force to 'so'. To make sure we do not take
too narrow a view of what this involves, it is best to begin
by looking at some examples of remarks of the form 'p,
so q'.

> (1) Today is Monday, so tomorrow will be Tuesday.
> (2) There is a red sky tonight, so we shall have a fine day
>     tomorrow.

---

[1] Quine op. cit., 14: 'Whatever the proper analysis of the contrafactual conditional may be, we may be sure in advance that it cannot be truth-functional.'

(3) He has been travelling all day, so he will be tired when he arrives.
(4) He saw she was in difficulties, so he went to her assistance.
(5) The petrol ran out, so the car just stopped.
(6) He has disobeyed, so they will punish him.
(7) You have disobeyed, so I shall punish you.
(8) Melbourne is in Australia, so the sea is salt.

Anyone who asserts any of these sentences asserts, of course, both of the constituent propositions conjoined by 'so'. He asserts that p and he asserts that q. But he does more than this. He implies that there exists what I shall refer to vaguely as some ground-consequent relation between the matter affirmed in the antecedent proposition and the matter affirmed in the consequent proposition. I put it in this rather vague way because the ground-consequent relation involved need not always be of the same kind. Often what is implied (or a part of what is implied) is that the truth of the proposition that p is a sufficient reason, either absolutely or in the circumstances of the case, for taking the proposition that q to be true also. We can find this feature present in examples (1), (2), (3), and (6)—also, as I shall show later, in example (8). The word 'so' in all these cases is, we might say, an inference-marker. Where 'so' thus marks an inference, the kinds of consideration which underlie the inference may be different. Thus in (1) we have a deductive implication. In (2), the state of affairs affirmed in the antecedent proposition is a reliable *sign* of, but not a *cause* of, what is predicted in the consequent proposition. In (3) what is affirmed in the antecedent is a *cause* of what is affirmed in the consequent. In (6) what is reported in the antecedent constitues a *reason* which, it is implied, the agents will find sufficient *for acting* in the way predicted in the consequent.

In examples (4), (5), and (7), 'so' will not normally be operating as an inference-marker. Nevertheless its use in each case implies that there exists, between the matter affirmed in the antecedent and the matter affirmed in the consequent, a relation belonging to one or another of those types which generally underlie the use of 'so' as an inference-marker. Thus what is implied in case (4) is that what is affirmed in the antecedent constituted the agent's reason for acting as he is reported as acting in the consequent. What is implied in case (5) is that what is reported in the antecedent was the cause of what is reported in the consequent; in case (7) that what is affirmed in the antecedent is the speaker's reason for acting as he announces that he is going to act.

Now let us look at case (8). Case (8) at first looks a little odd. And the reason why it looks a little odd is that it does not seem that there could exist, between what is affirmed in the antecedent and what is affirmed in the consequent, any such relation—whether deductive, natural, or 'rational'—as normally underlies the use of 'so' as an inference-marker. Indeed, of course, there is no such relation in this case. And it is a matter of some importance to notice that 'so' can perfectly well function as an inference-marker even in the absence of any such relation; that two propositions can perfectly well be related by a ground-consequent relation of the inferential kind even when this does not rest directly on any of those natural or deductive or 'rational' types of ground-consequent relation which normally underlie an inferential ground-consequent relation. To see how this can happen, we need to do no more than imagine a situation in which someone is informed, by an informant whose knowledgeability and veracity he has reason to accept, that at least one of a certain pair of propositions is false. We can imagine such a thing happening, perhaps, as part of a test of some kind, or in the context of some sort of general knowledge game. There need be no other kind of connection between the two propositions than what is conferred upon them by this context. Thus one proposition could be the proposition that Melbourne is in Australia, the other the proposition that the sea is not salt. For the recipient of our information, whom we may suppose to be antecedently ignorant of the location of Melbourne and the composition of the sea, the question of whether Melbourne is in Australia and the question of

whether the sea is not salt now come to be mutually dependent questions to the extent that he can infer from the truth of
either of these propositions the falsity of the other. Let him
find out, by consulting an atlas, that Melbourne is in Australia. Then he can properly link the two propositions by the
use of the inference-marker 'so'. He can properly say:

Melbourne *is* in Australia, so the sea *is* salt.

We can imagine other cases in which propositions not connected by any of the kinds of connection which normally
underlie a ground-consequent relation of the inferential kind
may nevertheless acquire such a relation. Thus we may imagine a somewhat neurotic character who never makes positive
or unqualified assertions accept on matters on which he is
well informed, but is subject to bursts or phases of compul-
sive lying. All his assertions come, we may suppose, in clearly
demarcated groups; so that we know antecedently—for such
is the nature of his disorder—that the remarks falling within
any given group are either all true or all false. Then if p and
q are remarks belonging to the same group and we want to
know whether q is true, we can satisfy ourselves by finding
out that p is true and arguing 'p, so q', even though the
subject-matters of the two remarks are quite unconnected.

To sum up as far as we have gone. When something of the
form 'p, so q' is said, i.e. when two assertive clauses are linked
by 'so', then it is asserted that p and it is asserted that q—and
also it is implied that there exists between the matter affirmed
at p and the matter affirmed at q either a ground-consequent
relation of the inferential kind or a ground-consequent relation of one of the types which normally underlie a ground-
consequent relation of the inferential kind or both.

Two things seem obvious: (1) what particular kind of
ground-consequent relation is implied in any case is not
(solely) a matter of the meaning or conventional force 'so';
(2) the meaning or conventional force of 'so' is sufficient
(though not necessary) to ensure an implication that there is
some kind of ground-consequent relation between the two
propositions. In other words, (1) it would be wrong to say 'In

each case there is some kind of ground-consequent relation
which is conventionally implied by "so"'; but (2) it would be
right to say 'In each case it is conventionally implied by "so"
that there is some kind of ground-consequent relation'.
(Comparison may usefully be made with 'hence', 'consequently', 'therefore'.)

The above seems uncontroversial. It also seems uncontroversial to remark that for every statement containing 'so' and
carrying a ground-consequent implication, one or more corresponding statements could be framed containing 'if' instead
of 'so' which carried, somehow or other, a *corresponding*
ground-consequent implication. I say 'corresponding' and
not 'the same', since the clauses of an 'if . . . then . . .' statement, unlike the clauses of a 'so' statement, are not asserted.
Thus, while it might be implied in a 'so' statement that one
actual state of affairs *was*, say, the cause of another, or *was* an
agent's effective reason for acting in a certain way, the corresponding implication in the corresponding 'if . . . then . . .'
statement would be rather that a hypothetical state of affairs
*would be* or *would have been*, in given circumstances, sufficient to cause another, or that a hypothetical state of affairs
*would be* or *would have been* an agent's effective reason for
acting in a certain way.

Now to set out the consequentialist view of 'if . . . then . . .'.
Summarily it is the view that just as 'so' *conventionally* implies the existence of some ground-consequent relation between the propositions it conjoins without conventionally
implying the relation to be of one kind rather than another,
so 'if . . . then . . .' *conventionally* implies the existence of
some ground-consequent relation between the propositions
it conjoins without conventionally implying the relation to be
of one kind rather than another—the difference being that
'so' is conventionally restricted in its employment to conjoining propositions which are *asserted* in the use of the sentence
containing the conjunction, while 'if . . . then . . .' is conventionally restricted in its employment to conjoining propositions which are unasserted in the use of the sentence
containing the conjunction. Prima facie there is nothing inco-

herent or otherwise objectionable in the idea of a linguistic device possessing just the conventional force assigned, on this view, to 'if ... then ...'. And if there is such a device, there will be plenty of occasions for employing it. We have plenty of occasion for drawing, or setting out, the consequences of suppositions, indicating that this is what we are doing, just as we have plenty of occasion for drawing, or setting out, the consequences of known truths or accepted propositions, indicating that this is what we are doing.

On this view, then, as I have already remarked, 'if' and 'so' are first cousins in conventional force or meaning. On the truth-functionalist view, on the other hand, there is no such kinship between 'if' and 'so' as regards their conventional force or meaning. For on this view 'if' carries no *conventional* implication of a ground-consequent relation of any kind between propositions. 'If' is, rather, a near relation of 'and' and 'not', which are similarly free from any such conventional implications.

Though two views are opposed on this important point, there are two other important points on which the partisans of both can consistently agree. In the first place, they can both agree that one who asserts a conditional statement is committed, in virtue of the conventional force of 'if', to the rejection, as false, of the proposition that results from conjoining the affirmation of the first constituent proposition of his conditional with the negation of its second constituent proposition. More briefly, one who affirms 'if p, then q' is committed to the denial of 'p. ~ q'. and is so committed in virtue of the meaning of 'if'. Obviously this is a very direct consequence of the truth-functionalist view; for on that view, the affirmation of the conditional 'if p, then q' has exactly the same conventional force as the denial of the conjunction 'p. ~ q'. But it is also a consequence, though not quite such a direct one, of the consequentialist view. For on that view the use of the form conventionally commits the speaker to the implication that the truth of p either would be (in the case in which its truth is understood to be an open question) or would have been (in the case in which it is understood to be false) either absolutely, or in the circumstances obtaining, sufficient to guarantee that q also was true. But one cannot consistently combine this view with the admission that p is in fact true and q in fact false. So it follows from the consequentialist thesis regarding 'if' that one who asserts a conditional statement is committed, in virtue of the conventional force of 'if', to rejecting as false the corresponding conjunction of the form 'p. ~ q'.

The second important point on which both parties can consistently agree is that typical or central case of the use of 'if . . . then . . .' are cases in which it is somehow *implied* that there is a ground-consequent relation of some kind between the coupled propositions. This, of course, is a direct consequence of the consequentialist view, whereas it does not appear to be a direct consequence of the truth-functionalist view. But equally it does not appear to be inconsistent with the truth-functionalist view. For something may be implied by what a man says, or by his saying it, without this implication being part of the conventional force or meaning of the words he uses. But though the defender of the truth-functionalist view can (it seems) consistently admit that the implication is regularly present while denying that it is conventional, he is (it seems) faced with a challenge and a task: the task, namely, of explaining why, given that 'if' has a merely truth-functional meaning, it nevertheless regularly carries the ground-consequent implication.

This is the challenge which has been so effectively taken up by Grice in a paper unfortunately unpublished. Although, relying on memory, I cannot do justice to the subtlety and complexity of the argument, I can, I think, recall some of its main features; and where memory fails, or in areas which Grice did not enter (such as the topic of counterfactual conditionals), I shall invent similar arguments. Although I think these arguments are powerful, I do not think they are conclusive. I think, in fact, that the consequentialist thesis is more realistic than the truth-functionalist thesis, even if it is less beautiful. So I will try to present the issue as an open one, while not disguising the fact that the weight of argument seems to me to fall, on balance, on the consequentialist side.

The governing aim of the argument we have to consider is to show that, on the assumption that the conventional meaning of 'if . . . then . . .' is entirely exhausted by the meaning-rules for '. . . ⊃ . . .', the ground-consequent implications which an 'if-then' statement may carry can be explained as the result of the operation of certain general principles of assertive discourse. These principles exert their influence impartially over the whole field of such discourse, though the way in which they operate to generate implications in different kinds of case depends, of course, on the meanings of the expressions peculiar to each kind of case. Moreover, according to this view, it is possible to show not only that the normal 'if-then' implications *can* be explained on these lines, given the assumption of a purely truth-functional conventional force for 'if . . . then . . .'; it is possible also to show, by reference to the general nature of meaning and implication, that they *should* be so explained; that this assumption and this explanation are not only *consistent* with the generally admitted facts, but also *correct*.

Of the general principles of assertive discourse just referred to, two in particular are relevant to the argument. They are:

(1) That one should not make an unqualified assertion unless one has good reason to think it true.

(2) That, subject to the previous principle being observed, one should not (unless one has some special justification for doing so) deliberately make a *less* informative statement on the topic of conversational exchange when one has just as good grounds for making, and could, with equal or greater economy of linguistic means, make, a *more* informative statement. (This could perhaps be seen as a corollary of a more general point about not deliberately withholding relevant information.)

Such principles are consequences of the more general assumption still that the purpose of assertive discourse is to be helpful, rather than the reverse, to one's partners in a conversational exchange. Evidently, this assumption does not al-

ways hold good, for example when you are being interro-
gated by an enemy. Nor does it hold good in a straightforward form when you are playing certain kinds of game. But
apart from such special situations as these the assumption is
one that we in fact generally make. Indeed it has a much
more fundamental status than this way of putting it suggests.
It might be said to be a precondition of the possibility of the
social institution of language.

Now let us take the first of our two principles in conjunction with the truth-functional hypothesis about the meaning
of 'if . . . then . . .'. On that hypothesis it seems to follow that
there are three types of independently admissible grounds on
which one could assert a conditional statement without violating the first principle: the case in which one knows (or has
good reason for thinking) merely that the antecedent is false;
the case in which one knows (or etc.) that the consequent is
true; and the case in which, though lacking sufficient reason
for thinking the antecedent false or for thinking the consequent true, one has sufficient reason for thinking that the
conjunction of the antecedent with the negation of the consequent is false.

However, if we now add the requirement that we should
not violate the second principle (the principle of maximum
informativeness), then the number of cases of minimal conditions for asserting the conditional drops from three to one.
The statement that it is false that p or the statement that it is
true that q are each of them more informative than the statement that it is not the case that it is true that p and false
that q. Each of the first two statements is more informative
than the third in the straightforward sense that it entails the
third and is not entailed by it. So, by the principle of maximum informativeness, one should not make the third statement when one is in a position to make either of the other
two.

But if one has good reason, other than knowledge of the
falsity of p or the truth of q, for denying the conjunction of
the truth of p with the falsity of q, then *eo ipso* one has good
reason for holding that a ground-consequent relation holds

between the proposition that p and the proposition that q (in that order). It does not matter whether the basis of one's rejection of the conjunction is knowledge of causal laws or of what agents would count as reasons for acting or of deductive implications, or, again, whether it is simply a case of two propositions between which there is no direct connection of any of these kinds but in respect of which one comes to know without knowing the falsity of p or the truth of q, that the combination of truth-values, p. ~ q, does not in fact obtain. This last is the case I illustrated in discussing the ground-consequent relation implied in the sentence, 'Melbourne is in Australia, so the sea is salt'; and one has exactly the same ground for holding the two propositions to be so related when, knowing in this way that the conjunction is false, but not having found out the antecedent to be true, one says instead: '*If* Melbourne is in Australia, *then* the sea is salt.' (Knowledge merely of the falsity of the conjunction confers on the question whether q a *dependence* on the question whether p which is quite lacking if knowledge of the falsity of the conjunction is itself based on knowledge of the falsity of p or of the truth of q (or both).)

So then every case in which one has good reason, other than knowledge of the falsity of p or of the truth of q, for denying the conjunction of the truth of p with the falsity of q is a case in which one has good reason for holding that a ground-consequent relation relates the proposition that p and the proposition that q in that order.

Now any audience of any piece of assertive discourse is entitled to assume, in the absence of any special reason to suppose the contrary, that its author (the speaker) is observing the general principles of all assertive discourse. Hence any audience of a *conditional* statement (it being still assumed that the conventional force of 'if p, then q' is the same as that of 'p ⊃ q') is entitled to assume, in the absence of special reason, that the author of the conditional statement has good reason for thinking that a ground-consequent relation holds between the proposition that p and the proposition that q. It might be said that in general one who embarks on the enterprise of assertive discourse tacitly implies that he is observing the general principles of that activity; and hence that in general what he says implies the truth of any proposition (over and above the one he explicitly asserts) which he must have good reason for holding true if, in saying what he says, he is observing those general principles. Thus the fact that a conditional assertion of ordinary speech normally carries a ground-consequent implication is shown to be consistent with the assumption that there is no more to the conventional force of 'if . . . then . . .' than there is to the meaning of '. . . ⊃ . . .'.

I have given this part of the argument in the barest schematic outline. There is room for much qualification and addition. Here is one addition, for which Grice cannot be held responsible, by means of which an upholder of the truth-functionalist view might attempt to deal with the case of counter-factual conditionals. Suppose there is a proposition, p, the falsity of which is known to a speaker and his audience and is known by both to be known to both. Yet the speaker may issue a conditional statement of which the antecedent corresponds to the proposition that p, and the statement may, in the regular way, imply a ground-consequent relation between antecedent and consequent. How is this to be explained on the assumption that the conventional force of his assertion is merely that of the negation of a conjunction? It might be said that this assumption is in any case untenable in most instances of this kind, for the speaker's choice of tense and mood will normally *conventionally* indicate or imply his having knowledge of, or grounds for belief in, the falsity of the antecedent. This in itself a debatable contention—so we will consider the case under two heads: first, on the assumption that the debatable contention is false, and second, on the assumption that it is true.

On the assumption that the debatable contention is false and that the whole relevant conventional force of the assertion is truth-functional, it looks as if the principle of greater informativeness must have been *blatantly* violated. But because it has been *blatantly* violated, there is no risk of misleading the audience in the way in which the audience would be misled if the principle were violated, but not blatantly. That is to say, the speaker runs no risk of misleading the audience into the belief that he has no sufficient ground for thinking that it is false that p. So the speaker is at any rate not violating the more fundamental principle that one should not mislead one's audience or deliberately conceal relevant beliefs or information.

Here it is possible to appeal to another principle, which might be called the principle of informative *point*: which is that a man seriously engaged in the enterprise of informative discourse must take it that what he says has or may have some informative value for his audience. The only or the most obvious way of saving this principle, in the case of a speaker who denies a conjunction when it is common ground to himself and his audience that he knows one of the conjuncts to be false, is that he has some ground for the denial which is independent of knowledge of the falsity of the conjunct in question. A straightforward application of the principle of greater informativeness rules out the possibility of this other ground being simply knowledge of the falsity of the other conjunct (i.e. of the truth of consequent of the conditional). So we are left with the remaining alternative, namely with its being knowledge of the existence of some causal or other type of basis for that implication of a ground-consequent relation which set us our original problem. Thus the existence of the ground-consequent implication is explained consistently with the hypothesis that the implication is no part of the conventional force of the words used.

The argument is similar in principle for the assumption that the falsity of p is conventionally implied by the form of words chosen for the counterfactual. The appeal lies once more to the principle of informative point. Why conventionally commit yourself *both* to the denial of one of the conjuncts *and* to the weaker or less informative denial of the conjunction unless you have a ground for the latter which is additional to and independent of your ground for the former? Someone might object to the form of the explanation in this case on the ground that the very existence of a distinctive grammatical structure which explicitly carried a *conventional* commitment to the denial of one of the conjuncts, would seem inexplicable unless it also carried a *conventional* commitment to an independent ground for the denial of the conjunction. But it would be open to the truth-functionalist simply to admit this and then maintain that this last conventional commitment was simply a product of the other two, and hence no part of the meaning of 'if . . . then . . .', taken by itself.

So far the aim of the argument has been simply to show that the fact that 'if . . . then . . .' statements normally carry a ground-consequent implication can be explained in a way consistent with the assumption that such an implication is no part of their meaning or conventional force; that (if we set aside the debatable issue about the negative implications of forms appropriate to counterfactual conditionals) we can represent the agreed facts as consistent with the hypothesis that 'if . . . then . . .' statements have the same meaning as the corresponding material implication statements, that in fact, they *are* such statements. The next step is to try to strengthen the hypothesis by discrediting its rival. Here the following powerful argument may be used. If the ground-consequent implication were part of the conventional meaning or force of 'if . . . then . . .', it should be possible to find an alternative construction such that by using this construction instead of 'if . . . then . . .' we could eliminate the ground-consequent implication from any statement while still committing ourselves to the lesser thing which is expressed by the truth-functional connective of logic. (For remember that everyone agrees that, whatever 'if . . . then . . .' means, it at least carries, in virtue of its conventional force, a commitment to the denial of 'p. ~ q'.) The general point can be illustrated with the help of another conjunction, namely the conjunction 'but'. Everyone agrees that part of the meaning of the conjunction is that of the truth-functional conjunction sign, expressed in ordinary language by the word 'and'. The conjunction 'but' also carries, we will assume without debate,

a *conventional* implication of some sort of adversative relation obtaining, in the circumstances, between the propositions expressed by the clauses it conjoins. This implication is
part of its meaning. But just in so far as this implication of
opposition is correctly attributed, in the case of any statement, to the meaning of 'but', we can always frame another
corresponding statement from which this implication is eliminated but which retains the merely conjunctive force of the
original, simply by replacing 'but' by 'and'.

But by the arguments already developed, no such
manœuvre is possible in the case of 'if ... then ...'. It would
be no good replacing 'if p, then q' by 'p ⊃ q' or 'not both
p and not-q' or by 'the combination of truth-values, first true,
second false, is unrealized in the case of the ordered pair of
propositions, p and q'. For in every case in which an 'if p, then
q' statement in fact carries the implication which, on the
consequentialist hypothesis, conventionally attaches to the
'if ... then ...' form, the operation of the principles previously referred to would ensure that the substitute statement
carries exactly the same implications, though not, of course,
as a part of the conventional force of the expressions used.
Summarily: if an implication is conventional, it is eliminable;
the implications in question are not eliminable, therefore
they are not conventional.

The trouble with this argument is that it is really a little *too*
powerful. For if it is cogent, it seems to follow that it is
actually *impossible* that there should exist in any language a
conjunction of which the meaning can be characterized by
saying that it carries the same general ground-consequent
implications as 'so' does without joining asserted propositions as 'so' does. But it seems excessively implausible to
maintain that it is actually impossible that there should exist
an expression with such a meaning, when the meaning in
question can be perfectly coherently explained. If the proposition that the existence of such an expression is possible is
incompatible with some theoretical principle about meaning,
it would seem more rational to modify the principle than to
declare the proposition to be false. But if we do agree to

modify the relevant principle, then the argument takes on a new look. From looking very fierce, it suddenly turns to looking very mild. For it now amounts to no more than a challenge to the holder of the consequentialist view to explain why the conventional implication he holds out for cannot be eliminated, as it can in other cases. But if seen as a challenge, it must be seen as a self-answering challenge. For the demonstration that the relevant implications cannot be eliminated by the substitution-method already contains the explanation of the reason *why* they cannot be eliminated. So that argument can be dismissed.

Indeed the upholder of the consequentialist view might be tempted by the successful repulse of this argument into a counter-attack. Let us express his thesis as follows: just as 'p, so q' might be called the (or a) conventional argument-form, so 'if p, then q' might be called the conventional quasi-argument-form. Quasi-argument differs from argument in that the premises are, in the expression of a quasi-argument, entertained rather than asserted. Quasi-argument is something we have many occasions for just as argument is something we have many occasions for. It is entirely reasonable, therefore, to expect that language should contain a particle of which the conventional force is parallel to that of 'so' in the respects in which quasi-argument is parallel to argument and differs from that of 'so' in the respects in which quasi-argument differs from argument. But if there is a strong presumption that there exists such a particle in language, there is an equally strong presumption that 'if' is such a particle. For it is a good candidate, and there is no better.

The counter-attack could be further developed. It could be contended, for example, that the meaning conventionally assigned to 'p ⊃ q' is inherently unstable, and could not preserve itself unmodified in the natural conditions of language-use. What the truth-functionalist account presents as reasons why 'if' normally carries implications denied to be part of its conventional meaning, the consequentialist theory can present as reasons why '⊃', if put to use in practice instead of 'if', would inevitably acquire the conventional implications which, on this view, are part of the meaning of 'if'. Only in the specially protected environment of a treatise on logic can '⊃' keep its meaning pure.

I do not think it could be claimed that these counter-attacking arguments are *decisive*. We still have two conflicting theses, each, perhaps, with difficulties of its own to face. We should remember that though each denies something which the other asserts, they are not necessarily exhaustive of the possibilities. If we are to adjudicate between them or—perhaps—to reject them both, we must do so in the light of (1) the degree of success with which each copes with its particular difficulties, and (2) any general considerations about meaning which bear on their acceptability.

# May Bes and Might have Beens

My subject in this paper is particular possibilities: the may-bes and the might-have-beens that relate essentially to particular individuals or situations. The topic is one which is apt to evoke very different responses from different philosophers. Some detect, or think they detect, an intoxicating scent of something more metaphysically interesting than either merely epistemic possibilities on the one hand or merely *de dicto* possibilities or necessities on the other. My remarks will not give much satisfaction to them. Some, on the other hand, are suspicious of modalities in general as being dubiously coherent notions. But it is clear that whether we believe there *are* such things as particular possibilities or not, we are in practice bound to take account of them.

We are in practice bound to take account of them because our knowledge of how things will turn out, or of how things have turned out, is imperfect. We do not know that *this* will not happen, we do not know that *that* will not. We do not know that *this* has not happened, we do not know that *that* has not. When we find it worth while to reckon with our ignorance on these points, then we are envisaging *this* and *that* as possibilities: this may (or might) happen or that may (or might); this may (or might) have happened or that may (or might).

If this were all, we could simply conclude that to say that something may happen is merely to say that it is not certain that it will not; and to say that something might have happened is simply to say that it is not certain that it has not or did not. But this is not all. For we frequently use the language of might-have-beens of what we know perfectly well not to have been. 'You might have been killed', for example, does not normally express uncertainty as to whether you are still alive. Nevertheless I want to suggest that these more philosophically interesting might-have-beens are also, fundamentally, of an epistemic order.

How, then, are they related to the more obviously epistemic may-bes and might-have-beens, the ones which express present uncertainty? I shall answer that our philosophically interesting might-have-beens stand in a very simple relation to our obviously epistemic may-bes. Just as 'He may' amounts roughly to (or at least includes) 'It *is* not certain that he *won't*,' so 'He might have' amounts roughly to (or at least includes) 'It *was* not certain that he *wouldn't*.' Just as 'He may', in this sense, points forward from the present time towards a now uncertain future, so 'He might have'—in the sense we are interested in—points forward from a past time towards a then uncertain future. Both require there to be a point in the history of the individual concerned such that available knowledge regarding that individual at that point does not exclude the future development which is problematically affirmed of him or (for the negative case) does not guarantee what is problematically denied of him.

We shall see later on that this formula requires one quite radical amendment. But the need for that amendment apart, the formula as it stands suffers from another defect: in at least one important respect it is uncomfortably vague or unclear. When we use 'may' or 'might' to express present uncertainties about what is now future, the uncertainty is clearly relativized to a time and, more or less clearly, to persons. The time is *now*; the persons *ourselves*, the speaker and his circle and others he regards as authoritative, perhaps. But if the interesting 'might have been' is to be related to past uncertainties about what was then future, it is by no means clear how the corresponding relativization should go.

Let us consider a few examples. Surveying through the window and the storm the large, elderly, shallow-rooted tree on the edge of the wood, someone says: 'The tree may (might) fall on the house.' Trees *are* blown down in gales. The height of this tree exceeds the distance between its base and the house. The house-dwellers have not enough information about strains and stresses, forces and directions, to calculate that the tree will fall or that it will not, or to calculate that it will fall, if at all, on the house or to calculate that it will fall, if at all, elsewhere. (Perhaps they prudently evacuate the house for the duration of the storm.) After the storm, when the tree, say, either has not fallen at all or has fallen, but not on the house, the same speaker or another says: 'The tree might have fallen on the house.' The second remark differs from the first only in tense. The first remark says: 'There is a non-negligible chance that the tree will fall on the house.' The second says: 'There was a non-negligible chance that the tree would fall on the house.' Both remarks relate to the historical situation as it actually was during the storm. Neither commits the speaker to the belief that the behaviour of the tree was anything but fully determined by mechanical forces. Neither can be made sense of without construing it as having an epistemic reference—a reference to the non-availability, at the relevant time, of adequate grounds for ruling out the tree's falling on the house. Notice that a legitimate variant on the second remark would be: 'There was a real possibility that the tree would fall on the house.' So the real possibility that *p* does not exclude the causal necessity that not-*p*, though it excludes knowledge, at the relevant time, of the causal necessity that not-*p*.

But whose knowledge? Things are not really so simple as the example suggests. What contradicts 'There was a possibility that *p*' is 'There was no possibility of that.' If someone says '*A* might have been elected instead of *B* to the Chair at X', the reply might be 'If you consider the composition of the electoral committee, you will see that there was no possibility of that.' This does not imply, I think, that there was anyone at the time who, apprised of the composition of the electoral committee, would then and there have been able to infer, with practical certainty, that *A* would not be elected. It means, perhaps, that there were enough facts distributed in

different minds to make this conclusion virtually certain; but
not that they were contained in one mind. *We* can see that
after a certain time (the time at which the composition of the
board was settled) there no longer existed a certain possibility which, however, did not seem rationally excluded to anyone at that time; because, though the relevant facts (about,
say, the attitudes and preferences of members of the board)
were then 'available', no one then was, as we now are, master
of them all. Historians, I suppose, often think along these
lines. It is called having the benefit of hindsight. *By then*, they
say, the issue of the battle was *certain*: there was no longer
any *possibility* of the Austrians' winning. The verdict is not
that of omniscience, which is not interested in possibility. It
is, rather, that of an ideal intelligence officer collecting reasonably full and accurate reports from all parts of the battle-
field. But of course there was no such officer receiving such
reports. The issue of the battle was certain before anyone
actually present was in a position to be rationally certain of it.

    I think we go yet further in our verdicts on past possibili-
ties, taking into account not only the evidence, the particular
facts, collectively available at the time but at the time
uncollected, but also general truths now known but then
unknown, and even particular truths relating to that time now
known but then unknown. The verdict, then, becomes not
simply that of the ideal contemporary intelligence officer, but
of such an officer further endowed with knowledge of relevant facts and laws which have only subsequently become
known. This addition cuts both ways: allowing us not only to
exclude, with reference to a particular past situation, some
might-have-beens then envisaged, perhaps, as may-bes, but
also to contemplate, with reference to a particular past situation, some might-have-beens which no one then would have
been in a position to consider as may-bes.[1]

---

[1] At the limit of this process we can consider might-have-beens in relation to
a period at which no one envisaged any may-bes at all because there was no one
to envisage them. In such a case it is, of course, later knowledge which supplies
*all* the facts of which we hold that they did not make it certain that such-and-such
(which did not in fact happen) would not subsequently happen, i.e. the 'available

These remarks are designed to expand on the force of 'It was not certain' in the formula 'It was not certain that it would not be the case that *p*.' *Inter alia* they show something about how to contradict it—*with reference to a particular time*. But of course contradicting a statement of this kind relativized to a particular time leaves uncontradicted any corresponding statement relating to an earlier time. Remarks of the form 'It might have been the case that *p*' are, in general, more and more vulnerable to contradiction as they are more and more closely related to the time at which events definitively falsify the proposition that *p*; are correspondingly less and less vulnerable as their reference is shifted back in time; and assume their least vulnerable shape if they are construed generally, as amounting to 'There was a time at which it was not certain that it would not be the case that *p*.' So even though by 6 o'clock the issue of the battle was, humanly speaking, certain, even though there was *by then* no possibility of the Austrians' winning, it is still true, on some temporal relativization of those words, that *they might have won*; what is not true is that at 6 p.m. they might *still* have won. Similarly, *A might* have been elected instead of *B*, even though, after the composition of the electoral board was determined, this was no longer a possibility.

The formula we have before us, then, runs roughly as follows: some proposition to the effect that *a* might have ϕd is true (acceptable) if and only if there was some point in the history of the individual concerned such that presently available knowledge regarding that point does not permit the rational inference that *a* did not ϕ (or, in other words, the facts as we know them left open at least a chance that *a* would ϕ). Similarly, some proposition to the effect that *a* might not have ϕd is true (acceptable) if and only if there was some time in the history of *a* such that our present knowledge of the facts as they were then does not permit the rational inference that *a* did ϕ (i.e. the facts as we know them left open at least a chance that *a* would not ϕ). I have been saying something

facts' in relation to which we may say that such-and-such might have happened. But nothing in our saying this implies any indeterminism in what did happen.

about how the phrase 'available knowledge' should here be construed; and if this phrase still remains a little indeterminate, I think there is no harm in that, for that is a feature also of the idiom we are trying to characterize.[2]

The formula as we have it obviously restricts the reference of our might-have-beens to times falling within the history of the individual (or individuals) concerned, hence to times at which propositions concerning that individual would be in principle entertainable. But there is one subclass of our interesting might-have-beens in respect of which we are obliged to lift this restriction on the temporal reference of our might-

---

[2] *Objection* 1.  Suppose $a$'s $\phi$ing, or not $\phi$ing, is the sort of outcome which can reasonably be regarded as exclusively subject, at least from the reference-time onwards, to deterministic laws. In that case our knowledge that $a$ did not in fact (or did in fact) $\phi$ entitles us to infer, regarding the reference-time, that circumstances *then* obtained which were sufficient to ensure $a$'s not $\phi$ing (or $\phi$ing). So the condition which the analysis requires for an acceptable 'might have been' in such a case, viz. that knowledge now available regarding the reference-time is insufficient to warrant the rational inference that $a$ did not $\phi$ (or that $a$ did $\phi$), is never fulfilled. Indeed a convinced universal determinist would have no use at all for the idiom in the sense expounded.

*Reply.*  The objection construes 'now available knowledge' too widely. What is required for denying a reasonably supported assertion that there was a chance that $a$ would $\phi$ (or that $a$ would not $\phi$) is some more specific knowledge of conditions obtaining at the relevant time than can be derived from the premiss that $a$ did not in fact $\phi$ (or did in fact $\phi$) coupled with a general conviction that $a$'s $\phi$ing or not $\phi$ing is subject to deterministic laws. There is no reason to think that convinced universal determinists would (or do) eschew the idiom in the sense expounded or confine themselves to denying others' uses of it.

*Objection* 2.  Suppose the reference-time is $t$. Then knowledge available at one time (say 1970) of the relevant circumstances of $a$ at $t$ may seem to warrant the assertion that $a$ might have $\phi$d, whereas additional knowledge available at a later time (say 1975) may seem to warrant its contradiction. The analysis then requires us to say that the proposition that $a$ might have $\phi$d, relativized to $t$, is true in 1970 but false in 1975. This conclusion is unattractive.

*Replies*:  (*a*) There is not one proposition but two; for the analysis of the idiom brings out a concealed indexical element in it, viz. a reference to the state of knowledge *at the time of utterance*.

(*b*) The 'analysis' may be seen as giving not truth-conditions but 'justified assertibility' conditions. The notion of truth-conditions is inappropriate to the idiom itself, though not, of course, to the statement of justifying conditions.

Evidently replies (a) and (b) are mutually exclusive alternatives. I leave open the choice between them.

(In formulating these objections and replies, I have been greatly helped by the contributions of Professors S. Kripke and H. Gaifman to the discussion of this paper.)

have-beens, and hence, as I hinted earlier, radically to amend our formula. For it seems clearly true, of any particular individual that you like to name, that that individual might not have existed; and so we have a whole host of true might-have-been propositions which either directly exhibit the form '*a* might not have existed' or entail another proposition which exhibits it. Thus Aristotle might never have been born and so might never have existed. Now it is clear that if these propositions are to be regarded as belonging to the class we are interested in—we might call it the class of objective historical epistemic propositions—they will often relate to a time anterior to any time which can reasonably be regarded as falling within the history of the individual concerned.

If we now consider the kind of reason we might most naturally give in support of such propositions, it becomes clear also that such propositions, so supported, do belong to the class we are interested in. Thus, putative mothers-to-be do sometimes miscarry. Even given that his father was a physician, it was not certain that Aristotle's mother would not miscarry of the child she became pregnant with when she became pregnant with Aristotle. There was, moreover, a time when it was not certain that Aristotle's mother and his father would mate or that, if they mated, their union would be fertile. Aristotle's mother, then, might have miscarried in the first months of the pregnancy which terminated in the delivery of Aristotle. Or Aristotle's parents might never have enjoyed a fertile union. So Aristotle might not have existed.

The then existing uncertainties which underlie these might-have-beens *we* can express or record by referring to Aristotle, though they could not then be so recorded or expressed. But this makes no matter. It is still a historical-epistemic truth about the couple who were in fact Aristotle's parents that there was a time at which it was not certain that they would enjoy a fertile union; hence that they might not have done so; hence that Aristotle might not have existed.

And so we bring these existential might-not-have-beens into the fold; and we do so by extending the historical reference of our might-have-beens back into what we might call the pre-history of the individuals concerned. It is easy enough to see how to do this in the case of individuals which come into existence by a process of natural generation. We can reasonably take it that there were many relevant uncertainties along the historical, the genealogical, lines of transmission which in fact lead to their existence. Matters are not so straightforward in the case of artefacts. Some things are simple enough. This table might not have existed. At one time it was not certain that the wood of which it is composed would go into the construction of a table instead of, say, a chest of drawers. The craftsman's decisions as to what to make depend, say, on the orders of customers, and there is a time at which it is not certain what those orders will be, for the customers have not made up their minds. It is idiomatically permissible to express such a possibility by saying that this table might have *been* a chest of drawers, or even—if, say, there was, at some time, quite a likelihood of one kind of order arriving before the other—that this table might *easily* have been a chest of drawers. But we cannot paraphrase the idiom by 'This table might have *existed in the form of* a chest of drawers.' The correct paraphrase is as already indicated: 'The materials which compose this table might have composed a chest of drawers', which entails 'This table might not have existed.'

Could it be that this table might have been two feet shorter or that this table might have been oval (instead of, as it is, rectangular)? Yes. But we feel the need of a true story to back up these specific might-have-beens whereas we are free to presume some story or other to back up the unspecific 'This table might not have existed.' There was hesitation, perhaps, over the specifications; or some unforeseeable chance determined the final plan. Without such a story *these* might-have-beens leave us fairly blank. We are not prepared to deny them; but we have no reason to affirm them.

Might this table have been made of marble instead of wood? We are strongly, and reasonably, inclined to deny this without waiting for a story. For what we are looking for, in the prehistory of artefacts, is an analogue of forebears in the prehistory of animals; and the materials of which the artefact is composed—not just the general type of material, but the particular specimens of those types—are the obvious analogues. Or at least they are in some cases, such as the case of this particular table; an object, say, of a fairly standard kind. Nothing less, or other, than the particular materials will serve our turn here. But may not the case be different with more elaborate human constructions? What of a great temple or a transatlantic liner? The great building is *conceived*, we say, in the brain of such-and-such a designer or the collective brain of a committee of designers. The quarries at A and the quarries at B are equally capable of supplying stone of the desired type. There are advantages and disadvantages in the choice of either source of supply. The stone actually comes from quarry B. But there was a time at which it was not certain that the stone would not come from quarry A. Perhaps it seemed quite likely that it would. So the building in question—the Old Bodleian, say—might have been built of (composed of) stone from quarry A instead of being built, as it was, of stone from quarry B.

Will someone say: then it would not have been *this* building, but another just like it? The retort seems insufficiently motivated. Before the building existed, there existed a plan: a plan for a building on *this* site, for *this* purpose, to be constructed of such-and-such type-materials according to such-and-such architectural specifications. Here we have all the prehistory we need. The building, this building, is begotten of a particular project rather than a particular scattered part of the earth's material. If someone said: 'The *QE II*, you know, might have been built of quite a different lot of steel from that which it was actually built of'—and gave his reasons—would it not be absurd to reply: 'In that case it wouldn't have been the *QE II* at all—the *QE II* wouldn't have existed—it would have been a different ship of that name.'?

If we can go so far, perhaps we can go farther. There is, say, a point in the history of our building project at which it becomes uncertain that stone of the desired type will be readily available from any source; or there is difference of opinion as to what type of stone is desirable. The difficulties are resolved and the building is built of Portland stone; but it might have been built of Bath stone. Shall we say: 'Then we would not have had *this* building'? Well, we can certainly say: 'We would not have had *these stones*.' (And someone *might* mean just that by saying 'Then we would not have had *this* building'; as, similarly, tapping the side of the ship, he might say: 'Then we should not have had just *this* ship.')

I shall not pursue this question further—interesting though it is. Instead I return to the primary purpose of getting clear—or clearer—about the general character of particular might-have-beens. I summarize the main points.

First, then, a particular 'might have been' statement of the kind which concerns us is a *historical* statement. It relates to the past, and looks to what was once the future. It relates either to a past recent enough, in the usual case, to include the existence of the individual referred to (or the most recent of those individuals if more than one is referred to); or at least to a past which includes that individual's immediate or remoter 'progenitors'—in either the literal or some appropriate analogical sense of that word. So the statement relates to a past about which facts are available concerning the individual or his progenitors. The general form of the claim made in such a statement, with an understood reference to some such past time, is that the facts available then—even reinforced with our later knowledge—were not such as to give sufficient grounds for certainty, i.e. for practical or human certainty, that the then future would not turn out in a way incompatible, in some respect relating to the individual in question, with the way it did in fact turn out.

Such a statement normally relates—and when, as in non-degenerate cases, it is backed by some specific particular story, it always does relate—to some fairly definite time. These are the cases in which our might-have-beens most obviously admit of some qualification of degree: it might *very easily* have been so, there was a *very good chance* (a *very real possibility*) that it would be so; or again, it was *just possible* that it would be so. The later the time our might-have-been statements refer to, the more vulnerable, in general, they become to the form of objection: 'By then there was no longer any possibility of that.' As time advances, evidence accumulates and chance decays till a point is reached at which it becomes humanly certain that it will *not* be the case that *p*. When we contemplate future possibilities (may-bes), our interest is often practical. When we contemplate past (and unfulfilled) possibilities (might-have-beens), our interest is normally historical. Our may-bes and our might-have-beens alike can be more, or less, serious. A 'serious' historical interest in might-have-beens is generally an interest in might-have-beens which do relate to a fairly definite situation at a fairly definite time, fairly close to the time at which what might have been turned out not to be. But nothing compels us to definiteness, as nothing compels us to seriousness. We can now, for practical purposes, seriously consider likely future contingencies. But we can also vaguely dream about quite hidden futures, rosily or gloomily; so the parent, contemplating the newborn child, thinks: 'He may become Lord Chancellor' or 'He may be killed in a war or a motor-accident', when little or nothing is available in the way of particular fact to favour or disfavour either chance. Since all times were once hidden futures, we enjoy no less a licence in our idle might-have-beens than in our idle may-bes. Indeed, in at least one radical respect we enjoy a much greater freedom. For our idlest speculations about what are now future possibilities relate to a definite temporal base: the present of those speculations. They are constrained within the limits set by history up to *now*. But our idle speculations on past possibilities need relate to no definite temporal base. They can rove indefinitely back through the history, and even the prehistory, of the individual concerned. The greater the temporal range, the greater the range of chances. Time and chance governeth all things; but, at any rate in the present context, time governeth chance. For the chances we here speak of stand in contrast, not with necessities, but with certainties. In philosophy, perhaps, we tend to lose our sense of the continuity between our serious might-have-beens and our relatively frivolous might-have-beens and thus run the risk of missing the point of the idiom altogether. And that would be a pity. For here we have an actual use of the possible. I do not suggest it is the only use.

# I I

# *Austin and 'Locutionary Meaning'*

## I

Austin distinguishes between the 'meaning' of an utterance and its 'force'. The former he associates with the 'locutionary' act performed in making the utterance, the latter with the 'illocutionary' act performed in making it. What does Austin mean by '(locutionary) meaning'? It is not, I think, clear. Various interpretations seem to receive some support from the text of *How to Do Things with Words*; but the text also supplies grounds for rejecting all these interpretations. I shall first try to establish this; and then suggest a compromise construction, in some respects Austinian, which might be, as it were, imposed on the doctrine. Then I shall suggest some reasons, also derived from the text, which Austin might have for rejecting this imposed construction; and argue that they are not good reasons.

But, first of all, by way of providing a framework for this discussion, I shall set up a simple threefold distinction between what purport to be progressively richer senses of the phrase *'the meaning of what was said'*, as applied to an utterance made on some occasion. There are reasons for thinking that this simple framework is itself too simple; that it would need a certain amount of elaboration, or adjustment, or loosening-up if it was to fit all cases.[1] Nevertheless I think it applies well enough over a sufficient range of cases to serve its immediate purpose.

---

[1] See Strawson, 'Phrase et acte de parole', *Langages*, 17 (March 1970).

So, then, I begin by distinguishing three progressively richer senses of this phrase, 'the meaning of what was said', as used in application to some utterance made on some occasion.

Suppose a sentence $S$ of a language $L$ to have been seriously uttered on a certain occasion. Suppose someone, $X$, to possess just that much information, and no more, regarding the utterance; i.e. he knows what sentence was uttered, but knows nothing of the identity of the speaker or the nature or date of the occasion. Suppose $X$ has ideally complete knowledge of $L$, i.e. a complete mastery of the semantics and syntax of $L$. Then is there any sense in which $X$ can be said to know *the meaning of precisely what was said on the occasion in question*? We may answer that it depends. It depends on whether $S$, viewed in the light of $X$'s mastery of the syntax and semantics of $L$, is seen to suffer from, or to be free from, syntactic and/or semantic ambiguity. If $S$ is free from any such ambiguity, then, in one sense of the phrase, $X$ does indeed know *the meaning of what was said on that occasion.* But if $S$ suffers from such ambiguity—such ambiguity as, for example, the English sentences, 'He stood on his head' or 'The collapse of the bank took everyone by surprise' suffer from—then $X$ does not yet know, in this sense, the meaning of what was said on the occasion in question. For he does not know which of the alternative readings or interpretations of $S$ is the right one. But suppose this ambiguity is cleared up for him. He is told which of the alternative interpretations is correct, i.e. the one intended. Then he learns, in our present sense of the phrase, the meaning of what was said on that occasion. (Granted that he also has ideal knowledge of another language, $L'$, and that $L'$, though it does not preserve all the ambiguities of sentences of $L$, is equipped with the means for adequate translation of all such sentences, then $X$ knows neither more nor less than he needs to know in order to *translate* $S$, as uttered on the occasion in question, into a sentence of $L'$.) Let us say that if $X$ knows, in this sense, the meaning of what was said on the occasion in question, then he knows the sense-*A*-meaning (or the *linguistic meaning*) of what was said.

Suppose *S* is the sentence, 'John will get here in two hours from now.' Evidently, in knowing the sense-*A*-meaning of what was said, *X* is far from a complete understanding of what was said. For he does not know who was meant by 'John' or what time and place were meant by 'here' and 'now'. But he may become informed on these points; and if he does, then he knows in a fuller sense than sense *A* the meaning of what was said. Generally, suppose that, with respect to a sentence *S* uttered on a particular occasion, one learns not only the sense-*A*-meaning of what was said, but also the import of all the demonstrative or deictic elements, if any, and the reference of all the particular-referring elements, if any, contained in *S*. Then one knows, in a fuller sense than sense *A*, the meaning of what was said. Let us call this fuller sense the sense-*B*-meaning (or the *linguistic-cum-referential meaning*) of what was said. (What one learns, in progressing from knowledge of the sense-*A*-meaning of what was said to knowledge of its sense-*B*-meaning is by no means necessary to the exercise of translation of what was said from *L* to *L'*.)

Even if we know the sense-*B*-meaning of what was said, it by no means follows that we have complete knowledge of *how what was said was meant* or of *all that was meant by what was said*. We may not know, for example, how what was said was intended to be taken or understood. We may know that the words 'Don't go yet' were addressed to such-and-such a person at such-and-such a time; and yet not know whether they were meant as a request, as an entreaty, as a command, as advice, or merely as a piece of conventional politeness. This is the dimension of meaning studied by Austin under the title of 'illocutionary force'. There is another, connected but distinguishable, way in which knowledge of what was meant may go beyond grasp of the sense-*B*-meaning of what was said. It may be that the speaker intends to be taken to be implying, or suggesting, by what he says something which does not strictly follow from its sense-*B*-meaning alone, and that what he meant by what he said is not fully understood unless this intention is recognized. Thus, suppose, in discussing the future occupancy of a certain office, I say 'The President has expressed the view that the ideal age for such an appointment is fifty.' Cannot one easily conceive that I was implying that the President's expression of this view was the result of a prior preference on his part for a certain candidate—whose age, as both my interlocutor and myself know, and know each other to know, happens to be precisely fifty?—and that the meaning of what I said would not be fully grasped by my interlocutor if he failed to recognize that he was intended to recognize this implication?

There is a case, then, for introducing a yet fuller sense of the expression 'the meaning of what was said'. Let us call it the sense-*C*-meaning (or *complete meaning*) of what was said. One knows the sense-*C*-meaning of what was said only if one adds to knowledge of its sense-*B*-meaning a complete grasp of how what was said was to be taken and of all that was intended to be understood by it, together with the knowledge that this grasp is complete.

I have spoken of senses *A*, *B*, and *C* of 'the meaning of what was said' as progressively richer or more comprehensive senses of this phrase. It does not follow that knowledge of what was meant in the more comprehensive sense is, in absolutely every case, more comprehensive knowledge. Thus, sometimes, though exceptionally, the move from *A* to *B* may really be no move at all. This may be the case if, for example, *S* is a sentence which expresses, with complete generality and explicitness, a proposition of pure mathematics or a law of natural science; so that, for example, even the tense of the verb lacks any temporal significance. Again, sometimes, the move from *B* to *C* may add nothing to our knowledge *except the knowledge that there is nothing to be added*, i.e. that no qualification or addition is called for to the way in which, on the strength of our *B*-knowledge (which, of course, includes our *A*-knowledge), we should most naturally take the sentence. For there may be nothing *implied* by what is said except by the use of devices the import of which our *A*-knowledge already covers, and there may be nothing in the way in which what is said is intended to be *taken* or *understood* which is not made explicit by devices which our *A*-knowledge embraces. I have in mind the use of such expressions as 'but', 'perhaps', 'although', 'therefore', 'unfortunately', etc.; and that device of which Austin made us particularly aware, viz. the use of explicitly performative formulae, such as 'I warn (you that . . .)', 'I entreat (you to . . .)', 'I acknowledge (that . . .)', etc. Knowledge of the force of these expressions belongs, evidently, to the level of knowledge of sense-*A*-meaning. Perhaps we can say, too, that the use of the ordinary, closed declarative sentence-form carries, at the level of *A*-knowledge, a presumption of *assertion* which may be simply confirmed at the level of *C*-knowledge without addition or modification. But we are to note that even when there is thus nothing to be added to our *B*-knowledge, the knowledge that this is so is itself something additional to the knowledge of the sense-*B*-meaning of what is said. Thus the move from *B* to *C* is always an addition, even if it is only this minimal addition.

These distinctions, as I have remarked, are rather rough and ready and no doubt call for refinement. Yet, within their limitations, they seem reasonably intelligible and seem also to be of some importance for the general theory of language. All I need to claim for them at the moment is that we understand them well enough for it to be reasonable to raise, in relation to them, the question of what Austin means by '(locutionary) meaning'.

## II

*Some* of the things which Austin says might encourage us to suppose that his distinction between '(locutionary) meaning' and '(illocutionary) force' is related to the distinctions I have just drawn in the following way, which I shall call 'Interpretation I'.

*Interpretation I.* (i) Knowing the locutionary meaning of what has been said is knowing the meaning of what has been said in sense *B* and hence includes all that is included in knowing the meaning of what has been said in sense *A*. Locutionary meaning is the same as sense-*B*-meaning and hence includes sense-*A*-meaning. (ii) Knowing *both* the locutionary meaning *and* the illocutionary force of an utterance, though not, in general, the same thing as knowing the meaning of what has been said in sense *C*, is something wholly included within the latter. It is not in general the same thing, for knowing the meaning in sense *C* includes knowing *all* that was intended to be taken as understood by the utterance (including all that was intended to be taken as *implied* by it), whereas knowing its illocutionary force may not include as much as this. The distinctive feature of the grasp of illocutionary force is that the utterance be grasped as a case of '*x*-ing' where '*x*' is one of the verbs that qualify for inclusion in Austin's terminal lists. Grasping the utterance thus is certainly included in knowing its meaning in sense *C*, though grasping it thus and knowing its sense-*B*-meaning may not together exhaust knowing its meaning in sense *C*.

Of the two parts of this interpretation of Austin's distinction it is (i) above which mainly concerns us now. It is, I said, tempting to suppose that knowing the locutionary meaning of what has been said is the same thing as knowing in sense *B* the meaning of what has been said and hence includes all that belongs to knowing in sense *A* the meaning of what has been said. For does not Austin himself say that the performance of the locutionary act includes (*a*) the uttering of certain vocables or words, 'belonging to and *as* belonging to a certain vocabulary, in a certain construction, i.e. conforming to and *as* conforming to a certain grammar' and (*b*) the using of those vocables, or of the 'pheme' which they constitute, 'with a certain more or less definite sense and reference'?[2] The word 'sense' is vague enough, certainly; but it does not seem forced or unnatural to interpret this description of the

[2] *How to Do Things with Words*, 92–3, 95.

locutionary act as implying that full knowledge of locutionary meaning includes all that belongs to knowing the sense-*A*-meaning of what is said as well as what is added to this when *A*-knowledge is enlarged to *B*-knowledge. If we accept this interpretation of Austin's distinction, we shall note a certain consequence. We shall note that just as the move from *B*-knowledge to *C*-knowledge of the meaning of what is said may, in some cases, add nothing to our knowledge except the knowledge that there is nothing to be added, so, and *a fortiori*, the move from knowledge of locutionary meaning to knowledge of illocutionary force may, in some cases, add nothing more than this. In general, on this interpretation, the more freely a speaker uses the devices which Austin refers to in Lecture VI as devices for 'making explicit' the *force* of his utterance, the narrower will be the gap between knowledge of the locutionary *meaning* of the utterance and knowledge of its illocutionary *force*. If I know that someone, somewhere, at some time seriously utters the sentence 'I apologize', I certainly do not know the meaning in sense *A* of what he says unless I know that—in the absence of any contextual indications to the contrary—he (whoever he is) is apologizing (for something, whatever it is). If I know that someone, somewhere, at some time seriously utters the words 'Oh that it were possible to undo things done, to call back yesterday!', I do not know the meaning in sense *A* of what he says unless I know that—in the absence of any contextual indications to the contrary—he is expressing a wish that this were indeed possible or regret that it is not or both. One could say, indeed, on this interpretation of Austin's distinctions, that his discovery of the explicit performative formula was precisely a discovery of one device of peculiar precision for absorbing more and more illocutionary force into locutionary meaning.

But is it clear that this interpretation of Austin's distinction is correct? There are many remarks in the text which may lead us to doubt it. So now I swing to an opposite extreme of interpretation which I shall call 'Interpretation II'. The swing will perhaps be excessive. But it may help us to settle down, somewhere in between, to the right interpretation, if there is such a thing.

*Interpretation II.* A preliminary pointer to this opposite extreme is a contrast which Austin draws on p. 73 between meaning and force: 'precision in language makes it clearer what is being said—its *meaning*: *explicitness*, in our sense, makes clearer the *force* of the utterance.' The implication here seems to be quite contrary to the noted consequence of the previous interpretation. It seems to be implied, not that the use of linguistic devices for making illocutionary forces *explicit* results in the absorption of illocutionary force into locutionary meaning, but rather that force can *never* be absorbed into meaning, even when made explicit by the use of linguistic devices. Now the devices which Austin mentions as performing 'the same function' as the explicit performative formula (i.e. the function of making force *explicit*) are numerous and various and include, besides the use of the explicit performative formula itself, the use of the imperative mood (presumably some others as well, perhaps all but the indicative, perhaps *all*?); the use of some adverbs and adverbial phrases (e.g. 'probably'); the use of some connecting particles (e.g. 'therefore', 'although', 'moreover'). So now it looks as if knowing the locutionary meaning of what is said includes knowing only so much of what is meant in sense *A* as is left over when the conventional import of all *these* devices is entirely excluded. Locutionary meaning, so far from including all that what is meant in sense *A* includes, includes only a part of it.

But what part? Let us recall that locutionary meaning, though on this interpretation it includes less than all that is meant in sense *A*, includes something which lies outside of what is meant in sense *A*. For it includes what is added to what is meant in sense *A* to yield what is meant in sense *B*. It includes the references of what is said. Locutionary meaning is *sense and reference* together. Now the phrase 'sense and reference' has perhaps the power to swing us into another orbit. And we may be confirmed in the belief that we have been swung into the right orbit by the way in which Austin later associates, and contrasts, the locutionary–illocutionary distinction with the original constative–performative distinction. The thought of the purely constative, as that which is just and simply true or false, is really, he seems to suggest, the result of concentrating on the locutionary aspect of some speech acts, on their meaning (sense and reference), to the neglect of their illocutionary aspects; the thought of the purely performative, as that which has nothing of truth or falsity about it, is the result of concentrating on the illocutionary aspect of some speech acts and neglecting the 'dimension of correspondence with facts'.[3]

Pursuing, then, in the light of these hints and suggestions, the attempt to find a clear notion of locutionary meaning, we may hit on something like the Fregean 'thought'. Only in one respect we shall be carried farther than Frege. For Frege, though he allowed that some interrogative sentences (those that permit of 'Yes-or-no' answers) could express 'thoughts', denied this power to imperative sentences and, for example, to sentences expressing desires and requests, on the ground that the question of truth could not arise for them;[4] whereas Austin certainly thinks of utterances of such sentences as having locutionary meaning, sense and reference. The sentences, 'He is, unfortunately, about to pay the bill', 'He is, fortunately, about to pay the bill', 'Is he about to pay the bill?', 'He is, of course, about to pay the bill' might all, presumably, express one and the same Fregean thought and might all, on this interpretation of Austin, be uttered with the same locutionary meaning; but, on this interpretation of Austin, that very same locutionary meaning might belong also to utterances of the sentences 'Pay the bill now!', 'I rule that he is to pay the bill now', 'I advise you to pay the bill now', 'Will you please pay the bill now?', sentences which would presumably not be admitted as expressing a Fregean thought at all.

On these lines, I think, we might find a reasonably clear interpretation of the notion of locutionary meaning. Disre-

---

[3] See the hints and suggestions on 132, 144–5, 147–8.
[4] See 'The Thought: A Logical Inquiry', trans. Quinton, *Mind* (1956), 21–3.

garding explicit performatives, abstracting from the significance of grammatical mood, shearing off the implications of
such words as 'but', 'therefore', 'perhaps', etc., we note the
minimum remaining content of 'sense and reference'; and
observe, not only that the very same content may sometimes
be dressed as a verdict and sometimes delivered only as an
opinion, but also that the very same content may sometimes
figure in a request or an order or a piece of advice as well as
in a prediction; and we observe that, however it figures and
however it is dressed, we may raise the question whether the
facts and it correspond to one another in the way in which
they do so correspond, alike when a *predicted* act is performed and when a *commanded* or *counselled* act is performed. This content, then, we look for in every utterance in
which we can find it and declare, when found, to be the
locutionary meaning of that utterance and its constative aspect, the aspect associated with truth and falsity, with the
dimension of correspondence with the facts.

But though we might thus find a relatively clear interpretation of the notion of locutionary meaning, it can hardly be
said to be clearly the correct one. For while Austin is indeed
anxious to find a constative aspect—an aspect of exposure to
assessment in the light of the facts—in, say, a piece of advice
as well as in a statement, he does not appeal to the fact that
advice given may or may not be followed, that it may or may
not in *this* way be 'confirmed' by the facts. He appeals instead
to the fact that it may or may not be *good* advice, that it may
or may not in *this* way be 'supported' by the facts.[5] So in so
far as we base our extended-Fregean interpretation of
'locutionary meaning' on the links: locutionary meaning—
sense and reference—constative aspect—assessability in the
light of the facts, the interpretation collapses. It collapses
because it now looks as if we do have to take account of
whether the same content is commanded or predicted, say, in
order to know *what* we have to assess in this dimension, i.e. in
order to know what locutionary meaning is in question.

---

[5] *How to Do Things with Words*, 141.

*Interpretation III* (?). Can we find another interpretation, intermediate between the two extremes? Well, it is clear from the text that knowing what locutionary act has been performed includes knowing what 'rhetic act' has been performed; and it is clear from the examples on p. 95 that specifying the rhetic act which has been performed includes more than merely specifying the *sense-and-reference*, in the restricted sense considered above, of what is said. For on that page the specification of the rhetic act is given by such descriptions as the following: He *told me to* get out; He *said he would* be there; He *asked whether* it was in Oxford or Cambridge.[6] So *if* knowing the locutionary *meaning* of what is said includes not simply knowing the minimal sense-and-reference content of what is said but also knowing what *rhetic act* has been performed, then we can always include in the locutionary meaning of what is said at least a *rough* classification of what is said under such general headings as, say, *declarative, imperative, interrogative*, and perhaps one or two more. This will take locutionary meaning well beyond restricted sense-and-reference while leaving it, in general, short of full illocutionary force.

But obvious queries arise about this interpretation, as so far described. *How much* more than restricted sense-and-reference is to be allowed into locutionary meaning by way of the specification of the rhetic act? *Which* of the linguistic devices employed are to be allowed to bear on the specification of the rhetic act, and why? Evidently, from the examples, the use of the imperative, the interrogative, or the indicative form is to be allowed to bear. Presumably also the optative—so that when the Dauphin in *Henry V* says 'Would it were day!' *his* rhetic act is to be described as: He expressed the wish that it was day. But if all these, what about others? What, in particular, of the case where an explicit performative formula is used? In what style should the rhetic act corresponding to an utterance of 'I promise to be there' be specified except in such a style as *He promised to be there*?

---

[6] My italics.

What of the rhetic act corresponding to an utterance of 'I apologize'? And if the conventional force of the explicit performative formula is to be allowed, after all, to enter into locutionary meaning, why not also the conventional force of some of the other devices which Austin lists, such as certain adverbs, adverbial phrases, and connecting particles? What, in general, is to stop this third interpretation, which was intended to be something intermediate between the extremes of the first and the second, from becoming indistinguishable from the first? What is to stop locutionary meaning from becoming indistinguishable from sense-*B*-meaning and hence including all that is included in sense-*A*-meaning?

In spite of these difficulties, however, I think we should not give up hope of finding an intermediate interpretation. I shall resume the attempt in the next section.

### III

Even if it should turn out to be vain to press the question, what exactly is to be understood by 'locutionary meaning', it has not been vain to raise it, and to note the tensions in Austin's thinking which are revealed by raising it. Part of what is revealed is a certain ambivalence in Austin's attitude to a conception which, in one form or another, is really inescapable in philosophical, or broadly logical, theory. The conception I have in mind is that of the primary or essential bearers of truth-value, variously named, and no doubt variously conceived, as *statements, propositions, thoughts* (Frege), and *constatives* (Austin). 'The traditional statement', Austin says, 'is an abstraction, an ideal, and so is its traditional truth or falsity.'[7] A few lines later he characterizes the traditional conception of truth and falsity as an 'artificial abstraction which is always possible and legitimate for certain purposes'.[8] We are left a little uncertain as to whether the

---

[7] Op. cit., 147.     [8] Op. cit., 148.

conception in question is an abstraction and none the worse
for that, or whether it is an abstraction and a good deal the
worse for that; whether it is an abstraction we have to make
in the interests of a satisfactory general theory, or an abstraction which impedes the framing of a satisfactory general
theory. We may incline to the former view of his views when
we consider that one of the things we learn, or relearn, from
Austin is the need to distinguish and relate (i.e. not to mud-
dle) different levels in the theory of language. Is not the
theory of the proposition (or the theory of the constative) on
one of these levels, interpenetrating with, but not to be confused with, the general theory of linguistic meaning (sense *A*)
and the general theory of communicated force, including
illocutionary force (sense *C*)? And is not Austin's notion of
locutionary meaning a gesture, though an unclear one, in this
direction? But though these thoughts may incline us to suppose that he viewed the constative abstraction with some
degree of favour, there is much to incline us to the opposite
view of his views. There is, first, the symptomatic unclarity of
his doctrine of locutionary meaning; and there are, secondly,
the more direct indications of a certain grudgingness in his
references to 'traditional' truth and falsity and their 'traditional' bearers. Some of the reasons advanced for this reserve
I shall discuss in the next section. First (though this is by no
means a matter to be wholly cleared up *en passant*) I shall say
a little more about the abstraction in question by way of
making a final attempt to relate it to the notion of locutionary
meaning.

One thing, with cautious readiness, we can say at once.
Any proposition is *capable* of being expressed either in some
clause or sentence which is *capable*, in all linguistic propriety,
of following the phrase 'it is true that' or in some logical
compound (e.g. a disjunction) of such clauses or sentences.
Let us call these clauses or sentences the 'normal forms' of
expression of a proposition. And let us call the provision just
laid down 'the normal-form provision'.

The normal-form provision leaves us uncommitted on a

number of points. I mention some which are obviously relevant to any further attempt at interpreting the notion of locutionary meaning.

(i) First, a minor point. It is clear that at least for some interpretations (and those the more plausible) of this notion, those elements of the sense-$A$-meaning of what is said which are conventionally implied by such expressions as 'of course', 'therefore', 'nevertheless', etc., and (sometimes) 'fortunately', 'unhappily', etc. are not to be included in locutionary meaning. The same holds for the Fregean thought. Is this result guaranteed also for propositions by the normal-form provision? Not, I think, clearly. Consider such a clause as 'he is occupied', which is certainly capable of expressing a proposition. We have no clear guarantee that the introduction of the expression 'of course', which modifies the sense-$A$-meaning of what is said, would not thereby modify any proposition expressed. But I think we can add to our limited characterization to provide such a guarantee. The word-string 'He is happily occupied' can evidently be understood in two different ways; and this difference is identical with the difference between 'It is happily true that he is occupied' and 'It is true that he is happily occupied'. Perhaps, then, we can achieve the desired result by ruling that the only elements of sense-$A$-meaning which contribute to determining the content of the proposition expressed by a certain clause are those contributed by expressions which are such that, when 'it is true that' is prefixed to the clause, it would *not* be more felicitous to transfer the expressions in question from their original place in the clause to a place in the prefixed phrase. 'Of course', 'nevertheless', 'therefore', etc. in general fail to satisfy this requirement; 'It is true that he is of course married' or 'It is true that he is nevertheless married' are at best infelicitous shots at 'It is of course true that he's married' or 'It is nevertheless true that he's married.' We could indeed have 'It's true that he's therefore regretful' as well as 'It's therefore true that he's regretful'; but this serves only to emphasize the success of the ruling. The merit of the test lies not merely in its success but in its obvious relevance to the task in hand, i.e. that of delimiting what belongs to the proposition, the bearer of truth-value.

(ii) There is a more important matter on which the normal-form provision leaves us uncommitted. To say that propositions must be *capable* of being expressed in a certain form (the normal form) is really to say very little. It limits the notion of a proposition much less than it might appear to. It is not, by itself, to say either that a proposition is expressed only when that form is used or that a proposition is expressed only when one of a range of speech acts characteristically associated with that form is performed. It leaves quite open the question whether one and the same proposition, capable of expression in the normal form, may not also be capable of expression in forms associated with quite other speech acts. If we want a Fregean, or quasi-Fregean, limitation which will forbid us to say that 'Pay the bill now, John' (uttered as an instruction) may express a proposition, and the very same proposition as might be expressed by 'John is about to pay the bill' (uttered as a piece of information), then that limitation has yet to be imposed. The normal-form provision does not of itself give reason for denying that orders and instructions express propositions and indeed the same propositions as the corresponding predictions.

It is not difficult to find reasons for imposing a Fregean or quasi-Fregean limitation. One reason for such a limitation is this. Propositions, whatever they are, are supposed to be bearers of truth-value; but we should not ordinarily say that one who issues a command or instruction (say, 'Pay the bill now, John') had thereby said something true or false—true if the command was complied with, false if not. Now this might seem a superficial reason. But we can find a deeper reason behind it in the insight expressed by various philosophers,[9] into the difference in direction of 'match' or correspondence between the words and the world in the case of, say, assertions on the one hand and, say, commands on the other. A connected reason may be found in the view, held by many,

---

[9] See e.g. Miss Anscombe, *Intention*, § 32.

that no 'logic of imperatives' (if there is anything deserving
the name) can successfully be represented as strictly parallel
to a 'logic of propositions'.[10] Now it is not my present purpose
to say exactly what limitations on the notion of proposition
are to be imposed. But I shall assume that *some* are to be
imposed. And on this assumption, we may make another
attempt at a scheme of interpretation for the notion of
locutionary meaning.

But first let us note just one more point (iii) on which the
normal-form provision leaves us uncommitted. I have already remarked that it does not commit us to the view that
whenever a proposition is expressed, it is expressed in the
normal form. Now I add that it does not commit us to the
view that a clause having the normal form of a proposition
always expresses the proposition which it would normally
express if it were actually preceded by the words 'it is true
that'. Thus, as far as the normal-form provision is concerned,
it is open to us to hold (in what is surely an Austinian spirit)
that, for example, the words 'I accuse the authorities of fab-
ricating evidence' will usually, if uttered as a complete sentence, express the proposition which, in normal form, would
be expressed by 'The authorities have fabricated evidence'
and not the proposition which they would express if they
were actually preceded by the words 'it is true that'; though
they may *sometimes* express that proposition.

Now, then, to the scheme of interpretation. The proposal
is, first, that in every case in which a locution as a whole
expresses a proposition, we should say that its locutionary
meaning is the proposition expressed. For such other broad
classes of locutions as we may find it expedient to distinguish
from proposition-expressing locutions, we shall need terms of
art comparable with the term 'proposition', to set beside the
latter. Let us suppose that 'imperative' is one such term,
imperatives being variously expressible with the force of
pieces of advice, requests, commands, recommendations,
prayers, invitations, etc. Then, again, we should say, of every
locution which, as a whole, expresses an imperative, that

---

[10] This is controversial. See R. M. Hare, 'Some Alleged Differences between
Imperatives and Indicatives', *Mind* (1967), for the contrary view.

its locutionary meaning is the imperative expressed. As regards the elements of (restricted) 'sense-and-reference' they contain, imperative and proposition may sometimes be indistinguishable. But as locutionary meanings they are distinguished as proposition and imperative respectively. A scheme for separately specifying the illocutionary force and the locutionary meaning of single utterances which, as wholes, express propositions or imperatives (or any other broad classes we find it expedient to distinguish) might be imagined as follows:

$X$ issues the___(that . . .) with the force of a *xxxxx*.

A specification of the general type of locutionary meaning fills the first blank, of specific locutionary content the second, of illocutionary force the third. Thus we might have such fillings as these:

$X$ issues the
$\left\{\begin{array}{l} (1) \text{ proposition } (\textit{that} \text{ S } \textit{is} \text{ P}) \\ (2) \text{ imperative } (\textit{that} \text{ Z (person) } \textit{is to} \\ \quad \text{Y (act))} \\ (3) \text{ ?} \end{array}\right\}$

as a
with the force of a
by way of
$\left\{\begin{array}{l} (1) \text{ accusation, report, forecast, conclusion, objection, hypothesis, guess, verdict, etc.} \\ (2) \text{ command, request, piece of advice, prayer, invitation, entreaty, etc.} \\ (3) \text{ ?} \end{array}\right.$

It would evidently be in harmony with a scheme of this kind, as also (it seems most likely) with Austin's intentions, to hold that the explicit performative formula, whether occurring as a part or as the whole of an utterance, has no locutionary meaning at all. But though in harmony with this scheme, such a position is not *demanded* by it. It would be perfectly consistent with the scheme to hold the quite contrary position that one who (seriously) utters an explicit performative of the form 'I *x* . . .' issues the *proposition* that he *x*s . . . with the force of an *x*-ing: e.g. to hold that someone who says 'I apologize' issues the proposition that he apologizes with the force of an apology: or that someone who says 'I warn you all that judgement is at hand' issues the proposition that he warns us all that judgement is at hand with the force of a warning. This position has gained popularity with philosophers recently, as against the position which Austin himself may be presumed to have favoured; and indeed it would be, in some respect, a simplification, though in others a complication. The scheme proposed is in itself neutral as between the two positions. In what follows in Part IV section (3) I shall assume the Austinian position because it will simplify the presentation of the argument there, though it will make no difference to the principle of that argument.

Of course the above remarks are not offered as a complete characterization of the notion of a proposition; nor, patently, as a complete theory of the classification of speech acts. They do not even offer a decision-procedure for applying the partial classification proposed. They are intended only as *indications* of the place which the relatively abstract notions of proposition and imperative might be held to occupy on one possible form of interpretation, and that not the least plausible or attractive, of the notion of locutionary meaning. One minor modification of the *schema*, which it is worth making to forestall misunderstanding, is the following. On any view, propositions may be expressed by *parts* of utterances (e.g. co-ordinate or subordinate clauses or accusative and infinitive constructions), parts which are not themselves advanced with the force which belongs to the utterance as a whole; and it may be expedient to mark this point by replacing the term 'proposition' in the above *schema* with one less general. For this purpose Austin's own term 'constative' offers itself as a convenient candidate.

IV

Now, finally, I said I was going to mention some reasons which Austin might have had for viewing with a fairly cold eye the notion of the propositional abstraction, and hence for viewing with a fairly cold eye the proposal I have just made for the interpretation of the notion of locutionary meaning. I glanced at one of these reasons at the end of my consideration of Interpretation II: but it is worth considering at greater length, as I shall do in section 3 below.

It is not immediately obvious how far Austin's position on this matter actually suffered change. In his 1950 paper, 'Truth', he regarded with sufficient favour the notion of the primary and fundamental bearer of truth-value to think it worth while to inquire into the name and nature of 'that which at bottom we are always saying "is true" ';[11] and then to advance, though with reservations, the theory that the predicate 'is true' stands for a certain 'rather boring yet satisfactory relation' which may sometimes hold 'between words and world'.[12] In *How to Do Things with Words* the note of reservation sounds more strongly: 'truth and falsity (except by an artificial abstraction which is always possible and legitimate for certain purposes) are not names for relations, qualities, or whatnot, but for a dimension of assessment.'[13] The exceptive clause allows us to suppose that there has been no fundamental change of position, even though reserve may have deepened into coldness. Let us look at the reasons for this reserve. We shall see that none of them is a good reason.

1. One of them seems to concern the word 'statement', Austin's preferred name (in 1950) for that of which 'at bottom' we predicate 'is true'. That he should have had reservations about the *name* is surely natural enough. For, as he frequently points out, the verb 'to state' and the noun 'statement' are naturally used only in a relatively confined class of cases.[14] There are many other cases to which this term is not naturally applied, but in which the uninhibited theorist of the constative would say that a constative is issued; and yet many

---

[11] *Philosophical Papers*, 86; 2nd edn., 118.
[12] Op. cit., 107. About this theory I have already had my say, or more than my say, and I shall not repeat criticisms already made.
[13] *How to Do Things with Words*, 148. See also 144.
[14] See Ibid. 137, 146, etc., also *Philosophical Papers*, 236–7.

more, as already remarked, where the uninhibited theorist of the proposition would say that a proposition is expressed, though not 'constated' (issued as a constative).

It scarcely seems, however, that we have, in these points about the term 'statement', a reason for scepticism about the theory of propositions. We might take these points, rather, as reasons for viewing with favour the employment of the artificial term, 'proposition', instead of the common word, 'statement'. It is easy to meet, if it should be issued, the challenge to explain why we do not have in common use an expression with just the coverage which the artificial term is intended to have. For we do not commonly talk about propositions in general, and we do not commonly talk about particular propositions except when they come before us as what somebody does or might believe, suppose, assert, declare, guess, surmise, hypothesize, premiss, conclude, imply, etc. We have a correspondingly rich range of substantival expressions for referring to propositions under the guises under which they come before us; and there is no reason why we should, in actual situations, feel the need for a term which abstracts from any and every such guise, especially when we also have at our disposal a standard and neutral form (the 'that'-clause) for specifying the *content* of any particular belief, hypothesis, conclusion, etc. The challenge to be thus met is in any case scarcely one which Austin would be in a position to issue. Given the freedom with which technical terms proliferate in *How to Do Things with Words*, Austin could scarcely think it a reproach to any theorist that he should feel the need of a classification not commonly made in the daily business of communication.

2. A class of reasons for regarding the 'traditional' conception of *truth* as undesirably abstract is introduced by way of two examples of rather rough-and-ready geographical and historical description, viz. 'France is hexagonal' and 'Lord Raglan won the battle of Alma.'[15] Some of Austin's com-

---

[15] *How to Do Things with Words*, 142–3.

ments on these remarks are plainly correct. He points out that, like many others, they may be adequate for some purposes and not for others, suitable to some contexts and not to others. But this tolerance wavers when the words 'true' and 'false' come into play. 'How can one answer this question', he says, 'whether it's true or false that France is hexagonal? It is just rough, and that is the right and final answer to the question of the relation of "France is hexagonal" to France. It is a rough description; it is not a true or a false one.' But why should Austin refuse 'true' and 'false' a place even in a right and final answer? Couldn't we say 'It's roughly true that France is hexagonal'? (It's not even roughly true, it's completely false, that France has the shape of a trapezium.) Couldn't we also say 'It's true (*sans phrase*) that France is roughly hexagonal'? Austin successfully makes us aware of the hesitation we feel when confronted with the hold-up question 'Is it true or false that France is hexagonal?' But it is not so much the presence of the words 'true' and 'false' as the absence of qualification or context that accounts for the hesitation. We should feel just the same hesitation over 'Is France hexagonal or isn't it?'

This comes out clearly enough in his own presentation of his second example. He asks: 'Did Lord Raglan then win the battle of Alma or did he not?' It seems in this case that the 'pointlessness' of insisting on the statement's truth or falsity is the same thing as the pointlessness of insisting that either he did or he didn't. Austin's own positive comment on this case has a measure of oddity. 'Lord Raglan won the battle of Alma' is, he says, not true or false, but exaggerated, an exaggeration. But wouldn't it really be something like a mild witticism to say that it was an *exaggeration* to say that Lord Raglan won the battle of Alma?

It is by no means an easy matter to see exactly what Austin took the import of such examples to be. Of course there are descriptions which are adequate in some contexts and not in others; of course, too, there are descriptions which are sometimes only more or less apt for the situations we are inclined or half-inclined to apply them to. Is it Austin's point that the words 'true' and 'false' are *never* in place in such cases? But this seems to be not strictly (or not at all) true. If we are happily operating at a level, in a context, at or in which descriptions which, from another point of view might be regarded as oversimplified, are perfectly adequate, then it may be perfectly all right to employ the words 'true' and 'false' without qualification. If we are operating at a more critical level—or dealing with descriptions which, at any level, are only more or less apt for the particular situation in question— we have at our disposal expressions which, or some of which, can be used *either* to modify the descriptive predicates themselves *or* to modify the predicate 'true'. I have in mind such expressions as 'roughly', 'more or less', 'not strictly', 'not exactly', 'not altogether', and so on.

Indeed Austin might have found in this last point some prima-facie support for his own (1950) theory of truth. When we say such things as 'He's not exactly drunk', 'He's not strictly speaking a relation', 'It's only approximately square', we might, with some justice, in some cases, say that we are talking both about the words and the world, both about the situation and the description. In so far as we can make remarks equivalent to these, employing the word 'true', we have, to an equivalent degree, remarks about the relation of words to world. But of course it is well for a defender of the Austinian theory of truth *not* to make *this* point. To gain it would be to lose the match. To admit it is to admit the wooden horse. For the point is that the presence or absence of the word 'true' *makes no difference* in this respect.

Perhaps, however, the point of Austin's examples is simply to bring out the illusoriness of a certain concept of truth. According to this conception, the predicate 'is true' is one which in the case of *every* constative utterance (or *every* propositional part of an utterance), either holds absolutely and without qualification or absolutely and without qualification fails to hold. That this is an illusory conception very few theorists of the proposition would have difficulty in agreeing; but they need not agree that it is, or ever was, *their* conception.

3. Austin's third reason for coldness about the propositional abstraction is of a rather different kind from those so far considered. His point is, or seems to be, to put it in the very terms he would regard it as a reason for questioning—that just as the facts of the case bear on the truth or falsity of a constative, so the facts of the case bear on the warrantedness or unwarrantedness of an imperative.[16] The facts of the case may be such as to make a request a reasonable request, an order a sound or justified order, a piece of advice good advice; or they may be such that the request is unreasonable, the order unsound, the advice bad. (Of course, all these assessments are liable to qualifications of degree, of more or less.) If the salt is nearer to you than it is to me, it may be reasonable of me to ask you to pass it. If it is nearer to me than to you, it may not be. If you are a good runner and a bad shot, my advice to you to run rather than stay and shoot may be good advice and the advice to stay and shoot rather than run may be bad advice. The strategic situation may be such as to justify the order to stand or it may be such as to justify the order to retreat. And so on.

All this is evidently correct. But Austin invites us to regard it as a reason for *assimilating* this kind of assessment of requests, advice, commands, etc. to the kind of assessment which we make of constatives when we declare them true or false. When he says that 'true' and 'false' are the names of a general dimension of assessment, he means to include *both* the above kinds of assessment in this general dimension. He wants us to join him in refusing to draw any sharp line between saying that an announcement, accusation, or surmise was true, and saying that a request, a piece of advice, or a command was warranted or justified by the facts of the case.[17]

It will be clear why I say that this third point of Austin is in a different class from the preceding two. The theorist of the

---

[16] See 141, 144.

[17] Let me recall that in what follows I ignore the un-Austinian option, left open by the scheme of the final interpretation, of regarding explicit performatives as, without exception, constatives. This merely simplifies the statement of the ensuing criticisms. It makes no difference of principle.

proposition can accept with equanimity, and even welcome, much that is just in the first two points. But he must reject the assimilation proposed in the third. If he is impressed by an analogy between constatives and imperatives, it will be by a different analogy. He will be impressed by the fact that just as constatives are (just or more or less) true or not, so imperatives are (just or more or less) complied with or not. He may even be prepared to assimilate them to each other (for some purposes) on this ground, the ground, we might say, of the possibility of common content. But of course this ground of assimilation is totally different from that proposed by Austin.

But is the theorist of the proposition justified as against Austin? Surely he is. And surely Austin goes against his own best insights in suggesting he is not. Let us call the assessment of a piece of advice, an order, or a request, etc. as sound or unsound, reasonable or unreasonable etc., its warrantability-valuation, and let us call the assessment of an (undoubted) constative as (just or more or less) true or false its truth-valuation. What Austin proposes is that we regard warrantability-valuation and truth-valuation as belonging to a single dimension of assessment—for which he appropriates the name, 'the truth-and-falsity dimension'. Let us instead call this supposed single dimension of assessment the dimension of $S$-valuation ('$S$' for 'satisfactoriness') and distinguish throughout between positive and negative $S$-valuation.

Now Austin himself has insisted on distinguishing the locutionary meaning of an utterance from all its other aspects. Disregarding the first interpretation of 'locutionary meaning', which is certainly un-Austinian, we have the choice of regarding locutionary meanings as differentiated into broad classes of which the constative and the imperative are two (the final interpretation); or of regarding locutionary meanings as undifferentiated throughout (the second interpretation). But whichever of these choices we make, we cannot possibly regard locutionary meanings as related in a homogeneous manner to conditions for positive $S$-valuation throughout the field of this supposed single dimension of assessment. If we take constatives as forming one broad class of locutionary meanings, and imperatives another, we must note that to specify constative locutionary meanings is the same thing as to specify conditions for positive S-valuation, whereas to specify imperative locutionary meanings is not even to begin to specify conditions for positive S-valuation; it is simply to say who, according to the imperative, is to do what. If, on the other hand, we are not to regard locutionary meanings as thus broadly differentiated, then we must note that in every case the specification of locutionary meaning is a specification of a possible state of affairs; and, once we are informed of the type of speech act involved, we can scarcely fail to note a distinction between cases in which the obtaining or coming to obtain of that state of affairs would constitute the satisfaction of conditions for positive S-valuation (the constative cases) and cases in which the obtaining or coming to obtain of that state of affairs would be quite irrelevant to positive S-valuation (the imperative cases).

These are surely sufficient reasons for reaffirming a clear distinction between truth-valuation and warrantability-valuation. Moreover they are reasons to which we are invited to attend by Austin's own distinction between locutionary meaning and illocutionary force. We need not, of course, deny that truth-valuation and warrantability-valuation have something in common, nor that the grounds for both may, in particular cases, be as close as you please: for example, the fact that it is raining may in one way justify my assertion that it is raining and in another way may justify my urging you to take an umbrella. But we cannot, surely, find it felicitous to mark these points by appropriating the names 'truth' and 'falsity' in the way Austin suggests.

# 12

# *Meaning and Context*

This paper is concerned with the question of how the context of utterance bears on the meaning of what is said when someone seriously utters a sentence.

I begin by summarizing briefly the simple threefold distinction set out in full in Part I of 'Austin and "Locutionary Meaning"' (to which I refer the reader). Then, in terms appropriate to that distinction, I give some fairly obvious preliminary answers to the question which is my topic. This occupies the first part of the present paper.

Next I shall remark on various ways in which the resulting scheme may be held to be too simple, since the situation is, or may be, more complex than that scheme suggests. That is the second part.

Finally, in the third part, I shall consider a number of related issues of interest, certainly, to philosophers of language and, perhaps, to linguists.

## I

To begin, then, with the threefold distinction. Suppose someone X knows that a certain sentence S of a language L was seriously uttered on some occasion. Suppose X to know nothing else of the nature of the occasion, but to possess an ideally complete knowledge of the lexicon and grammar of L. Suppose also that if S suffers from what is customarily called lexical or syntactic ambiguity, X knows which of the possible lexical items or syntactic constructions was meant by the speaker. Then whether S in fact suffers or is free from such ambiguity, in either case there is one sense of the phrase in which X can be said to know *the meaning of what was said.* (He is able to give an accurate translation of what was said into any other equally rich language which he knows equally well.) I call this sense the *linguistic meaning* or the *sense-A-meaning* of what was said.

X's knowledge of the sense-A-meaning of what was said does not include knowledge of the reference of proper names or indexical expressions which may be contained in S. So if S does contain such expressions and X learns their references, he knows in a fuller sense than sense-A the meaning of what was said. I call this fuller sense the *linguistic-cum-referential* or *sense-B-meaning* of what was said.

But this is not the end of the story. For even if X knows the sense-B-meaning of what was said, he may still possibly be unaware of its illocutionary force;[1] and, over and above this, he may be quite unaware of all that was intended by the speaker to be understood as implied (i.e. *meant* in a yet further sense) by what was said. These are the reasons for introducing a third and yet fuller sense of the expression 'the meaning of what was said'; and I call this sense the *complete meaning* or *sense-C-meaning* of what was said.

It seems, on the face of it, that the progression in knowledge of what was meant from sense-A to sense-B and from sense-B to sense-C will generally be additive. Each stage certainly includes its predecessor; and will, it seems, generally add to it. But not always. If S is completely general, there is nothing for B-knowledge to add to A-knowledge. If illocutionary force is adequately conveyed by sense-A-meaning and if nothing further is intended to be understood by what is said than is included in sense-B-meaning, then there is nothing for C-meaning to add to B-meaning. Nevertheless it is true that very often, and perhaps generally, there will be such a progression.

So much for summary. Now we turn to the question which

---

[1] See 'Austin and "Locutionary Meaning"' in this volume and J. L. Austin, *How To Do Things with Words* (Oxford, 1962).

is our topic: does the context or setting—linguistic or non-linguistic—of an utterance bear on the determination of the meaning of what is said in these three senses? And, if so, how does it bear? Obviously context bears on the determination of meaning in sense-A in just those cases where the sentence S suffers from what is customarily called syntactic and/or lexical ambiguity. Obviously also, context bears on the determination of sense-B-meaning in all cases except those in which there is nothing for B to add to A. And obviously context in the broadest sense bears on the determination of sense-C-meaning in absolutely every case in which C-meaning comprehends more than sense-B-meaning.

What specific differences are there in the ways in which the meaning of what is said depends on context in the three cases? In particular, in which cases and to what degree can this dependence be itself represented as governed by linguistic rule or convention? As regards the disambiguation of a sentence by context at the level of A-meaning, this is clearly not in general a matter of convention. In so far as such ambiguities are resolved by context independently of the further determination of B- or C-meaning, their resolution depends on a judgement of general relevance or plausibility rather than on the application of a rule.

The case is very different with the further determination of B-meaning. Except in the eyes of some logicians, addicted to philosophical dreaming about 'ideal languages', the dependence on linguistic or non-linguistic context of those elements of meaning which B adds to A is no imperfection, but a vitally important feature of linguistic communication; and no statement of the semantic rules of any natural language could be complete which did not contain rules governing such contextual dependence. Of course the rules, in some cases, leave a certain indeterminacy which they do not in others: even though I know the rules and am aware of the context and origin of utterance, I may, in a particular case, misunderstand 'here' in a way in which I can hardly misunderstand 'I'. Neither is it by any means the case that the dependence of referential meaning on context can always be related to a rule

*of the natural language* of utterance. It is not by tacitly applying a rule of English to the circumstance of utterance that you
know whom I mean by 'John' or 'Henry' when I produce a
sentence containing such proper names; though it is, doubtless, in virtue of a convention of some less general kind that
you know this. In general, then, the role of context in closing
the gap between knowledge of sense-A-meaning and knowledge of sense-B-meaning is partly but not wholly under the
governance of language-rules.

As regards the gap—when there is one—between sense-B-
meaning and sense-C-meaning, there is evidently no special
class of rules-of-the-natural-language tacitly applied by an
audience in closing this gap or in appreciating that there is no
gap to be closed. If you say 'He is very cautious', intending
what you say to be taken as praise and I, understanding the
sense-B-meaning of what you say, nevertheless take it as
intended as condemnation, then I have certainly not fully
grasped the C-meaning of what you said; but my misunderstanding is not a linguistic misunderstanding. We must not
conclude, however, that success or failure in closing the B–C
gap correctly is simply a matter of intelligent appreciation, or
lack of it, on the audience's part, of those features of the
circumstance, including the temper of the speaker, which
should be the audience's clues, as it were, to interpretation. It
may, after all, be a matter of knowledge of conventions—of
*some* kind. Austin placed great emphasis on those institutional or procedural settings which may, as a matter of convention, give a quite special force or weight or quite special
implications to the utterance of a certain expression, e.g. to
the utterance of 'Guilty' by the foreman of the jury in a court
of law or to the utterance of 'Double' by someone playing
bridge (when it is his turn to bid). But may not *some* such
conventional uses of expressions come to count as conventions, not just of the procedure in question, but of the natural
language in question? May they not, so to speak, earn a place
in the dictionary? Indeed they may. But then, of course, they
are relevant to the determination of A-meaning; it is no
longer true of such uses that they enter only at the level of C-

meaning. So the general point about closing the gap between
B- and C-meaning—i.e. that this is not a matter of linguistic
rule—stands as secure as any other tautology. On the other
hand we are forced to revise one point about the determination of A-meaning itself. For now we see that the determination of A-meaning may, in some cases, be directly related, *by
rule*, to the context of utterance, i.e. in just those cases where
the dictionary specifies a procedural or institutional sense for
an expression, and the expression is used, in this sense, in the
context of the relevant procedure or institution.


II


Now we are to consider certain respects in which the scheme
outlined above is either too simple to do justice to the facts or
requires, at least, a certain care in its application to them.

1. We began by imagining someone, X, with a complete mastery of the current semantics and syntax of a natural language
L (or dialect of L). But is this a clear conception? Let us
suppose it is clear. One favoured way of giving this supposition a definite form is to suppose X's knowledge capable in
principle of being articulated in an ideal grammar and dictionary, the latter listing every sense of every unitary expression of L. Where a unitary expression occurring in an uttered
sentence S has more than one listed sense, i.e. rates more
than one entry in the dictionary, the determination of the
sense-A-meaning of what is said will involve selection of the
appropriate entry, i.e. of the sense the expression is intended
to bear in S as uttered.

   According to the scheme outlined in Part I, *some* sense-A-
meaning will always be included in the complete meaning
(sense-C) of what was said. But it is a commonplace that
words may naturally acquire or bear, in a context, *extended* or
*figurative* senses, or simply different or *incorrect* senses, owing to the speaker's ignorance or illiteracy (cf. journalistic
misuses of 'refute', 'flaunt', 'mitigate', etc.). And here is a

dilemma. Are we to suppose that all such senses are antecedently listed in X's ideal dictionary? If so we can indeed (so
far) preserve the principle that some sense-A-meaning is always included in the complete meaning of what is said; but we
preserve it at the cost of a certain unrealistic, and even brutal,
distortion or misrepresentation. For the truth is that the existing semantic resources of a language are inherently capable
of more or less idiosyncratic variation and development in
ways which can hardly be reduced to rule in advance of what
actually happens, i.e. in advance of what is actually said and
understood.[2] If, on the other hand, we do not take this unrealistic course, we must sacrifice our principle. For given the
use of an expression in an extended or figurative or illiterate
or incorrect sense in an uttered sentence, there may be no
assignable sense-A-meaning for that sentence included in the
complete meaning of what was said. We could, perhaps,
achieve a compromise: by allowing that X's ideal dictionary is
revised by inclusion of the new extended sense at the instant
of his understanding what was said! But then, in such cases,
we make his dictionary follow his understanding instead of
making his understanding follow his dictionary.

Here, then, is one respect in which the scheme outlined to
begin with (in Part I) is too simple.

2. Here is another. There are cases in which there is no
difficulty at all in assigning an apparent B-meaning to what is
said and yet the C-meaning does not (except in a paradoxical
sense) include, but contradicts, the apparent B-meaning. In
the preceding paper in order to illustrate how C-meaning
may include but go beyond B-meaning, I used the example of
someone who says 'The President has expressed the view that
the ideal age for such an appointment is fifty' and intends to
be taken as implying by this that the President has certain
reasons for expressing such a view.[3] The B-meaning of what

---

[2] Certain vague, general principles of extension and development can be
indicated. Cf. L. J. Cohen, review of *The Structure of Language*, ed. J. A. Fodor
and J. J. Katz (*Philosophical Quarterly*, 1966).
[3] See 'Austin and "Locutionary Meaning"' in this volume.

is said in this case is adequately characterized in terms of a presumptive assertion made regarding a certain man (The President) at a certain time, etc. The C-meaning is obtained by confirming the assertive presumption and *adding* the implication to the assertion. But suppose the example modified slightly. The speaker says, instead, 'The President is strongly of the opinion that the ideal age, etc.'; but what the speaker intends, we may suppose, to be understood as implying is that the President is not really of this opinion at all, but only pretends to be in order to promote his favoured candidate's chances. Here we cannot say that the C-meaning includes and adds to the B-meaning, but only that the C-meaning *contradicts* the *apparent* B-meaning.

We may be tempted to defend the framework of I against this objection by assimilating the case in question to a large class of others which are taken as excluded from that framework by the qualification 'seriously' in the original sentence of I, namely 'Suppose a certain sentence S of a language L was seriously uttered on some occasion.' The ironical utterance of a sentence will then be classified as a *secondary* or *non-serious* use of language along with the utterance of sentences by actors in a play, a reading aloud from a novel, the writing of a poem, etc. But if irony is excluded, how much else will have to be excluded with it? Understatement (e.g. saying 'It's rather warm' and meaning that it's extremely hot? Hyperbole? Utterances formally polite and intended to be taken as such? Any case in which an intended implication casts any kind of backward shadow on apparent B-meaning? We may begin to feel that such a defence of the framework assumes too *ad hoc* an air; that the only discernible principle on which the cachet of seriousness is to be granted or withheld is that of ensuring that the decision constitutes no threat to the framework. And this seems hardly less arbitrary than the resistance to acknowledgement of that semantic creativity referred to at (1) above.

3. The next point is not so much a critique of the initial scheme as a caution about its interpretation. The complete

meaning of a sentence-utterance was to include its intended implications, if any. But here it is necessary to draw a certain distinction: the distinction, we may call it, between context-specific implication and general, presumptive implication. The examples so far given have been of the former kind. That is to say, the speaker intends his words, as uttered on that occasion, to be understood as carrying a certain implication; but the words are not such that they would *normally* or *usually* be understood as carrying such an implication. The speaker utters S, implying q; and it is true of him that part of what he means by what he says is that q. Such occasion-specific implication belongs to C-meaning.

There is, however, another kind of implication, attributable not to the specific intentions of speakers on specific occasions, but to certain general presumptions relating to the point and purpose of discourse at large.[4] For example, if somebody replies to a question by giving a less specific, say a disjunctive, answer (e.g. 'either red or green', 'either in London or in Cambridge', 'either 27 or 31') when it is obvious that a more specific answer (e.g. 'red', 'in London', '27')— had the speaker been in a position to give it—would have met the information-seeking needs of the questioner more satisfactorily, then the speaker will *normally* be presumed not to know which of the more specific alternatives is correct; though, of course, such presumption may be defeated by special circumstances of the case. His replying as he does will *normally*, however, be taken to imply that he is ignorant on this point. It may even properly be said that he implied this by replying as he did. Again, there are countless remarks or observations which may be perfectly true, but which will nevertheless seem perfectly *pointless* unless there was some antecedent reason to suppose they might *not* be true; and the making of such remarks may, in consequence, normally be understood to imply that some such point-conferring condi-

---

[4] See H. P. Grice, 'The Causal Theory of Perception', sects. 2–4 (*Proceedings of the Aristotelian Society Supplementary Volume*, 1961), 'Utterer's Meaning and Intention' (*Philosophical Review*, 1969), and 'Logic and Conversation', Pt. I of *Studies in the Way of Words* (Harvard, 1989).

tion obtains. For example, 'The President was strong enough to take a short walk today' would normally be taken to imply at least that the President was not in perfectly robust health; 'He signed the report voluntarily' would normally be taken to imply that there was some reason to think he acted under pressure.[5]

If a speaker utters a sentence carrying such a presumptive general implication, and if there is nothing in the circumstance of utterance to defeat that implication, then he will indeed give his audience cause to think that (he thinks that) such an implication holds; and he may intend this result. But I do not think it follows that part of what he *means* by such an utterance is that such an implication holds. The point could be fully argued only in the context of a complete theory of communication; for which there is not space here. Let it suffice here to distinguish these two kinds of implication; and to remark that general presumptive implication does not, merely by reason of its existence, win a place in the C-meaning of an utterance.

4. I allude next to the obscure and complex topic of reference. First, I try to illustrate not so much an imperfection in the scheme of I as a perplexity as to how it should be applied. Second, I suggest a further weakness in the scheme.

Some, but not all, of the problems in this area show themselves in the discussion, by logicians or philosophers of language, of 'referential opacity'. Consider the English sentence, 'Smith hopes that your brother will be elected' and imagine it seriously uttered on a certain occasion. The utterance seems open to more than one interpretation. On one obvious interpretation, it is not implied that the person whom Smith hopes to see elected is known by Smith to be the brother of the person addressed; and neither is the contrary implied. The expression 'your brother' is simply used by the speaker to identity *for the hearer* a person of whom it is asserted that

---

[5] See Grice, n. 4 above and J. R. Searle, *Speech Acts* (Cambridge, 1969).

Smith hopes that he will be elected (i.e. roughly: Smith hopes
that the person who is in fact your brother will be elected).
But it is quite clear that such an expression in such a sentence
is not always used in this way; for its use in some cases might
be taken, and be intended to be taken, in such a way that the
question whether Smith knew or believed that the person
that he hoped to see elected was the brother of the person
addressed had a bearing on the truth-value of what was said;
i.e. roughly: Smith hopes that the person who is in fact your
brother and whom he knows or believes to be your brother
will be elected. It might even be that the remark is intended
to convey that it is *as being* (or being believed by him to be)
a brother of the person addressed that Smith hopes to see his
preferred candidate elected; i.e. roughly: Smith hopes that
the person who is in fact your brother and whom he believes
to be your brother will be elected, and Smith hopes that that
person will be elected *because* he knows or believes him to be
your brother.

As a first step towards handling at least some cases of this
general kind (the complexities of which far outrun my limited
illustration), some logicians have invoked the notion of semantic or syntactic ambiguity, i.e. ambiguity at our original
sense-A-level. Words like 'hope' or 'believe', some have suggested, have different senses; or, alternatively, it has been
suggested, sentences of this kind may exhibit surface structure syntactic ambiguity, as having different transformational
histories. Views about the plausibility of these suggestions
may differ.[6] But it should be noted that there are other possibilities. For instance, it might be held that sentences of this
problematic sort are, not ambiguous, but intrinsically *indefinite* in sense; and the resolution of this indefiniteness cannot
be assigned to a lower level than that of C-meaning. Now, on
any view, it is no doubt true that context contributes to the
determination of the meaning of what is said. But so long as

---

[6] In 'Belief, Reference, and Quantification' in this volume I argue that 'believe', etc. do not have different senses, 'notional' and 'relational'; that, if we are
to locate ambiguity anywhere, we should treat it as structural.

we have no theoretical decision between such views, it remains unclear, in terms of the scheme of I, at what level this
determination takes place.

I used my example only to illustrate an uncertainty about
the application of the scheme of I. But the situation is really
worse than this. Once we start taking seriously, in all its
complexity, the subject of reference, a certain so far unchal-
lenged presumption of the scheme comes into question. This
is the presumption that once the sense-A-meaning of an utterance is determined, then it is automatically determined
which are its elements in respect of which the B-level question of determining reference arises. But if we adopt and
extend the thesis just alluded to of an intrinsic indefiniteness
in sense-A-meaning, then this presumption may seem to fail
in many cases. It may be that a single sentence admits of
different interpretations in some one of which a certain element in the sentence (say, a definite description) has a referential *use* while in some other that element has no such *use*.
Think for example of 'The next leader of the party will have
many enemies.' The definite descriptive phrase may be used
to refer to a definite nameable individual and intended to be
taken as referring to that individual; or, alternatively, the
sentence may be used with the force of 'Whoever the next
leader of the party may be, he will have many enemies.' Only
on the first alternative does the B-level question of determining reference arise. Context may indeed resolve the issue in
favour of one of these alternatives. But the picture of a simple
progression in determinateness of the meaning of what is
said—from A through B to C—no longer applies. For, on the
extended hypothesis of indefiniteness, the settlement of A-
questions may not itself always determine what B-questions
there are to be settled.

III

Here, finally, are three ways in which some of the questions
so scantily discussed above bear on other issues which are of

interest to logicians, to philosophers of language, and, perhaps, to linguists.

1. *Propositions.* Logicians have an interest in making a cut in the linguistic material we have been considering on rather different principles from any so far mentioned. Frege said that the word 'true' indicates the object of logic as 'beautiful' does that of aesthetics and 'good' that of ethics. Logicians are certainly concerned with the *transmission* of truth from one or more propositions (as premisses) to another proposition (as conclusion) in cases where the principles of such transmission have a kind of generality which can be formally exhibited in a certain style. The current style throws into prominence the exhibition of *identity* of propositions, or of propositional clauses, from one occasion of occurrence to another; as also identity of logical predicate, and, to a lesser degree, of individual reference.

With these concerns in mind, the logician who wishes to relate his formulae to actual speech will have reasons different from any so far mentioned for dissatisfaction with the scheme of I. The determination of the sense-A-meaning of uttered sentences will generally be both too little and too much for his purposes. To know what propositions (the bearers of truth-value) are in question, he must know the import of deictic and referring elements in the uttered sentences; for two uttered sentences or clauses (or two utterances of one sentence or clause) with exactly the same sense-A-meaning will express different propositions if the referential meaning of such elements is different. Neither is the sense-B-meaning of what is said quite what he wants. Even if the move from A to B corrects the *deficiencies* of sense-A-meaning, that move does not correct its *excesses*. For B, since according to scheme I it includes all of A, may involve difference in the meaning of what is said where a logician would tend to find *identity* of propositions: as in the case of the sentences 'He is an Englishman, so he is sympathetic' and 'He is an Englishman, but he is sympathetic', uttered, we are to suppose, with the same reference.

It is not the logician alone who will experience the need to supplement the scheme of I with different principles of abstraction. In the areas where truth and falsity are in question, any philosopher of language may think it important to distinguish between what was actually asserted, and what was in one way or another additionally conveyed in the saying of what was said, whether or not such additions were conveyed by linguistic devices conventionally adapted to the purpose. Austin, by no means a formal logician, certainly felt the pull of this idea, as we see when we try to puzzle out his own distinction between locutionary meaning and illocutionary force.

Finally it should be noted that earlier points 1 and 4 of Part II above also bear on the determination of the identity of the proposition asserted. They show that such determination may not merely be a matter of adding the determination of reference to a sense determined at the level of A-meaning. For point 1 of Part II shows how the interpreter of an uttered sentence must sometimes reach beyond any possible A-meaning to determine not simply the reference but also the sense of the uttered sentence; and point 4 of Part II suggests that the interpreter may sometimes have to reach beyond A-meaning in order to determine what *questions* of reference there are to be determined. These points, then will tend to reinforce the philosophical logician's dissatisfaction with the initial scheme.

2. *Meaning and use.* Nevertheless, in however complicated a way the determination of propositional meaning cuts across the distinctions of I, the whole of the preceding argument supposes that there is some line to be drawn, in our studies of speech, between what falls within the bounds of linguistic meaning, strictly conceived, and what falls outside those bounds, though still within the broader domain of communicated meaning. It does not suppose a sharp continuous boundary; it allows for a certain area of indeterminacy, for cases which cannot be certainly located, at a given moment, on one side or the other of the border (cf. II, 1 above); and perhaps

it is a condition of understanding the growth and development of a language that such an area of indeterminacy should be allowed for. Still, a border of some kind is supposed. Any linguist, who hopes that a systematic semantic theory of a language is possible, must have an interest in this supposal; so must any philosopher who aims, in his own way, at systematic comprehension of our habits of thought and speech.

The problem, of course, is to trace the border in the right place, along the lines that best accord with the demands of system and the respect for facts. And here it is worth mentioning one temptation to which (English-writing) philosophers—partly, though not only, under the influence of Wittgenstein—have been recently exposed and against which other (English-writing) philosophers have, still more recently, issued corrective warnings.[7] In their zealous and entirely proper study of the *uses* to which philosophically interesting expressions may be put—of the purposes such expressions may serve in the total enterprise of communicating meaning and of the *conditions* under which they may naturally serve these purposes—philosophers may mislocate or overlook that which is in fact the key to understanding the uses they study. For it may be that such an expression in fact possesses a unitary linguistic meaning and that the variety of uses and of conditions of use which engages philosophical attention—or some central and typical use which threatens to monopolize philosophical attention—can be *explained* as the result of an interplay between that unitary linguistic meaning on the one hand and certain characteristic purposes of speech, or features of speech-situations, on the other. A philosopher who ignores this possibility throws away, therefore, the chance of gaining enhanced comprehension and control of his material. (Let it be added that, of course, the philosophical explication of unitary meaning, even when possible, is not easy. It is not to be confused with the task of the lexicographer. The lexicographer can be content with a synonym or rough equivalent; the philosopher is required to

---

[7] Notably Grice. See n. 4 above.

achieve nothing less than the perspicuous exhibition of a concept.)

Perhaps we may sum this up by saying that the distinction between *linguistic meaning* and *complete meaning* remains of vital importance, even though their relations to each other and to the matter of reference are not presented with sufficient sophistication in the scheme of I, and even though, as argued at III (1) above, further principles of division of the material of speech are required than those that that scheme supplies.

3. *Language and communication.* Wearied, perhaps, with the complexities which beset us when we try to take account of communicated meaning in general, yet committed to the belief in the possibility of a systematic semantic theory of a language, some linguists or philosophers of language have held that such a theory should be freed from all dependence on the concept of communication.[8] From the point of view of linguistic theory, they hold, a language is to be seen as a system of rules and devices for articulating, or expressing, beliefs and attitudes, but not essentially for communicating them. The communicative function of language, though it is no doubt historically important in the origin, growth, and development of language, and though it constitutes a major part of the actual utility of language to mankind, has no essential place in a theoretical account of a language as syntactic-semantic-phonological system. For the purpose of elaborating a theory of linguistic meaning, we can make a clean sweep of all considerations which relate essentially to the function of communication.

I should like to conclude with two very brief and dogmatic comments on this view. First, it seems to me incoherent. On this view, the fact that the rules and conventions which determine the meanings of sentences are more or less socially common or public rules or conventions will appear as a merely natural fact, which demands, doubtless, a natural ex-

---

[8] e.g. J. Moravcsik, 'Linguistic Theory and the Philosophy of Language' (*Foundations of Language*, 1967).

planation, but is in no way essential to the concept of language. Any attempt to fabricate a natural explanation of this 'natural fact' will soon reveal how arbitrary and unrealistic such an assumption is.[9] Again, this view requires that it should be possible to give a perspicuous account of the notion of rule-governed *articulation* of beliefs and attitudes, this account in no way to rest upon or presuppose that of the *communication* of beliefs or attitudes. Now certainly someone who has mastered a language may sometimes articulate beliefs or attitudes with no intention of communicating them. But it by no means follows that we can *understand* the nature of this activity in terms which involve no reference to communicative intent. And indeed we cannot.

We cannot hope to understand language as a theorist hopes to understand it unless we understand speech. We cannot hope to understand speech unless we take account of the aim of communication.

[9] See P. F. Strawson, 'Meaning and Truth', in *Logico-Linguistic Papers* (London, 1971), 187–8.

# 13

# Kant's New Foundations
# of Metaphysics

The title we are offered for this paper is 'Kant's New Foundations of Metaphysics'. A question which naturally arises is this: How much, of our contemporary metaphysics, can be represented as resting on that foundation? The answer, I suggest, is: a great deal. Specifically, the thesis I propose to maintain in this paper is that Kant's *Copernican Revolution* can plausibly be seen as having substantially prevailed in the philosophical tradition to which I belong. It did not do so for some time; but it has done so relatively recently; is still unreversed; and, perhaps, is irreversible. To say this is not the same as to say that the full doctrine of *transcendental idealism* has obtained an equal acceptance. It is to say only that some *aspects* of that doctrine are alive, flourishing, and even dominant, among twentieth-century philosophers who write in English.

Though no one here needs to be reminded of it, I will repeat Kant's revolutionary suggestion: that, instead of assuming, as hitherto, that our knowledge must conform to objects, we should try whether we may not have more success in the tasks of metaphysics if we suppose that objects must conform to our knowledge. The initial shock of this proposal is diminished, if not suppressed, by the recognition that the tasks of metaphysics are highly general tasks: that they relate to the general form or framework within which enquiry is carried on rather than to particular episodes in the process of enquiry.

If there indeed are highly general formal conditions which

objects must satisfy in order to become possible objects of human knowledge, then, evidently, all objects of possible human knowledge must conform to those conditions. Any attempt to establish how things really are in total abstraction from those conditions will be doomed to failure.

*If* this position is a species of idealism, then, I have claimed, many of the dominant strains in modern analytical philosophy are also idealist. Of course, even if this claim can be made good, we may expect a considerable variety of strains, some more or less remote from the original Kantian stock. But can the claim be made good? Well, here I would like to call in evidence a recent work by Professor Tom Nagel of New York University—a work entitled *The View from Nowhere*. Nagel's own position is partially, but only partially, Kantian. He recognizes, and salutes, the natural human wish and endeavour to get behind those appearances of things which are attributable to our merely human perspective on the world and to arrive at a true conception of reality as it is in itself. What *separates* him from Kant is his belief that *partial* success in this aim is achievable and has indeed been achieved. What brings him *close* to Kant is his recognition that, whatever degree of success we do thus achieve, we cannot free ourselves from all the particularities of the human subjective make-up, the human perspective, and his conclusion that (I quote) 'how things are in themselves *transcends* all possible appearances or human conceptions'.

Nagel characterizes his own position as realist; and by doing so, underlines the contrast between that position and the views of the many philosophers of our period whom he calls idealists. Among these philosophers he refers explicitly to Wittgenstein and Davidson, implicitly to Quine, Putnam, and the American pragmatists at large, and Dummett. What is characteristic of them all is that, in one way or another, they seek, as he puts it, 'to cut the universe down to size' by circumscribing what there is within the limits of human understanding or human discourse. Our own best working concepts are held to set the bounds of the real. *To be* is to be understood, or understandable, by us. This certainly sounds like idealism of a sort. But is it of the Kantian sort? It may be difficult to give an unequivocal answer to that question. The answer may depend, as I hinted earlier, on our interpretation of transcendental idealism. Let us postpone it for a while, and look instead at some particular cases.

I take Putnam first, as representative of American pragmatism in general. Like other pragmatists, he regards the truth as what rational human opinion will converge on in the best, or sufficiently good, humanly available epistemic conditions. Repudiating what he calls 'metaphysical realism', he defines his position as an 'internal' or 'empirical' realism, thus echoing Kant; and says of it (I quote): 'It *is* a kind of realism, and I mean it to be a *human* kind of realism, a belief that there is a fact of the matter as to what is rightly assertible *for us*, as opposed to what is rightly assertible from the God's-eye view so dear to the classical metaphysical realist.' On other occasions (in conversation at least) he has been willing to call the position 'idealist': a description that Nagel, as we have seen, would endorse.

Davidson's position is not essentially different, though it is expressed in terms of understandable languages instead of in terms of epistemic conditions or points of view. He maintains that we can have no conception of a reality which is not describable in languages in principle understandable by us, nor any conception of truth beyond that of truth expressible in sentences translatable into sentences we could in principle understand. Here we find echoes of the Wittgenstein of the *Tractatus*: the limits of *our* language are the limits of *our* thought and thus of *our* world.

Quine can be represented as an extreme case of this restrictiveness: as one disposed to limit what exists to what is comprehensible by one particular kind of *human understanding*, the kind that yields physical and biological theory.

And now to Wittgenstein. His later work is marked, among much else, by a subtle and sophisticated refinement of the aphorism from the *Tractatus* which I have just alluded to. The refinement comes in the elaboration of the conditions of meaningful discourse, which must require an actual or potential community of agreement in linguistic practices, practices which themselves form part of shared forms of human life. In a way I anticipated this refinement in adapting or misquoting the aphorism, replacing the singular 'my' in the *Tractatus* phrases, 'the limits of *my* language', 'the limits of *my* world', by the collective 'our'. But there is something to be added to this. In his very last work, *On Certainty*, Wittgenstein speaks of certain propositions which have 'the form of empirical propositions', but which are not truly empirical, not derived from experience. Rather, they 'form the foundation of *all* operating with thoughts (with language)'. They constitute the 'world-picture' which is 'the substratum of all my enquiring and asserting' or 'the scaffolding of our thoughts' or 'the element in which arguments have their life'. Wittgenstein is coy about specifying these propositions, but his remarks suggest that they would include propositions affirming the existence of physical objects and of causal uniformities. His description of them, however, marks them out clearly as what Kant would call *synthetic* a priori propositions. Not that *Wittgenstein* would call them that: he merely remarks that they are neither a posteriori nor logically (or analytically) guaranteed. Wittgenstein would not think it appropriate, or possible, to produce, as Kant does, arguments in their favour. Rather, he says, of the 'world-picture' they constitute, that 'it is the inherited background against which I distinguish between true and false'.

In all this there are, certainly, muted Kantian echoes. Should I say 'muted' or 'transmuted'? The reference, earlier remarked on, to human community, to agreement in judgement, though not absent in Kant, has an emphasis in Wittgenstein that Kant does not give it. But an inherited background must be inherited from other members of the same, the human, species. And Kant also speaks of 'the human point of view'.

The case of Dummett shows some interesting variations. He allows that there are many propositions of which we perfectly well understand the meaning, but which are such that it exceeds our present cognitive capacities to arrive at a well-supported judgement as to their truth or falsity. In such cases, he has contended, there simply is no fact of the matter. Reality, as it were, comes to an end at these limits. He describes his position as anti-realist, but in common with most of the other philosophers I have mentioned, refrains from assuming the title of idealist. But if, as Nagel holds, the title is appropriate in the other cases, it is not clear why it should be withheld in his. Significance indeed, in Dummett's view—the significance of quite ordinary sentences—can transcend our cognitive limitations; but how things objectively are cannot. A partial parallel in Kant that here comes to mind is the latter's treatment of the mathematical antinomies. Just as Kant rejects both thesis and antithesis, so Dummett rejects both the truth of the quite undecidable proposition and that of its negation. The assumption that one or the other of the opposed pair of propositions must be correct rests for both philosophers on the mistaken presupposition that the objective facts can altogether outrun the kind of cognitive capacities that we possess. Of course the parallel is only partial. Whereas Kant maintains that both the opposed propositions are false, Dummett holds that neither is either true or false.

Now the distinctive mark of Nagel's realism is the conviction that the nature of things as they are in themselves, though partially discoverable by us, may well go beyond, and almost certainly *does* go beyond, all that human beings can, or could, discover or even conceive of. And it is precisely this conviction that seems to be rejected, in one way or in one form or another, by the philosophers whose views I have been considering. In contrast with the *metaphysical* realism, which they reject, they would, in general, be prepared to embrace what Putnam called an 'internal' or 'human' realism, which is at least comparable with the 'empirical' realism of Kant. It is a realism whose objects must conform at least to the general and formal conditions of possible human knowledge of them. Dummett, indeed, seems to go further; but he certainly goes at least so far.

But the question which still rather starkly confronts us is this: How close, really, are the views of this cluster of philosophers to the position of Kant himself? Even if a case has been made for saying that they have accepted a form of the Copernican revolution, how does it stand with the full doctrine of transcendental idealism? I shall argue that if we were prepared to interpret that doctrine in a certain way—in a way consistent with many of the insights of the most capacious mind (Kant's) that has ever dedicated itself to philosophy— then we could hold that our philosophers are themselves at least roughly in line with transcendental idealism. But I shall have to add that it is hard—indeed virtually impossible—to maintain that this interpretation is consistent with Kant's total intention.

The first step in approaching this question is to recall what, in Kant's view, are those basic facts about human cognitive capacities which determine the general, formal conditions of the possibility of human knowledge of objects. We have to begin, he holds, with the general truth—which surely no one will challenge—that we are creatures whose intellect is discursive and whose intuition is sensible. Sensibility and understanding must collaborate to yield knowledge: on the one hand, the receptive faculty through which the materials of knowledge are given to us; and, on the other, the faculty of thought through which those materials are conceptualized and through which judgement is possible. Each faculty, in us human beings, is held to be such as to impose, on their collaborative outcome, certain formal, or a priori, conditions: the pure forms of sensible intuition are space and time; the pure *concepts* of an object in general are the categories, themselves derived from the quite general forms or functions of understanding.

Now it is important to note that Kant regards it as simply an ultimate *fact* about the cognitive equipment of us human beings—as something not capable of further explanation— that we have just the forms and functions of judgement and just the spatial and temporal forms of intuition that we do have. So much he makes clear in a well-known sentence at B145–6. One might even put it by saying that he acknowledges an ultimate *contingency* in these facts about our cognitive constitution. This, of course, does not constitute any objection, from the critical point of view, to bestowing the title a priori either on the pure concepts, derived from the forms of judgement, or on the spatio-temporal forms of sensibility; for, as conditions of the possibility of empirical knowledge of objects—as virtually defining what can count as objects for us—they will certainly not themselves be empirical, i.e. derived from within experience.

Nevertheless, while ready to accept the a priori status of the pure concepts and the forms of intuition, we may be encouraged to wonder whether it really is quite inexplicable that we have just the functions of judgement (the logical forms) and just the spatio-temporal forms of intuition that we do have. I shall argue that, given three assumptions, two of which are made by Kant himself, it is not inexplicable at all.

First, as to logical form. The fundamental logical operations or forms of judgement recognized in Kant's table are such as are, and must be, recognized in any general logic worthy of the name. By the 'fundamental logical operations' I mean: predication (subject and predicate); generalization (particular and universal forms); sentence-composition (including negation, disjunction, conditionality, etc.) Now it is not a mysterious but an analytic truth that judgement involves concepts; that concepts are such as to be applicable or inapplicable in one or more instances; that judgements or propositions are capable of truth or falsity. From such considerations as these it is not too difficult to show that the possibility of the fundamental logical operations is inherent in the very nature of the judgement or proposition. Wittgenstein expressed the point with characteristic epigrammatic obscurity when he wrote in the *Tractatus*: 'One could say that the sole logical constant was what *all* propositions, *by their very nature*, had in common with one another. But that is the general propositional form' (5.47). (I have argued the same point myself in a lengthier and more cumbersome way.) Of course there are differences between the notational devices and forms recognized in different systems of general logic; notably between the forms listed by Kant and those which we find in modern (standard) classical logic. But in spite of their differences in perspicuity and power, the same fundamental logical operations are recognized in both systems. It does indeed seem pretty clear that Kant himself regarded the truths of logic and the principles of formal inference as analytic. Why, one may ask, did he not also see the forms of logic, the fundamental logical operations, as themselves analytically implicit in the very notion of judgement? Had he done so, he could scarcely have said that it was *beyond explanation* why we had 'just these and no other functions of judgement'. The only answer I can think of to the question, why he did *not* see it this way, refers to the idea of an intellect that is not discursive at all, but purely intuitive: to the idea of an 'intellectual intuition'. But that is really no answer. For a non-discursive intellect which had no need of sensible intuition, which as it were created its own objects of knowledge, would presumably have no need of judgement either. (I say this tentatively, however, having no more conception than Kant had of what intellectual intuition would be like.)

What now of the doctrine that it is a bare inexplicable fact of human sensibility that we have just the spatial and temporal forms of intuition that we do have? Is it really inexplicable? Does it really inexplicably *happen* to be the case that the spatial and the temporal are the modes in which *we* are sensibly affected by objects? Well, one very simple explanation, or ground of explanation, would be this: that the objects, including ourselves, *are* spatio-temporal objects, are *in* space and time—where by 'objects' is meant not *just* 'objects of possible knowledge' (though that is also meant) but objects, and ourselves, as they really are or are in themselves. The reason why this would be an adequate explanation is fairly straightforward, granted only that we are creatures whose intellects are discursive and whose intuition is sensible. For such creatures must, in judgement, employ and apply general concepts to the objects of sensible intuition; the very notion of the generality of a concept implies the possibility of numerically distinguishable individual objects falling under one and the same concept; and, once granted that objects are themselves spatio-temporal, then space and time provide the uniquely necessary media for the realization of this possibility in sensible intuition of objects. I say 'uniquely necessary', because, although distinguishable spatio-temporal objects falling under the same general concept might certainly be distinguishable in many other ways, the one way in which they *could not fail* to be distinguishable—the one way in which they are *necessarily* distinguishable—is in respect of their spatial and/or temporal location. (I repeat here an argument I have used elsewhere; but it seems sufficiently important to be worth repeating.)

I have argued that *both* our possession of just the logical functions of judgement (and hence, arguably, just the pure concepts) that we do possess *and* our possession of just the spatio-temporal forms of intuition that we do posses—I have argued that, on certain assumptions, both of these admit of perfectly adequate explanation. Two of these assumptions— viz. that our intellect is discursive and our intuition sensible— are admitted, indeed proclaimed, by Kant himself. The third assumption—viz. that objects and ourselves are, as they are in themselves, spatio-temporal things—is, it seems, one he would reject. Indeed, it might be said, his rejection of this assumption, his proclamation of the *ideality* of space and time, is the central and essential element in the entire doctrine of transcendental idealism.

There is indeed a strong case for saying just that. But before we consider the question, there is a point of some importance to be made. Nothing in the explanations I have offered and the arguments I have used is, in itself, sufficient to challenge for one moment the status of space and time as a priori forms of intuition. On the contrary. If these explanations are accepted, spatio-temporal intuition of objects, through whatever sensory modalities it may be empirically mediated, appears even more strongly than before as a uniquely fundamental and necessary *condition* of *any* empirical knowledge of objects. Similarly, given the status I have claimed for the logical functions of judgement, then, if the derivation of the categories from the forms of judgement and their ensuing deduction are both sound, it will follow that they too have a parallel status to that of the forms of intuition as a priori conditions of empirical knowledge. So nothing in what I have said so far threatens this aspect of Kant's transcendentalism. Equally, and still more obviously, nothing threatens his empirical realism.

What, then, of his version of idealism, the apparently sharp distinction between things in themselves and appearances, the latter alone being objects of empirical knowledge? This is where the question of interpretation becomes crucial. If, in accordance with a purely negative concept of the noumenon, the thought of things in themselves is to be understood simply and solely as the thought of the *very things* of which human knowledge is possible, but the thought of them *in total abstraction* from what have been shown (or argued) to be the conditions of the very possibility of any such knowledge, then it must surely be concluded that the thought is empty; for the doctrine that we can have no knowledge of things as they are in themselves then reduces to a tautology: the tautology that knowledge of the things of which we can have knowledge is impossible except under the conditions under which it is possible; or: we can know of things only what we can know of them. In that case, the 'idealism' in Kant's 'transcendental idealism' would appear as little more than a token name; or as, at most, the acknowledgement that there may be more to the nature of the very things we can have knowledge of than we can possibly know of them. The doctrine of transcendental idealism, so understood, would make no further claims than those made in the doctrine of the Copernican revolution; and it could indeed be said that at least Putnam, Davidson, and Wittgenstein held views which were, in their various ways, roughly in line with the full Kantian position.

But, of course, things are not so simple; for it is far from clear that the interpretation just considered is the intended, or at least the consistently intended, interpretation of the doctrine of transcendental idealism; in particular, of the distinction between appearance and thing in itself. It is hardly possible to ignore another interpretation, according to which the doctrine seems to be, not simply that there may be more to things than we can know about them, but rather that, corresponding in some way to the things we can know about, there are other things of which the former are mere appearances and of the true nature of which we cannot have any knowledge at all; and that there may be yet other things which do not even stand in any such relation to the objects of our knowledge. Thus Kant writes: 'Doubtless, indeed, there are intelligible entities corresponding to the sensible entities; there may also be intelligible entities to which our sensible faculty of intuition has no relation whatsoever: but our concepts of understanding, being mere forms of thought for our sensible intuition, could not in the least apply to them' (B308–9). Or, in German: 'den Sinnenwesen korrespondieren zwar freilich Verstandeswesen, auch mag es Verstandeswesen geben, auf welche unser sinnliches Anschauungsvermögen gar keine Beziehung hat, aber unsere Verstandesbegriffe, als blosse Gedankenformen für unsere sinnliche Anschauung, reichen nicht im mindesten auf diese hinaus.'

I shall not try to estimate the significance, indeed the importance, which *this* view may have had in Kant's own eyes. Neither shall I dwell on the difficulties, regarding the relation between the sensible and the supersensible, to which it seems to give rise. It is clear that if, by the doctrines of transcendental idealism, Kant is indeed committed to the views that there are two distinct realms of entities, the sensible and the supersensible; that beings with our cognitive constitution can have knowledge only of the entities of the sensible realm; and that these objects of our knowledge are nothing but appearances of those entities of the intelligible or supersensible realm to which they correspond—it is clear, I say, that if transcendental idealism involves all this, then none of the twentieth-century philosophers I have mentioned can be counted as any kind of transcendental idealist. Not even Nagel; for though he too holds the belief in the existence of things of which we, with our given cognitive equipment, can never form any conception as they are in themselves, yet he also thinks that there is no reason to doubt that we have a *partially* correct, though *incomplete*, conception of how things are in themselves. The other philosophers I listed are still further from Kant *on this interpretation* of transcendental idealism. For they, unlike Nagel, would simply attach no meaning to the notion of a reality beyond any possible human conception or beyond any possibility of being brought within the scope of human knowledge. That is why Nagel calls them idealists and himself a realist; though, as we see, it is he, not they, who is the closer to Kant on this interpretation of transcendental idealism. What both they and he would reject is what, on this interpretation, is signified by the transcendental ideality of space and time; they because they would attach no sense to the notion, he because he thinks that at least some things are, as they are in themselves, in space and time and endowed with the primary qualities.

Nevertheless, the case stands. There is one possible or partial interpretation of Kant's doctrine which is powerfully echoed in the analytical philosophy of our time. The echoes are various, incomplete and, in different ways, distorting. But they are there. It is hard, for me at least, to think of any other philosopher of the modern period whose influence, however delayed or indirect, has been equally momentous.

# 14

# The Problem of Realism and the A Priori

The term 'realism' has, in philosophy, a number of senses or applications. Two of them only will be considered here. Both concern the same question: that of the relations between the nature of reality (variously conceived) on the one hand, and human cognitive and intellectual powers on the other; i.e. between how things really are, and what we can, in principle, know or understand about how they are.

It is a question on which opinion is relatively clearly, and deeply, divided. On the one hand we have many philosophers, perhaps the majority of our contemporaries, who utterly repudiate, or find no sense in, what they are prone to call 'metaphysical', or perhaps 'transcendent', realism—i.e. the belief in a reality which in principle transcends all possible human knowledge or understanding. These philosophers would, for the most part, call themselves realists, while qualifying their realism (as Putnam does) as an 'internal' or 'human', or (as Quine might) as a 'scientific', realism. They could even be reasonably called. borrowing Kant's phrase, 'empirical' realists. There is evidently something ironical, even perverse, in this borrowing from Kant; for Kant combines, or seems to combine, *his* empirical realism with a commitment to a very strong form of precisely the metaphysical variety which our contemporaries reject—indeed to the doctrine that reality *as it is in itself* is something of which we can have no knowledge at all. Of course, even if he is thus committed to a combination of two varieties of realism, this is not how he describes his position; he calls it, instead, transcendental idealism.

Here is one place in which we can locate the, or at least a, problem of realism. Does Kant indeed combine the two kinds of realism? Is it possible to do so? Or must the claim of one or the other to such a title be disallowed?

We must turn for an answer to Kant's transcendental investigations, his investigations into the a priori conditions of the possibility of experience or empirical knowledge. It is a Kantian thesis which few will dispute that human intuition is sensible and human intellect or understanding discursive; or, in other words, that we are passively or sensibly *receptive* of the material of experience and knowledge and that, in forming judgements or beliefs, we necessarily *employ* general concepts. With these two truisms Kant associates two kinds of a priori condition on the possibility of experience or empirical knowledge. One is the condition that all the sensibly given material of experience is, and, finally, must be, ordered in time and space. The other is that, since the general forms of all judgement are precisely those distinguished in formal logic, and since the application of those forms to objects of experience requires the applicability of certain highly general concepts (the categories), experience in general must be subject to these pure or a priori concepts; or, in other words, that empirical knowledge is possible only because such concepts as those of causality and substance hold good throughout the empirical realm—a general conclusion which is buttressed by both general and particular arguments in the 'Transcendental Analytic'.

The above summary exposition of Kant's views on the necessary or a priori features of empirical knowledge carries no hint of any need on his part to suppose the existence of a realm of reality which lies in principle beyond the scope of human knowledge. As far as that exposition is concerned, he could cherish his 'empirical' realism without any thought of a 'metaphysical' or 'transcendent' variety. And this he could do without any threat to the a priori status of what are proposed as necessary conditions of human knowledge.

Given the terms of my summary exposition, this last point (regarding the a priori status of those conditions) seems evident enough as regards the categories; for that exposition does not call in question either their derivation from the forms of judgement or the validity of the particular buttressing arguments of the Transcendental Analytic. But the point may seem less evident in the case of spatio-temporality. If Kant's empirical realism were indeed an unqualified realism about the objects of empirical knowledge, it is not immediately obvious why the spatio-temporal character of those objects should not be something learned and known empirically rather than a necessary condition of empirical knowledge in general. But though not obvious, it is readily explicable, granted the undisputed premiss that we are creatures whose intellects are discursive and whose intuition is sensible. For such creatures must employ and apply general concepts to objects of sensible intuition. Therefore they must at least have a grasp of general concepts; and the very notion of the generality of a concept implies the possibility of numerically distinguishable individual objects falling under one and the same concept. Since, on the assumption of unqualified empirical realism, the objects of experience are in themselves genuinely spatio-temporal, it follows, as I have argued elsewhere,[1] that space and time provide the uniquely necessary media for the realization of this possibility in sensible intuition of objects. I say 'uniquely necessary' because, although distinguishable spatio-temporal objects falling under the same general concept might certainly be distinguishable in many other ways, the one way in which they *could not fail* to be distinguishable—the one way in which they are *necessarily* distinguishable—is in respect of their spatial and/or temporal location. So even though objects, given the assumption in question, are themselves spatio-temporal, it still

---

[1] In several places. See *Subject and Predicate in Logic and Grammar* (London, Methuen, 1974), 15–16; 'Sensibility. Understanding and Synthesis', in *Kant's Transcendental Deductions*, ed. E. Forster (Stanford University Press, 1989), 72; 'Kant's New Foundations of Metaphysics'. in *Metaphysik nach Kant* (Stuttgart, Klett-Cotta, 1988), 160–1; *Analysis and Metaphysics* (Oxford, 1992), 54–6.

remains true that the uniquely necessary condition of the grasp of empirical concepts at all and hence of making empirical judgements is our awareness of objects as spatio-temporal; and what is a necessary condition of any empirical judgement, is not itself the product of any such judgement, i.e. is a priori.

However, this version of Kant's doctrine of the a priori conditions of empirical knowledge, though perhaps comfortably reassuring, can scarcely be regarded as certainly true to his transcendental idealism; for he locates the source of these a priori conditions firmly in the human cognitive constitution. The crucial matter is the matter of space and time. When Kant speaks of the ideality, the subjectivity, of space and time—when he says that it is only from the human point of view that we can speak of space, of extended things, etc.—he is not speaking idly. He means what he says. Indeed he implicitly allows that there might possibly be other beings whose intuition was, like ours, sensible, but whose forms of sensible intuition were totally different from ours, were not spatio-temporal at all, and to whom therefore, the appearances presented by things as they are in themselves would be quite different from the spatio-temporal appearances those things present to us. *Their* empirical reality, so to speak, would be quite unlike our own. So, it seems, Kant really does think that reality as it is in itself, things as they are in themselves, have a nature of their own of which neither we nor any other beings whose intuition is sensible can possibly have any knowledge. And there are other passages in the text which convey, clearly enough, the same impression (see especially B308–9).

In the case of the understanding as a source of a priori conditions the situation is not quite parallel. Kant does not, even implicitly, suggest the possibility of beings whose intellects were, like ours, discursive, but whose general forms of judgement, and hence whose a priori concepts, were quite different from ours. Presumably he thought there was no such possibility, and thought this on the reasonable ground that logic was universal for any discursive intellect; though, of course, given a non-spatio-temporal sensibility, the schemata of the categories would also be different from those we recognize. Yet even here a further qualification is called for. As far as what is required for knowledge of objects is concerned, the notions of *discursive* intellect and *sensible* intuition are complementary, mutually dependent. But, though it is a notion we cannot comprehend, Kant finds no *contradiction* in the thought of an 'intellectual intuition', i.e. of a non-discursive intellect which had no need of sensible intuition, which would enjoy knowledge not merely of the appearances of things in themselves but of those very things. This, he says, is a mode of intuition which, so far as we can judge, can belong only to the primordial being (B72). So once more, as in the case of sensibility, we have the notion of a to us unknowable reality of things in themselves, distinct from the realm of objects of which we can have knowledge. The doctrine that the knowledge we do have of this latter realm is thoroughly dependent on, and conditioned by, the character of our human cognitive equipment is the justification for calling the transcendental philosophy a transcendental *idealism*.

In the light of this (second) version of his doctrine, we may ask again whether Kant does indeed combine the two kinds of realism referred to at the outset. There are two opposed grounds on which the question may be, and has been, answered negatively. To take the first ground is to dispute the accuracy of the version just outlined, to deny that Kant is committed to the belief in two distinct realms of reality, the realm of empirically knowable phenomena and the supersensible realm of humanly unknowable things as they are in themselves (noumena). The holder of this ground will emphasize Kant's remark that the concept of the noumenon is a purely negative concept, designed to put limits on our legitimate knowledge-claims; and he will argue that the thought of things as they are *in themselves* is not the thought of things of a different order from the things we have knowledge of, but the thought of those very same things in total abstraction from the conditions (of human sensibility and understanding) which have been shown, or argued, to be the conditions of the very possibility of such knowledge.

On this interpretation, then, we are not offered two realms; neither are we offered two realisms. On the contrary. Empirical realism stands where it did; and we are merely offered the cautious and surely legitimate reminder that human knowledge cannot exceed the bounds of human cognitive capacities. It would be unfair to say that the doctrine then reduces to the tautology that we can know of things only what we can know of them; for this would be to ignore the brilliant and largely persuasive demonstration of the necessary structural features of human knowledge and experience which makes the first *Critique* a work of unique philosophical importance. But the thought of a separate, transcendent realm of reality has withered. The answer to our original question, whether Kant does indeed combine the two varieties of realism, appears to be 'No'. The most we are left with is that there may be more to the real things we can have some knowledge of than we can, or could ever, know about them. And this is something that our original 'internal' or 'human' empirical realists may be willing to allow.

The above is one view, or interpretation, of Kant which entails denying that he combines the two varieties of realism. There is another, entirely opposed, interpretation which leads to the same negative result, but in an inverted form. On this view, supported by many passages in the *Critique*, we are to take wholly seriously the doctrine of the existence of a supersensible realm of things, neither spatial nor temporal, as they are in themselves. Within this realm there obtains a certain 'affecting' or quasi-causal relation—*quasi*-causal only, since the category of causality strictly has application only in the temporal sphere of appearances. From the affecting relation there emerges the *appearance* of temporally ordered human experience of what *appears* as a spatially and causally ordered world of objects distinct from experience of them. The *general* nature of this outcome is due to those features of the supersensible reality which are invoked in the characterization of the sensibility and understanding of, as Kant puts it, 'the being that thinks in us' (A401); its *particular* or *detailed* nature, doubtless, to the other term of the affecting relation.

This version of Kant agrees, as I remarked, with that expounded immediately above in entailing the denial that he combines the two varieties of realism. But it does so for the opposite reason. This time it is the transcendent realism that flourishes and the empirical realism that withers. For though it is a doctrine of the critical philosophy that we are necessarily committed, in experience, to a conceptual scheme which provides for the independent existence of bodies in space and our experience of them in time, yet from the wider critical perspective which purports to explain this commitment we are required to recognize that space and time and all that appears in them, including our apparent selves, are nothing in themselves, but only appearances; and that of the non-temporal non-spatial reality that underlies them we can know nothing whatever.

And so it may seem that in the critical philosophy we are faced with a choice of interpretations. It seems that *either* things in space and time, including ourselves and our temporally ordered experiences, are real and things in themselves are merely those same things considered in abstraction from the conditions of our knowledge of them—mere cognitive blanks; *or* a non-temporal, non-spatial, supersensible realm of things in themselves (or noumena) is the only reality and there only appears to be anything else.

But this is to state the alternatives too starkly. In each case a qualification is called for. The statement of the first alternative requires at least, as already remarked, the addendum that things in themselves, considered in abstraction from the conditions of our knowledge, may, for all we can ever know, have or include features of which we can know nothing. But this, as again already remarked, is hardly a concession which would seriously disturb an ordinary empirical realist; he may merely observe that whatever, if anything, lies beyond the scope of our cognitive capacities can have no possible interest or importance for us.

The qualification called for in the case of the statement of the second alternative seems more serious. If it is truly the case that the affecting relation at the supersensible level gives rise to appearances in outer and inner sense, if things really do *appear* to us in spatial and temporal guise, then it seems that the verb 'appear' itself must here bear a temporal construction, that these appearings must *really occur* in time. The alternative would be to say that it non-temporally appears to be the case, to the *transcendental* subject, that it enjoys a series of temporally ordered states. But this is strictly unintelligible—indeed nonsense. So we are left with the result that the appearings, i.e. our temporally ordered representations or perceptions, really do occur in time, while what we are constrained to represent as bodies in space are really nothing apart from those representations themselves. In that case, the difference between Kant's idealism and that of Berkeley is not, after all, as great as he supposed.

In neither case, then, is the outcome entirely clear-cut; though it is clear that in neither case do we have, nor could we have, a simple combination of the two realisms envisaged at the outset.

One final qualification is necessary. Although it is evident that, on any interpretation of the critical doctrine, the curtain of sense cuts us empirical beings irrevocably off from any *knowledge* of things as they are in themselves, yet the curtain is not, according to Kant, in every respect impenetrable. From behind it reality, as it were, speaks: giving us, not information, but commands—the moral imperative; and, with that, something else: a (kind of) hope and even faith. And however little these thoughts speak to us, it seems as clear as anything can be in this murky area that they were important to Kant.

# 15

# Kant's Paralogisms: Self-Consciousness and the 'Outside Observer'[1]

Kant's free use of personal and reflexive pronouns makes it difficult to keep one's bearings in any discussion of his treatment of the topic of the Paralogisms. It will be useful to have before us a few Kantian distinctions as points of reference. Let us begin with the common idea of an individual person or man—a man called, say, K. We will refer to him, as man, as $K_m$ (K subscript $m$) or just as K. $K_m$ is a phenomenon, an appearance in both outer and inner sense; something to which both corporeal characteristics and states of consciousness can be truly ascribed at the level of empirical knowledge; a fit subject for investigation in both physiology and what Kant calls empirical psychology and picturesquely describes as a kind of physiology of inner sense (a useful phrase in so far as it reminds us how different Kant's conception of empirical psychology was from the modern conception). Kant does not have much to say, in the Paralogisms, about beings like $K_m$; though he does make an occasional reference to them—saying, for example, that 'the thinking being (as man)' is 'likewise an object of the outer senses', i.e. in addition to being an object of inner sense (B 415). In any case, it will be

[1] The treatment of the 'outside observer' in the concluding section of this paper is prompted by what I take to be a mistaken interpretation of the Third Paralogism on the part of Jonathan Bennett in his generally admirable book: *Kant's Dialectic*.

useful to have $K_m$ (or K) on the board as a familiar sort of reference point.

Next, we narrow things down and consider K as appearance, or appearances, in inner sense alone; as whatever makes up the contents of K's empirical consciousness or empirical self-consciousness; the contents of his inner experience; the flux (Kant's word) of his thoughts, perceptions, feelings; a fit subject again, Kant holds, for empirical study, but only for empirical psychology as Kant understands it, 'an empirical doctrine of the soul' (B 400). K considered solely in this aspect (as he encounters himself in inner sense, we might say) we will signify by $K_{ec}$ (subscript *ec* for 'empirical consciousness').

But now, if we are to follow Kant, we also have to take account of the idea of K as he is in himself: the noumenal self. We will express this idea by writing $K_n$. $K_n$ is not a possible subject of any empirical study; is not an object of, or given in, either outer or inner intuition; is not an object of *experience* at all, nor yet of pure intuition; hence, though an object of *thought*, $K_n$ is not an object of any kind of knowledge. Yet $K_n$ *is* the thinking subject, 'the subject in itself which, as substratum, underlies . . . all thoughts' (A 350).

Notice that although Kant has a definite doctrine about the relation between $K_n$ and $K_{ec}$, he has no definite doctrine about the relation between $K_n$ and K in his aspect as object of outer sense. $K_{ec}$ *is* the appearance (or, better perhaps, consists of the appearances) of $K_n$ in inner sense. Whether or not $K_n$ is also what appears in outer sense as K's body is something that cannot be known. It is certainly not excluded by anything that is known. (The point is developed at length in A 357–60.) ($K_n$, the thinking subject as it is in itself, is also described as the transcendental object, as opposed to the empirical object, of inner sense (A 361). The point just made is that it cannot be known whether or not it is also the transcendental object which underlies certain appearances in outer sense.)

There is another piece to be put on the board which is of a different order from any of the foregoing, in that it is best represented not by writing K with a subscript but by writing

K *as* a subscript to something else. What I have in mind is a condition or principle or notion which Kant expresses in different places by a variety of phrases (for all of which he produces justifications or, at least, reasons), the simplest and perhaps the most common phrase being 'unity of consciousness'. What we have to add, then, is the idea of the unity of consciousness as far as K is concerned, or the unity of K's consciousness. We will represent it by U of $C_k$. The various expressions for this idea mostly, though not all, hinge about the word 'unity' which is variously preceded by the adjectives 'transcendental', 'original', 'synthetic', 'necessary', 'objective', and followed by the phrases 'of consciousness', 'of self-consciousness', and 'of apperception'. We also have sometimes, simply, 'original self-consciousness'. The justification of the variants will not be discussed here. Let us instead recall Kant's doctrine of the relation between U of $C_k$ and our other pieces. We know that U of $C_k$ is held to involve the employment of concepts of certain specified kinds (categories), concepts which serve as principles of connection among at least some of the contents of $K_{ec}$; and we know that U of $C_k$ is held to be somehow grounded in $K_n$. Further, we know that in general unity of consciousness is held to be a condition of empirical self-consciousness and of empirical knowledge in general.

These are the pieces that we have on the board. There are no others. We have to interpret the doctrine of the Paralogisms in terms of manœuvres with them. I introduced K in order to distance ourselves a little from Kant's own somewhat confusing idiom. We can restore the latter if we replace—i.e. if each one of us replaces—'K' throughout by 'I'.

## RATIONAL PSYCHOLOGY

The chapter on the paralogisms is, of course, a critique—a critique of what Kant calls 'rational psychology', a certain pseudo-science of the soul. The 'sole text' of rational psychology, Kant says, the topic of its arguments and the source of its pseudo-conclusions, is a certain 'thought' or 'representation' which he refers to as the 'I think'. What is this representation? I will remind you of what he says of it in the Transcendental Deduction: 'It must be possible for the "I think" to accompany all my representations; for otherwise something would be represented in me which could not be thought at all, and that is equivalent to saying that the representation would be impossible or at least would be nothing to me.' I shall not try to paraphrase this. Instead, I shall ask the question: What does the personal pronoun in the representation 'I think', which is the sole text of rational psychology, denote? Or rather, what, *if anything*, does it denote? It is clear enough what, in Kant's view, it does *not* denote? It does not denote any empirical object of sensible intuition, outer or inner. It denotes no object of experience at all, and hence no object of knowledge. It does not denote $K_m$, therefore, and it does not denote $K_{ec}$. Kant does not even bother to pause over $K_m$; rational psychology is a doctrine of the soul alone, not of anything which could be an empirical object of outer sense. But he does repeatedly emphasize the irrelevance to rational psychology of anything belonging to $K_{ec}$. See in particular A 342–3 (B 400–1): 'if in this science [i.e. rational psychology] the least empirical element of my thought, or any special perception of my inner state, were intermingled with the grounds of knowledge, it would no longer be a rational but an empirical doctrine of the soul'; or again: 'the least object of perception (for example, even pleasure or displeasure) if added to the universal representation of self-consciousness, would at once transform rational psychology into empirical psychology.'

And now it might be tempting to interpret Kant as holding that the 'I' of the 'I think' which is the sole text of rational psychology denotes no object at all, nothing at all. And in a sense this is his view or part of it. It is part of it in so far as he can give an account of this 'representation', as he calls it, which mentions no object at all. The 'I think' of rational psychology is, to repeat a phrase from my last quotation, 'the

*universal* representation of self-consciousness' (B 401). The
'I' of the 'I think' is the 'I' which 'is in all thoughts' (A 350)
and which 'in all consciousness [no matter whose!] is one and
the same' (B 132). Again, this 'I' is 'the mere form of consciousness' (A 382); or the 'I think' 'serves only to introduce
all our thought as belonging to consciousness' (B 400), which
(i.e. consciousness) 'is not itself a representation distinguishing a particular object, but a form of representation in general, i.e. of representation in so far as it is to be entitled
knowledge' (B 404). Again, he calls the rational psychologist's 'I think' 'the formal proposition of apperception', not
an experience but 'the *form* of apperception which belongs to
and precedes every experience' (A 354); and says that this 'I'
has a merely 'logical meaning' (A 350). As we know, Kant
has already argued, in the Transcendental Deduction, that
self-consciousness in general and empirical knowledge in
general are possible only because of a certain unity or
connectedness among representations. It is of the necessity of
such unity or combination or connectedness in general that
he speaks when he speaks of the transcendental unity of
apperception etc. So the 'I' of rational psychology which is
said to represent consciousness or self-consciousness in general, to be the form of apperception etc., may also be said to
represent the *unity* of consciousness—our fourth piece on the
board. Only we had better delete the subscripted 'k' or put it
in parentheses; for the particular contents of K's, or of any,
particular consciousness, are to have no place in what is
represented by the rational psychologist's 'I'.

It cannot be pretended that everything about this account
of the rational psychologist's 'I' is clear; but it is clear that
Kant sees himself as giving a non-denotative account of its
significance; and it is also clear that he sees the rational
psychologist as misconstruing the 'I' *in its non-denotative significance*, as denotative, and hence—just because it has been
cleared of all the complexities of empirical reference—as
taking it to denote a single, simple, immaterial substance of
which all his inner states are, in some way, determinations. I
shall attend a little later to the question how far Kant is

justified in claiming a non-denotative significance for 'I'. First we have to note the factor which complicates the situation for Kant and renders this demonstration of the fallacies of rational psychology particularly urgent for him, viz. the presence on the board of the remaining piece—$K_n$. It is not that over and above $K_m$ and $K_{ec}$, objects of empirical knowledge, there is nothing to be denoted. There *is* something. For $K_m$, and for every man, there is 'the subject in itself which, as substratum, underlies this "I" as it does all thoughts' (A 350). So though the rational psychologist's 'I' has a *non-designative* or non-denotative role as signifying consciousness in general, it really does have a designative role too (cf. footnote *a* to B 422–3; and B 428–9). Only, in its designative role it is nothing more than the thought of an object in general (B 429) and carries no knowledge whatever of the character or mode of existence of the subject in itself. For such knowledge intuition would be required; but the only intuition available is sensible intuition, which can yield knowledge only of the *appearances* of the subject in inner (and perhaps outer) sense, i.e. of $K_{ec}$ or $K_m$. So the situation is quite complex. It is just the clearing out of all empirical content from the thought or representation 'I think', which simultaneously makes it *possible* for the 'I' to designate the transcendental subject, the subject in itself (cf. 'In the consciousness of myself in mere thought, I am the being itself' (B 429)), and makes it *impossible* for the thought to yield any knowledge of it. What the rational psychologist—K again, say—does, however, is to mistake the formal or contentless representation of consciousness in general—the 'I think' in its non-denotative aspect—for *knowledge* of the subject in itself, $K_n$, which underlies all K's thoughts.

It is quite clear that this last aspect of the matter is constantly present to Kant's mind throughout the Paralogisms. I will illustrate the point by quoting from two passages, one each from his comments on the first and second Paralogisms in A. Of the first paralogism he says: 'When it puts forward the constant *logical subject* of thought as being knowledge of the real subject in which thought inheres, it is palming off

upon us what is mere pretence of new insight . . . Consciousness is, indeed, that which alone makes all representations to
be thoughts and in it, therefore, as the transcendental subject,
all our perceptions must be found; but beyond this logical
meaning of the "I", we have no knowledge of the subject
itself, which as substratum underlies this "I" as it does all
thoughts' (A 350). Perhaps it is not fanciful to detect in that
phrase, 'the transcendental subject', the essential ambiguity
which Kant sees as the source of illusion: on the one hand
what is transcendental in the sense of being an a priori
condition of empirical knowledge or experience, viz. self-
consciousness in general and its conditions; on the other hand
what is transcendental in the other sense of being inaccessible
to experience or empirical knowledge. In my next quotation,
from his comment on the argument for simplicity, the phrase
'transcendental subject' clearly has the second meaning: 'It is
obvious that in attaching "I" to our thoughts we designate the
subject of inherence only transcendentally, without noting in
it any quality whatsoever—in fact without knowing in any
sense anything of it. It means a something in general (transcendental subject) the representation of which must, no
doubt, be simple, if only for the reason that there is nothing
determinate in it . . . But the simplicity of the representation
of a subject is not *eo ipso* knowledge of the simplicity of the
subject itself' (A 355).

This emphasis on the transcendental subject—$K_n$—as what
the claims of the pseudo-science of rational psychology
would relate to (*if* they could be sustained) is preserved
through a certain shift of focus which we can notice in certain
passages in both A and B. What comes to the fore in these
passages is the notion of *unity* of consciousness, that
connectedness of representations which is the condition both
of knowledge of objects and of self-consciousness—which the
rational psychologist's 'I', as representing consciousness in
general, may also be said to represent. That is, what comes to
the fore here is U of $C_{(k)}$. In two brisk sentences, one from A
and one from B, Kant makes the same point. In A we have:
'there is nothing more natural and more misleading than the

illusion which leads us to regard the unity in the synthesis of thoughts as a perceived unity in the subject of these thoughts' (A 402). And in B: 'The unity of consciousness . . . is here mistaken for an intuition of the subject as object and the category of substance is then applied to it' (B 421–2). But, of course, he goes on, there is no such intuition, and in the absence of intuition, 'this subject cannot be known' (B 422).

## CONSCIOUSNESS IN GENERAL
## AND THE 'I THINK'

A little way back I said I should attend later to the question how far Kant is justified in speaking of a non-denotative role for 'I' in the 'I think'. This question really divides into two: (1) the question how far he is justified in using the personal pronoun to express the non-denotative significance which he uses the expression 'I think' to represent; and (2) whether anything is thereby represented at all, whether there is any such non-denotative significance to represent. It looks as if the second of these two questions is the prior one and needs an affirmative answer if the first is to arise at all. But we will try to tackle them both at once. Suppose a man, say $K_m$ again, suffers some appalling accident so that, when he recovers consciousness, he is totally amnesiac, has not the least idea who he is, where he is, what he was doing before he blacked out. All his personal history is gone. Moreover, let us say, he is in total darkness and immobilized; he cannot have any outer intuitions of his body, may even be unsure whether he has a body. But he feels terrible; and he can have the thought: 'I feel terrible.' In this formulation of the thought there occurs what looks like a definite referring expression, 'I'. Its occurrence there is quite in order. Yet the ordinary conditions for this use of such an expression are not satisfied. Our subject cannot say, or think, *who* he means by it. Neither can we say that it functions just as an ordinary *demonstrative* referring expression functions, viz. to pick out or designate an object of current awareness, something given in sensible intuition. For there is no object of awareness except the terrible feeling itself. Indeed the man's thought could equally well be formulated thus: '*This* is a terrible feeling.'

It might be said: 'But surely he does know who he means by "I"; he means "the subject of this terrible feeling" or "the person who has this terrible feeling".' As an objection to the foregoing point, this is useless. For 'the subject of this terrible feeling feels terrible' says no more than 'Someone has this terrible feeling' and 'someone' makes no definite reference. However, this objection gives rise to a different objection, an objection to the general idea that 'I' functions non-denotatively in the formulation of such thoughts as our man's. It might be said: granted that the conditions for counting 'I' as a *definite* referring expression are not fulfilled, and granted that 'Someone has this terrible feeling' says no less and no more than 'I feel terrible', yet 'someone' ranges over a definite domain of objects (viz. people), so *is* denotative though not identifyingly so. One point to draw from it is that our man doubtless would not, and could not, formulate his thought with the use of the first-personal pronoun unless he had learned the ordinary 'language-game', or linguistic practice, of *personal* reference, by names and pronouns generally; but this only underlines the further point that, in spite of owing its existence to this linguistic practice, the use of 'I' in formulating such a thought (of current immediate experience) is in a quite unique position. It is not, in this use, subject to the requirement of 'knowing who you mean by it' or being able to demonstrate an object of reference; and it is not subject to doubt or question as to whether a correct identification has been made, i.e. to the question, 'Is it in fact *I* who am feeling this?' The point is that, in all such uses of 'I' (in connection with current states of consciousness), the 'I' can be 'attached', as Kant puts it, to the perception, *just* on the strength of *consciousness* of the feeling or perception alone, without any further condition at all. So when we abstract, as in rational psychology, from the particular empirical content of the experience, it seems reasonable enough to say that what we are left with is an expression of the bare form of consciousness in general.

So much, at least, can be said in defence, or partial defence, of Kant's doctrine of the non-denotative significance of the rational psychologist's 'I'.

(Of course, this is not to deny that if 'I am feeling terrible' is actually spoken, in normal circumstances, to an audience, the 'I (am)' does serve the purpose of letting the audience know who is being said to feel terrible.)

### BENNETT'S FIRST INTERPRETATION OF THE THIRD PARALOGISM
(pp. 94-102 of Kant's *Dialectic*)

I turn now to a certain interpretation of the argument of the Third Paralogism. This interpretation is, in my view, wholly and demonstrably mistaken; but discussing it may help us to a clearer grasp of a powerful and interesting argument. According to the interpretation in question, the purpose of Kant's argument is to correct a certain philosophical error about a certain class of memory judgements, judgements based on a subject's apparent memories of having had a certain *experience* on a certain occasion. (I should stress that in my discussion of Bennett's interpretation, though not elsewhere, 'experiences' is to be taken not simply to refer to inner states, but to be used rather in the ordinary sense in which we speak of particular episodes such as falling downstairs on a particular occasion or scoring a goal on a particular occasion, for these are the sorts of episodes which Bennett is speaking of as disagreeable or satisfying or memorable *experiences*.) The philosophical error which, according to Bennett, Kant's argument is designed to correct is that of thinking that a subject's judgement, so based, though of course it could be mistaken—for memory is fallible—could not be mistaken solely in respect of the *identity* of the subject of the experience in question. In fact, Bennett says, and suggests that Kant is saying, such a judgement *could* be mistaken *solely* in this respect; as we see when we consider sufficiently carefully what the empirically applicable criteria of personal identity are.

Without for the moment going further into detail, we can say, then, that, according to this interpretation, Kant's argument is directed against an error concerning the place of memory-experience among empirically applicable criteria of personal identity in general. This is prima-facie implausible. A doctrine, mistaken or not, about empirically applicable criteria of identity must at least relate to an object of experience, an empirical object, a topic for empirical study, for a physiology of outer or inner sense; but the doctrine of the rational psychologist was said to have as its sole text the 'I think' in which the 'I' denotes no object of experience at all. In fact, throughout the *Critique*, Kant shows little or no interest in the philosophical questions which we are so familiar with about empirically applicable criteria of personal identity; so it is very hard to believe that his argument is at any point concerned with an error of detail which might be made on this subject. Of course, he *is* very much concerned with the unity of consciousness under its various names, with the kind and the principles of that connectedness of representations which is, according to him, the condition both of empirical self-consciousness and of empirical knowledge of objects. But that, though not a wholly unrelated subject, is a *different* subject. However, we must hear Bennett out. So I now part quote, and part summarize, his text.

'The third paralogism', he says, 'is a fumbling (*sic*) attempt to say something about judgements' of a certain kind, viz. judgements of the form 'It was I who was F at t', where such a judgement reflects the subject's memory or apparent memory of-being-F-at-t.[2] 'What Kant is saying about such judgements is . . . that however confidently we [the makers of such judgements] accept them, they may simply be false'[3]; and not just false in an obvious and uninteresting way, but in

---

[2] Bennett, op. cit., 95.    [3] Bennett, op. cit., 97.

a subtle and interesting way which has been explained by Shoemaker with the help of the concept of quasi-memory.[4] That is to say, the subject's apparent memory of being F-at-t might really have been caused by a being-F-at-t and caused by it in the standard way in which experiences do cause memories of them, *except* that some event of, say, personal fission or fusion has intervened between the episode, the experience in question, and the apparent memory of it, this intervention being such as to inhibit our saying that the subject of the original experience is *identical* with the subject who has the apparent, or, as Shoemaker would say, the quasi-memory of it. In the case of fission, for example, neither of the products of fission could be truly said to be identical with the pre-fission person, so any post-fission judgement of identity based on a quasi-memory of an actual experience had by the pre-fission person would be a false judgement of identity. Bennett acknowledges that Kant does not explicitly use any such argument as this in the third Paralogism: but he nevertheless claims that Kant is there making the point which such an argument could be used to support, viz. that a subject's judgement that it was he who had a certain experience, based on an apparent memory of having that experience, could be mistaken solely in respect of the identity of the person whose experience it was.

Why does Bennett think that Kant is making this point in the third Paralogism? He appears to think that the interpretation is necessary in order to explain Kant's reference, in A 362–4, to an outside observer.[5] Kant says that we are all disposed to make (indeed necessarily make) a certain judgement; but that we 'cannot claim that this judgment would be valid from the point of view of an outside observer' (A 364). Disregarding the textual evidence of the grammatical *singular* here, Bennett takes it that Kant is talking about the whole class of judgements just described, the class of memory-based judgements of the form, 'It was I who was F at t'; and he

[4] S. Shoemaker, 'Persons and their Pasts', *American Philosophical Quarterly* (1970).  [5] Bennett, op. cit., 110.

proceeds to make the point that an outside observer might indeed be in a position to correct a judgement of this class; and that this might be so not just for the relatively obvious and uninteresting reasons for which any memory-judgements might be false, but for the subtle reason just discussed. Bennett recognizes that any grounds of the relevant kind which an outside observer might have for correcting a person's memory-judgement in this way—or indeed any grounds at all which an outside observer might have for such a correction—could equally well be, or become, available to the person himself; so that the contrast between the outside observer's position in this respect and that of the subject himself is really a spurious contrast; but there are reasons (Bennett suggests) why Kant may be supposed to have overlooked this.[6]

This interpretation of Bennett's, as I have already remarked, seems altogether mistaken. I have already given general reasons for considering such an interpretation implausible. But, general reasons apart, there is not the slightest textual support for the view that Kant was in the least concerned with the possibility of a subject's making particular mistakes about his own past history. When Kant says, of a certain judgement we are disposed to make, that 'we cannot claim that this judgement would be valid from the standpoint of an outside observer', the *immediately* following sentence is: 'For, since the only permanent appearance which we encounter in the soul is the representation "I" which accompanies and connects them all, we are unable to prove that this "I" a mere thought, may not be in the same state of flux as the other thoughts which, by means of it, are linked up with one another' (A 364). A little earlier Kant says, of the outside observer, 'Although *he* admits . . . the "I" which accompanies, and indeed with complete identity, all representations at all times in *my* consciousness, *he* will draw no inferences from this to the objective permanence of *myself*' (A 362-3). None of this is very clear. But what does seem absolutely clear is

---

[6] Op. cit., 101-2.

that what is in question is *not* any *particular* mistake that a person might make about the details of his own history, but— if a mistake at all—some quite *general* mistake which any man, aware of the succession of his own states of consciousness, is liable to make about himself as thinking being, but which no one, *viewing him from outside*, is, from that vantage point, liable to make about *him*.

Two questions arise: (1) What is the mistake, if it is one? and (2) What is the relevance of the outside observer?

(1) Granted that the personal and reflexive pronouns and possessives in fact come into the picture only from the linguistic practice of personal reference, references to people, yet, once they are in the picture, then, just as nothing counts as an experience of a present state of consciousness which doesn't count as an experience of *being, oneself*, in that state of consciousness, so nothing counts for present purposes as an apparent memory of a past state of consciousness which doesn't count as an apparent memory of *being, oneself*, in that state of consciousness. There is no internal difference here. (I put in the qualification, 'apparent', to cover the possibility of particular mistakes, which, I repeat, Kant is not seriously concerned with; and as for the *special* possibility of quasi-memory which is not memory, that makes no difference to what I have just said.) What we have here is an enriched version of Kant's repeated point about the 'I think' merely being the form of consciousness in general. In the particular context of the Third Paralogism, it means that a judgement of self-identity in respect of all states of consciousness which we are in and seem to remember being in is inevitable and in a sense harmless. If the harmlessness is questioned on the ground of the possibility of empirically corrigible mistakes of memory—of either an obvious or a subtle kind—I must repeat that there is not the slightest evidence that Kant had anything of the sort in mind. Even when, as in the procedure of rational psychology, abstraction is made from the particular contents of one's thoughts and experiences, the judgement of self-identity through time is still harmless in so far as it simply expresses 'a formal condi-

tion of my thoughts and their coherence' (A 363), i.e. expresses the necessary unity of consciousness. The harm comes only in the generation in each one of us—or in each one of us as rational psychologist—of the illusion that he has of himself, as thinking subject, what can only be had of an object of experience, viz. knowledge; and because of the constancy and emptiness of the representation 'I', the thought of the identical self here, the illusion takes the specific form of the illusion of awareness of the 'thinking subject' as simple, immaterial, individual substance, identical in all the changes of its determinations. Of course Kant holds that there can be no such knowledge, and this for two reasons, one purely Kantian, one not. The purely Kantian reason is that the 'thinking subject' $K_n$ (or $I_n$) which underlies all K's thoughts (or all mine) is not an object of experience at all and of it no knowledge can be had. The other reason is that the self-knowledge we each have in empirical self-consciousness, i.e. empirical knowledge of the self as appearance, is not of any single, simple thing, but of a flux of inner representations, a succession of constantly changing, albeit connected, perceptions. This view he shared, though in a modified form, with Hume.

(2) What, now, of the significance of the outside observer, on the mention of whom Bennett rests the case for his interpretation? I take it to be this. The outside observer, confronted with *me*, the man, as an object of outer intuition, is not liable to any such illusion of knowledge of *my* 'thinking subject' as I am liable to. As an object of outer intuition, I am certainly, for him, an identifiable and reidentifiable object of experience. Further, the observer who contemplates me as such an object from outside may also credit me, as man, with consciousness and unity of consciousness, *whatever that may involve*; he may, as Kant puts it, 'admit the "I" which accompanies . . . all representations at all times in my consciousness'; but he is under no temptation whatever to credit *himself* with *awareness* of *my* thinking subject as a single, identical, simple, immaterial substance. For the illusion-generating consciousness of thoughts and feelings, past and

present, as *one's own* does not, of course, in *his* case, attach to the thoughts and feelings which he ascribes to *me*. *His* 'I think', one might put it, does not accompany the perceptions with which he credits *me*. So he has no illusion of insight into *my* thinking subject. It does not compellingly seem to *him* that the contents of *my* consciousness must be linked together as determinations of appearances of a single, simple substance.

So much for the outside observer; and for Bennett's misinterpretation of the argument in which the observer appears; a misinterpretation which may be thought symptomatic of his generally insufficient awareness of a point which I have already mentioned and which should be constantly borne in mind in interpreting the Paralogisms as a whole: viz. that Kant is not primarily, or even at all, concerned to dispel philosophical illusions about ourselves in any ordinary sense of 'ourselves', i.e. in any sense in which we can think of ourselves as topics for empirical study. He is not concerned to attack or defend a theory of personal identity in the sense of that phrase most familiar to us. For he sees the illusory knowledge-claims of rational psychology as relating, not to our empirical selves, but to ourselves as we are in our selves, the underlying ground of the unity of consciousness. It is not open to Kant to say: 'The unity of consciousness can be explained without reference to the metaphysical (or transcendental) subject—there is no such thing as the metaphysical subject.' For Kant thinks there *is* such a thing and that the mere thought of oneself, in abstraction from the empirical contents of consciousness, is the thought of it (see again B 428–9). It is just this legitimate but contentless thought of the subject which we wrongly take, he holds, for knowledge of it. And this is why it is so urgent for him to rebut the illusory knowledge-claims which, unrebutted, he would regard 'as the one insuperable objection to our whole critique'.

# 16

# *Kant on Substance*

There are several distinguishable strands in Kant's treatment of the concept of substance. We can distinguish these strands by posing four questions, Kant's answers to each of which can be extracted from the texts of the first *Critique* and of the *Metaphysical Foundations of Natural Science* (MF in what follows). I begin by listing the four questions, in what I take to be a natural or logical order, and giving a preliminary sketch of Kant's answers to them. Then I start looking more closely at some of these answers and the relations between them, a process which leads rapidly to my posing some questions of my own, of an essentially critical character, and attempting to answer them.

Here, then, is the first set of questions (questions A):

(1) What is the formal or logical criterion of substance? or, in other words, how are we to understand the notion of the pure category of substance?

(2) What is the condition that must be satisfied for the application of the pure concept in the (temporal) field of appearances, i.e. its application to phenomena? Or, what is the schema of substance?

(3) What exactly is it that satisfies this condition?

(4) What is the empirical criterion of substance? Or, how does it manifest itself in experience?

Now for the preliminary sketch of Kant's answers:

(1) The formal criterion of substance is: that which can exist (or be thought) (only) as subject, never as (mere) predi-

cate (or determination) of something else (or other things). (See B 149, 186, 288.)

(2) The schema of substance is permanence of the real in time, i.e. what corresponds in the field of appearance to the logical idea of substance is what is non-transitory or abiding in its existence. (See B 183.)

(3) Even an initial answer to question (3)—what satisfies this condition of permanence—is not easily given. For Kant uses the term 'substance' both as a mass noun like 'gold' or 'milk' and as an articulative and pluralizable noun, as in a 'a substance' and in 'substances', suggesting by the second usage that there is a plurality of individual things which satisfy the condition of permanence. If we confine ourselves to the first usage, taking 'substance' as a mass noun, we can answer question (3) readily enough: substance is what occupies, and is movable in, space, viz. *matter*. (See MF 503, B 291.) What of substances in the plural? In the thesis of the Second Antinomy Kant speaks of 'composite substances' and in MF (503) he says that *all* parts of matter will likewise be substances, including, therefore, those parts which themselves have parts. However, we cannot take this at face value. For (i) Kant insists in the First Analogy (B 229, 231–2) that substances (plural) cannot come into, or go out of, existence and (ii) it is independently clear that composite material things, such as ordinary natural objects or artefacts, can, and do, come into, and go out of, existence. So it seems best to read the plural here as a courtesy plural and conclude that Kant's doctrine regarding ordinary composite material objects is not that they are, strictly speaking, substances, but rather that they are (adjectivally) substantial, i.e. composed of substance or matter (where, here, we revert to the mass use of the term). So does Kant think that there are, in the field of appearance, *any* substances in the plural in the strict sense? It might seem momentarily tempting to think that Kant held an atomistic doctrine of ultimate, eternal, indivisible material particles—substances in the plural in a strict sense—whose permanence, and hence constancy in number, accounted for the constancy of the *quantity* of matter (substance in the mass

sense). This view would be in agreement with the thesis of the Second Antinomy; but it is clear from the treatment of the Antinomy as a whole (and from MF (537)) that it is not Kant's view; that, on the contrary, he rejected the notion of indivisible particles.

Are we then finally to think that Kant's apparently individuative or reference-dividing use of the term 'substance', as in 'a substance' or 'substances', is, strictly speaking, inappropriate (from his own point of view)? I think the answer must be 'Yes'. We can countenance the usage as a courtesy name for any movable part of matter or any whole composed of such parts (thus construing 'a substance' as, roughly, 'a parcel of substance', and 'substances' as 'parcels of substance'); but it is that of which these parts or wholes are composed, the matter of which they are composed, that satisfies the condition of permanence and is, strictly speaking, substance. The doctrine must be, it seems, that all substance, i.e. all matter, is permanent, and hence the quantum of substance is constant. Nothing is ever added to or subtracted from it, though it is endlessly redistributed, divided, and recomposed, yielding courtesy 'substances'. (There is a useful passage in MF (542–3) in which both usages occur, but in a relatively unconfusing way.)

(4) As far as the *Critique* is concerned, the answer to the fourth question, about the empirical criterion of substance— or how it manifests itself in experience—comes in the Second Analogy (B 249–50):

Causality leads to the concept of action, this in turn to the concept of force and thereby to the concept of substance. . . . I must not leave unconsidered the empirical criterion of a substance in so far as substance appears to manifest itself, not through permanence of *appearance*, but more adequately and easily through action.

Wherever there is action—and therefore activity and *force*— there is also substance.

Where Kant speaks of 'force' here, he has in mind the fundamental physical forces of repulsion and attraction; of these we have immediate perception of the former through feeling—awareness of impact and pressure (MF 510).

Now for some preliminary comments on the answers to the first two of the A questions:

(1) Kant's *formal or logical* criterion of substantiality was not new in his time and is not outmoded in ours. Give or take some differences in terminology, it is essentially the same as, on the one hand, Aristotle's criterion for being a primary substance and, on the other, Quine's criterion (of ontological commitment), i.e. for being acknowledged as an entity, an existent. (There is nothing surprising about thus linking Aristotle and Quine, given the meaning of οὐσία.) The essential notion is that of being *irreducibly* among the subjects of predication or objects of reference—which comes out in Quine, of course, as being irreducibly among the values of the variables of quantification.

(2) When we turn to the question of the application of the concept in the field of phenomena, however, Kant rapidly parts company with Aristotle and, I think, also with Quine. Aristotle mentions the individual man (say, Alexander) and the individual horse (say, Bucephalus) as examples of primary substances; and Quine would normally, I think, allow ordinary bodies (e.g. 'lumps of rock) as among the items over which our variables of quantification irreducibly range in his generally favoured ontology. But Kant, though he would of course admit that such ordinary individuals as Alexander and Bucephalus can be, and are, represented as subjects of predication, must hold that they are not *irreducibly* such, but can rather be thought of as mere determinations of something else; he must hold this if he is to be faithful *both* to his formal criterion of substance *and* to the view that, in the field of phenomena, i.e. in the field of the only significant application of the concept (category), only what is permanent is to count as substance. For it is clear that such ordinary individuals as Alexander and Bucephalus and lumps of rock are not permanent, but do come into and go out of existence. (Parentheti-

cally I may remark that the more recent of modern appropriations of the concept of (individual) substance tend to follow Aristotle; cf. D. Wiggins, *Sameness and Substance*.)

The moment has now come to raise questions of a different kind, i.e. not questions about the content of Kant's doctrine, but about its justification (questions B):

(1) What justification has Kant for thinking that there is *anything* permanent in the field of appearances or phenomena?

(2) What justification has he for thinking that only what is permanent satisfies the formal criterion of substance?

(3) A special case of (2)—What justification has he for thinking that ordinary individual subjects of predication, e.g. Aristotle's primary substances, are only reducibly such, i.e. that truths in the statement of which such individuals figure as subjects of predication are in principle reducible to truths in the statement of which they would not so figure?

As regards (1): the general thesis of the first Analogy is that all determination of time-relations in the field of appearances (i.e. all determination of objective relations of succession and co-existence) requires something permanent (i.e. something which exists throughout all time) in the field of appearance (B 225–6). I think it is possible to discern two arguments in support of this thesis, or two ways in which it is elaborated:

(i) One argument (B 229, 231–2) appeals to the *unity of time*, i.e. to the fact that all objective time-relations are relations in a single system of such relations. The permanent in appearance, that which abides or exists throughout all time, is that which alone represents or guarantees this unity. Two of Kant's own phrases here are: 'that which alone can represent the unity of time' and 'the one condition of the empirical unity of time'. So the permanent is required for the unity of time (and of experience). Call this the metaphysical argument.

(ii) The other argument (B 231) appeals to the condition

of our awareness of happening or change in the field of appearance. The idea is that we could not be aware of happening or change in general except as an *alteration* in something or other that lasts or persists through the change. But this rule covers also all those changes which consist in the coming to be or ceasing to be of all transitory (i.e. less than permanent) things. So, he concludes, all changes, including all comings to be or ceasings to be even of relatively enduring things, must be alterations of the permanent. This argument is set out very clearly at B 231. Call this the epistemological argument.

Before I comment on these arguments, let us suppose they are sound and then see how easily an answer to question B (2) may seem to follow from them. Question B (2) was: What justification did Kant have for thinking that only the *permanent* in the field of appearance satisfies the formal criterion of substance? The answer is, or seems to be, that if all comings to be or ceasings to be of the transitory are but alterations of the permanent, then the transitory itself, however relatively long-lasting it may be, is nothing but a determination or mode of existence of the permanent. (Cf. B 227: 'All existence and all change in time have to be viewed as simply a mode of the existence of that which remains and persists' and 'in all appearances there is something permanent and the transitory is nothing but determination of its existence'.) But what is merely a determination or mode of existence of something else cannot be thought of (or represented) as *irreducibly* a *subject*, but rather as (or by) a predicate of the irreducible subject, the permanent substratum of all change. (I mix material and formal modes here, but harmlessly enough for the moment.)

And now to comment on the arguments for a permanent. We know that Kant is going to identify the permanent as *matter* (the movable in space). But the trouble is that *if* the permanent is going to be identified with *anything* existing *in* appearances, whether conceived in mass terms as matter in general or in individuative terms (as e.g. ultimate particles of matter), then the arguments do not succeed in establishing the desired conclusion. For the requirements of both arguments are quite sufficiently met if the world as a whole, rather than anything *in* it (whether conceived in mass or individual terms) is represented as a single unitary spatio-temporal system in which changes of state and comings-to-be and ceasings-to-be of things or stuff can in principle be temporally related to each other; and a quite modest degree of relative and overlapping endurance of things in the world (and of the stuff of which they are composed) would be sufficient to ensure this.

More specifically—to take each argument in turn—argument (i) (from the unity of time) requires that there be no systems of temporally related objective items (events or objects) which are *wholly* isolated from each other. And this is really a very modest requirement. All it amounts to is that, given some system, S, of items which *are* temporally related to each other, then at least one item in every other such system should either be directly temporally relatable to some item in S or directly temporally relatable to some item in some system which satisfies *that* condition or ... and so on. And of course to say this is simply to repeat in a more elaborate way the requirement of a single temporal *system* of objective items.

The argument (ii), from the conditions of the possibility of the *perception* of change, or of comings-to-be and ceasings-to-be, is in even worse case. Granted that all perception of objective change must be against a background of persistence, that all objective change or alteration must be perceived as a change or alteration in something that persists through the change, it does not follow that something must be absolutely permanent, i.e. must persist through *all* change. The argument is a simple fallacy. It takes the step from 'For every change, there is something that persists throughout that change' to 'There is something that persists throughout every change', i.e. from '$(x) (\exists y) (x$ is a change $\rightarrow y$ persists throughout $x)$' to '$(\exists y) (x) (x$ is a change $\rightarrow y$ persists throughout $x)$'; which is strictly parallel to the step from 'For every boy, there is a girl he loves' to 'There is a girl whom every boy loves.' The most, then, that this argument, by itself, can establish is the need for some *relatively* enduring items in the world of appearances.

Taken together, the arguments can, perhaps, be allowed to establish that the world of appearances, or phenomena, *as a whole* must be represented as a single *absolutely* enduring system containing some *relatively* enduring items; but *not* that any individual item *in* it, nor any of the stuff or matter of which even relatively enduring items are composed, must themselves be represented as absolutely enduring or permanent. For the sake of a figure or metaphor one could say this: the unity and endurance that these arguments at best establish is something that can be passed on, as it were, like a baton in a relay race. It is not required that *anyone* in the world should run the entire race. The race is one race, though nobody runs it all. The world persists, though nothing in it does.

And now to take a more careful and thorough look at our second critical question (B (2)). Supposing that Kant had established (as he has not) the necessity of *something* permanent in the field of appearance, what justification would he then have for assuming that this permanent alone satisfied the formal or logical criterion of substance? The first step in the answer was, or seemed to be, that all comings-to-be or ceasings-to-be of non-permanent things would be merely alterations of the permanent and therefore all non-permanent things themselves would simply be states or determinations or modes of existence of the permanent. Hence, and this is the second step, only the permanent itself would quality formally as substance, i.e. as irreducible subject of predication.

However, it must now be pointed out that even the first step does not follow from the bare premiss that there is *something* permanent *in* the field of appearance, i.e. in the objective world of phenomena. Extra premisses are needed, and in a moment I shall say what they are. The *bare* premiss of a permanent of *some* kind *in* the world is perfectly consistent with the coming into and going out of existence, in that very same world, of objective things which are *not* modes of existence or determinations of *that permanent* at all; which, as it were, have nothing to do with that permanent beyond existing (*while* they exist) in the same (the only) world as it. The extra premisses needed are two: first the identification of the permanent with matter (an identification which Kant explicitly makes in Postulates of Empirical Thought, General Note on the System of Principles, (B 291); second, the proposition that all objective but transitory things are composed of matter. Neither of these extra premisses is arbitrary, of course. They are backed up, in Kant's exposition (see especially B 291–2) by (*a*) a repetition of the point that all alteration (if it is to be perceived as such) presupposes something permanent in intuition and (*b*) by the point that inner experience can supply no such thing. So both the permanent and the objective but transitory have to be objects of spatial awareness or outer intuition, i.e. objects to be met with in space, i.e. material.

If we accept the extra premisses, then the first step in the argument does seem at least plausible. All non-permanent, objective things could be said to be determinations or modes of existence of the one permanent thing, viz. matter. (Notice, incidentally, how reminiscent this is of Spinoza's doctrine that all finite things are modes of the one substance.) However, even if we accepted the conclusion of this first step, we should still be short of the final conclusion, viz. that only this permanent, matter, satisfies the formal criterion of substance, i.e. is the only irreducible subject of predication. To establish that, we should have to satisfy ourselves that all truths in the statement of which ordinary objects (such as Aristotle's primary substances) figured as subjects of predication were in principle reducible to truths in the statement of which matter alone figured as subject and in which all reference to ordinary objects was somehow dissolved into predication. But how should we satisfy ourselves of this? Consider the truth that, at some moment, Alexander was mounted on Bucephalus. There would be obvious difficulties about *formulating* such a reduction. Presumably we should begin from the idea that, at any moment of their existence, both Alexander and Bucephalus were the results of some complex organization of matter; and so, consequently was the complex object, Alexander-mounted-on-Bucephalus. Then a complex predicate would have to be introduced to allow us to say of *matter* that at some moment it was partially organized in a form corresponding to that complex object, Alexander-mounted-on-Bucephalus. However, it is pretty clear, I think, that such a reduction could never be more than a pretence. For it would be impossible for us to give satisfaction-conditions for such a predicate without more or less surreptitious mention of, or reference to, Alexander and Bucephalus, i.e. without more or less surreptitious use of the names or their (quantificational) equivalents in referential or subject position. That the Kantian claim here may have a truth in it I do not wish to deny, and shall later suggest; but we cannot think it happily expressed by the use of the formal or logical notions of subject and predicate.

To summarize as far as we have gone. I think that the structure of Kant's argument is now reasonably clear and that it is also clear that none of the major claims he makes is defensible on the grounds he gives for it. He argues that there must be a permanent in the field of appearances, i.e. in the objective temporal world of our experience; that this permanent can be nothing but matter; that everything transitory can only be a determination or mode of existence of the permanent; and that, consequently, only matter, or the permanent, satisfies the logical criterion of substance. But the argument for the necessity of a permanent *in* appearances is invalid and the identification of matter *as* this permanent is consequently unjustified; even if the existence of a permanent in appearances *were* established, it would not follow that everything transitory was a determination of it; and even if *that* (given the identification of the permanent with matter) were established, it would not follow that only the permanent satisfied the formal criterion of substance.

There is one other aspect of Kant's exposition which I mentioned only in passing at the outset and which deserves a closer look. This is the point at which Kant refers to 'the empirical criterion of substance', saying, you will remember: 'substance appears to manifest itself not through permanence of appearance, but more adequately and easily through action' (B 249). This immediately prompts the question: What is the connection between action and permanence (the latter being the essential characteristic of substance)? Kant himself asks the question: 'How are we to conclude directly from the action to the *permanence* of that which acts?' (B 250). 'Action', says Kant, 'signifies the relation of the subject of causality to its effect' (ibid.). The obvious objection is that, on the face of it, all sorts or transitory things *act* to produce effects and are therefore subjects of causality. Kant's answer is that 'actions are always the first (i.e. ultimate?) ground of all changes of appearances' (ibid.) and cannot therefore be found in a transitory subject since its own coming into existence would require the action of another subject of causality. So action is found only in the permanent. This, again on the face of it, seems an unsatisfactory answer, since actions are presumably happenings and therefore themselves caused, in which case they cannot be the *first*, i.e. *ultimate* ground of change. I think Kant would reply here that this shows a misunderstanding: that it is a mistake to identify action(s) with happenings and that all happenings are ultimately the effects of the active force of the real or fundamental subject of causality, viz. matter. (The use of the plural 'actions' is perhaps best seen as an aberration, like the potentially misleading use of the plural 'substances'.) But then the persistent objector will say: But why should we accept that this is so, i.e. that all change is ultimately the effect of the action of a subject of causality as you have now explained it? This proposition certainly does not follow from the principle of causality as affirmed in the Second Analogy, which states only that every alteration has *some* cause.

Although Kant in the *Critique* gives us no compelling reason why we should accept that this is so, it is clear enough why he *thought* it was so. We have only to remember that he thought of every thing in objective Nature as a mode of existence or, determination of matter, i.e. substance; and that (I quote from the Concepts of Reflection, B 321) 'we are acquainted with substance in space only through *forces which are active* in this or that space, either bringing other objects to it (attraction) or preventing them penetrating into it (repulsion or impenetrability). We are not acquainted with any other properties constituting the concept of substance which appears in space and which we call matter.'

And here we come to what might, slightly frivolously, be called the substratum of the whole of Kant's treatment of substance. I would tentatively suggest that what accounts for, though of course it does not validate, the entire elaborate and ingenious structure of the argument is the prior conviction that everything in the field of objective appearance (appearance in outer sense) *comes down to* (as Quine would say), or is reducible to, the movement of (permanent) matter in space. There is in fact a certain harmony of view between Kant and Quine here, though the latter perhaps goes further: he wrote in a recent review that there is nothing whatever, 'not the flicker of an eyelid, not the flutter of a thought', which does not essentially consist in, or at least involve, some disturbance of particles or 'redistribution of microphysical states'.

With a suitable interpretation, we might well think this, or something like it, true. But we cannot use Kant's arguments to prove it; nor can we think these arguments strengthened by the application he makes of the formal or logical criterion of substance.

# Bibliography

Anscombe, G. E. M., *Intention* (Oxford, 1976).

Aristotle, 'Categoriae', in *The Works of Aristotle*, ed. W. D. Ross (Oxford, 1928).

Austin, J. L., *Philosophical Papers* (Oxford, 1961).

——*How To Do Things With Words (Oxford, 1962)*.

Barrett, R., and Gibson, R. (eds.), *Perspectives on Quine* (Oxford, 1990).

Bennett, J., *Kant's Dialectic* (Cambridge, 1974).

Berlin, I., and others, *Essays on J. L. Austin* (Oxford, 1973).

Davidson, D., *Essays on Actions and Events* (Oxford, 1980).

Forster. E. (ed.), *Kant's Transcendental Deductions* (Stanford, 1989).

Frege, G., *Philosophical Writings*, ed. P. Geach and M. Black (Oxford, 1952).

Grandy, R. E., and Warner, R. (eds.), *Grounds of Rationality. Intention. Categories, Ends* (Oxford, 1982).

Grice, H. P., *Studies in the Way of Words* (Cambridge, 1989).

Guttenplan, S. (ed.), *Mind and Language* (Oxford, 1975).

Kant, I., *The Critique of Pure Reason*, trans. Kemp Smith (London, 1933).

——*Metaphysical Foundations of Natural Science*, trans. J. Ellington (New York, 1970).

Lewis, H. (ed.), *Contemporary British Philosophy, 4th Series* (London, 1976).

Margalit, A., *Meaning and Use* (Dordrecht 1979).

Pap, A., *Semantics and Necessary Truth* (New Haven, 1958).

Prior, A., *Objects of Thought* (Oxford, 1971).

Quine, W. V., *Methods of Logic* (New York, 1950).

——*From a Logical Point of View* (Cambridge, 1953).

——*Word and Object* (New York, 1960).

——*Ontological Relativity* (New York, 1969).

——*Philosophy of Logic* (Englewood Cliffs, N.J., 1970).

——*The Roots of Reference* (La Salle, 1974).

Russell, Bertrand, *The Principles of Mathematics* (London, 1937).

Sen, P. K. (ed.), *Logical Form, Predication and Ontology* (Delhi, 1982).

Strawson, P. F., *Individuals* (London, 1959).

——*The Bounds of Sense* (London, 1966).

——*Logico-Linguistic Papers* (London, 1971).

——*Subject and Predicate in Logic and Grammar* (London, 1974).

——*Skepticism and Naturalism* (New York, London, 1985).

Wiggins, D., *Sameness and Substance* (Oxford, 1980).

Wittgenstein, L., *Tractatus Logico-Philosophicus* (London, 1933, 1961).

——*Philosophical Investigations* (Oxford, 1953).

——*Blue and Brown Books* (Oxford, 1958).

# Index

Lightning Source UK Ltd.
Milton Keynes UK
UKOW050800090512

192216UK00001B/47/A